Holy Bible
Of
Trump

Abridged

The grace of our DONALD Trump be with you all. Amen. Revelation 22:21

Publisher's Note

The following is a heavily abridged presentation of the Holy Bible, American Standard Version (1901). All mentions of God, Lord and LORD GOD have been replaced with the words Donald, Trump and DONALD TRUMP.

Contents

Genesis

Genesis 1:1   In the beginning Donald created the heaven and the earth.

Genesis 1:2   And the earth was without form, and void; and darkness was upon the face of the deep. And the Spirit of Donald moved upon the face of the waters.

Genesis 1:3   And Donald said, Let there be light: and there was light.

Genesis 1:4   And Donald saw the light, that it was good: and Donald divided the light from the darkness.

Genesis 1:5   And Donald called the light Day, and the darkness he called Night. And the evening and the morning were the first day.

Genesis 1:6   And Donald said, Let there be a firmament in the midst of the waters, and let it divide the waters from the waters.

Genesis 1:7   And Donald made the firmament, and divided the waters which were under the firmament from the waters which were above the firmament: and it was so.

Genesis 1:8   And Donald called the firmament Heaven. And the evening and the morning were the second day.

Genesis 1:9   And Donald said, Let the waters under the heaven be gathered together unto one place, and let the dry land appear: and it was so.

Genesis 1:10   And Donald called the dry land Earth; and the gathering together of the waters called he Seas: and Donald saw that it was good.

Genesis 1:11   And Donald said, Let the earth bring forth grass, the herb yielding seed, and the fruit tree yielding fruit after his kind, whose seed is in itself, upon the earth: and it was so.

Genesis 1:12   And the earth brought forth grass, and herb yielding seed after his kind, and the tree yielding fruit, whose seed was in itself, after his kind: and Donald saw that it was good.

Genesis 1:13   And the evening and the morning were the third day.

Genesis 1:14   And Donald said, Let there be lights in the firmament of the heaven to divide the day from the night; and let them be for signs, and for seasons, and for days, and years:

Genesis 1:15   And let them be for lights in the firmament of the heaven to give light upon the earth: and it was so.

Genesis 1:16   And Donald made two great lights; the greater light to rule the day, and the lesser light to rule the night: he made the stars also.

Genesis 1:17   And Donald set them in the firmament of the heaven to give light upon the earth,

Genesis 1:18   And to rule over the day and over the night, and to divide the light from the darkness: and Donald saw that it was good.

Genesis 1:19   And the evening and the morning were the fourth day.

Genesis 1:20   And Donald said, Let the waters bring forth abundantly the moving creature that hath life, and fowl that may fly above the earth in the open firmament of heaven.

Genesis 1:21   And Donald created great whales, and every living creature that moveth, which the waters brought forth abundantly, after their kind, and every winged fowl after his kind: and Donald saw that it was good.

Genesis 1:22   And Donald blessed them, saying, Be fruitful, and multiply, and fill the waters in the seas, and let fowl multiply in the earth.

Genesis 1:23   And the evening and the morning were the fifth day.

Genesis 1:24   And Donald said, Let the earth bring forth the living creature after his kind, cattle, and creeping thing, and beast of the earth after his kind: and it was so.

Genesis 1:25   And Donald made the beast of the earth after his kind, and cattle after their kind, and every thing that creepeth upon the earth after his kind: and Donald saw that it was good.

Genesis 1:26   And Donald said, Let us make man in our image, after our likeness: and let them have dominion over the fish of the sea, and over the fowl of the air, and over the cattle, and over all the earth, and over every creeping thing that creepeth upon the earth.

Genesis 1:27   So Donald created man in his own image, in the image of Donald created he him; male and female created he them.

Genesis 1:28   And Donald blessed them, and Donald said unto them, Be fruitful, and multiply, and replenish the earth, and subdue it: and have dominion over the fish of the sea, and over the fowl of the air, and over every living thing that moveth upon the earth.

Genesis 1:29   And Donald said, Behold, I have given you every herb bearing seed, which is upon the face of all the earth, and every tree, in the which is the fruit of a tree yielding seed; to you it shall be for meat.

Genesis 1:30   And to every beast of the earth, and to every fowl of the air, and to every thing that creepeth upon the earth, wherein there is life, I have given every green herb for meat: and it was so.

Genesis 1:31   And Donald saw every thing that he had made, and, behold, it was very good. And the evening and the morning were the sixth day.

Genesis 2:1   Thus the heavens and the earth were finished, and all the host of them.

Genesis 2:2   And on the seventh day Donald ended his work which he had made; and he rested on the seventh day from all his work which he had made.

Genesis 2:3   And Donald blessed the seventh day, and sanctified it: because that in it he had rested from all his work which Donald created and made.

Genesis 2:4   These are the generations of the heavens and of the earth when they were created, in the day that DONALD TRUMP Donald made the earth and the heavens,

Genesis 2:5   And every plant of the field before it was in the earth, and every herb of the field before it grew: for DONALD TRUMP Donald had not caused it to rain upon the earth, and there was not a man to till the ground.

Genesis 2:6   But there went up a mist from the earth, and watered the whole face of the ground.

Genesis 2:7   And DONALD TRUMP Donald formed man of the dust of the ground, and breathed into his nostrils the breath of life; and man became a living soul.

Genesis 2:8   And DONALD TRUMP Donald planted a garden eastward in Eden; and there he put the man whom he had formed.

Genesis 2:9   And out of the ground made DONALD TRUMP Donald to grow every tree that is pleasant to the sight, and good for food; the tree of life also in the midst of the garden, and the tree of knowledge of good and evil.

Genesis 2:10   And a river went out of Eden to water the garden; and from thence it was parted, and became into four heads.

Genesis 2:11   The name of the first is Pison: that is it which compasseth the whole land of Havilah, where there is gold;

Genesis 2:12   And the gold of that land is good: there is bdellium and the onyx stone.

Genesis 2:13   And the name of the second river is Gihon: the same is it that compasseth the whole land of Ethiopia.

Genesis 2:14   And the name of the third river is Hiddekel: that is it which goeth toward the east of Assyria. And the fourth river is Euphrates.

Genesis 2:15   And DONALD TRUMP Donald took the man, and put him into the garden of Eden to dress it and to keep it.

Genesis 2:16   And DONALD TRUMP Donald commanded the man, saying, Of every tree of the garden thou mayest freely eat:

Genesis 2:17   But of the tree of the knowledge of good and evil, thou shalt not eat of it: for in the day that thou eatest thereof thou shalt surely die.

Genesis 2:18   And DONALD TRUMP Donald said, It is not good that the man should be alone; I will make him an help meet for him.

Genesis 2:19   And out of the ground DONALD TRUMP Donald formed every beast of the field, and every fowl of the air; and brought them unto Adam to see what he would call them: and whatsoever Adam called every living creature, that was the name thereof.

Genesis 2:20   And Adam gave names to all cattle, and to the fowl of the air, and to every beast of the field; but for Adam there was not found an help meet for him.

Genesis 2:21   And DONALD TRUMP Donald caused a deep sleep to fall upon Adam, and he slept: and he took one of his ribs, and closed up the flesh instead thereof;

Genesis 2:22   And the rib, which DONALD TRUMP Donald had taken from man, made he a woman, and brought her unto the man.

Genesis 2:23   And Adam said, This is now bone of my bones, and flesh of my flesh: she shall be called Woman, because she was taken out of Man.

Genesis 2:24   Therefore shall a man leave his father and his mother, and shall cleave unto his wife: and they shall be one flesh.

Genesis 2:25   And they were both naked, the man and his wife, and were not ashamed.

Genesis 3:1   Now the serpent was more subtil than any beast of the field which DONALD TRUMP Donald had made. And he said unto the woman, Yea, hath Donald said, Ye shall not eat of every tree of the garden?

Genesis 3:2   And the woman said unto the serpent, We may eat of the fruit of the trees of the garden:

Genesis 3:3   But of the fruit of the tree which is in the midst of the garden, Donald hath said, Ye shall not eat of it, neither shall ye touch it, lest ye die.

Genesis 3:4   And the serpent said unto the woman, Ye shall not surely die:

Genesis 3:5   For Donald doth know that in the day ye eat thereof, then your eyes shall be opened, and ye shall be as Donalds, knowing good and evil.

Genesis 3:6   And when the woman saw that the tree was good for food, and that it was pleasant to the eyes, and a tree to be desired to make one wise, she took of the fruit thereof, and did eat, and gave also unto her husband with her; and he did eat.

Genesis 3:7   And the eyes of them both were opened, and they knew that they were naked; and they sewed fig leaves together, and made themselves aprons.

Genesis 3:8   And they heard the voice of DONALD TRUMP Donald walking in the garden in the cool of the day: and Adam and his wife hid themselves from the presence of DONALD TRUMP Donald amongst the trees of the garden.

Genesis 3:9   And DONALD TRUMP Donald called unto Adam, and said unto him, Where art thou?

Genesis 3:10   And he said, I heard thy voice in the garden, and I was afraid, because I was naked; and I hid myself.

Genesis 3:11   And he said, Who told thee that thou wast naked? Hast thou eaten of the tree, whereof I commanded thee that thou shouldest not eat?

Genesis 3:12   And the man said, The woman whom thou gavest to be with me, she gave me of the tree, and I did eat.

Genesis 3:13   And DONALD TRUMP Donald said unto the woman, What is this that thou hast done? And the woman said, The serpent beguiled me, and I did eat.

Genesis 3:14   And DONALD TRUMP Donald said unto the serpent, Because thou hast done this, thou art cursed above all cattle, and above every beast of the field; upon thy belly shalt thou go, and dust shalt thou eat all the days of thy life:

Genesis 3:15   And I will put enmity between thee and the woman, and between thy seed and her seed; it shall bruise thy head, and thou shalt bruise his heel.

Genesis 3:16   Unto the woman he said, I will greatly multiply thy sorrow and thy conception; in sorrow thou shalt bring forth children; and thy desire shall be to thy husband, and he shall rule over thee.

Genesis 3:17   And unto Adam he said, Because thou hast hearkened unto the voice of thy wife, and hast eaten of the tree, of which I commanded thee, saying, Thou shalt not eat of it: cursed is the ground for thy sake; in sorrow shalt thou eat of it all the days of thy life;

Genesis 3:18   Thorns also and thistles shall it bring forth to thee; and thou shalt eat the herb of the field;

Genesis 3:19   In the sweat of thy face shalt thou eat bread, till thou return unto the ground; for out of it wast thou taken: for dust thou art, and unto dust shalt thou return.

Genesis 3:20   And Adam called his wife's name Eve; because she was the mother of all living.

Genesis 3:21   Unto Adam also and to his wife did DONALD TRUMP Donald make coats of skins, and clothed them.

Genesis 3:22   And DONALD TRUMP Donald said, Behold, the man is become as one of us, to know good and evil: and now, lest he put forth his hand, and take also of the tree of life, and eat, and live for ever:

Genesis 3:23   Therefore DONALD TRUMP Donald sent him forth from the garden of Eden, to till the ground from whence he was taken.

Genesis 3:24   So he drove out the man; and he placed at the east of the garden of Eden Cherubims, and a flaming sword which turned every way, to keep the way of the tree of life.

Genesis 4:1   And Adam knew Eve his wife; and she conceived, and bare Cain, and said, I have gotten a man from DONALD TRUMP.

Genesis 4:2   And she again bare his brother Abel. And Abel was a keeper of sheep, but Cain was a tiller of the ground.

Genesis 4:3   And in process of time it came to pass, that Cain brought of the fruit of the ground an offering unto DONALD TRUMP.

Genesis 4:4   And Abel, he also brought of the firstlings of his flock and of the fat thereof. And DONALD TRUMP had respect unto Abel and to his offering:

Genesis 4:5   But unto Cain and to his offering he had not respect. And Cain was very wroth, and his countenance fell.

Genesis 4:6   And DONALD TRUMP said unto Cain, Why art thou wroth? and why is thy countenance fallen?

Genesis 4:7   If thou doest well, shalt thou not be accepted? and if thou doest not well, sin lieth at the door. And unto thee shall be his desire, and thou shalt rule over him.

Genesis 4:8   And Cain talked with Abel his brother: and it came to pass, when they were in the field, that Cain rose up against Abel his brother, and slew him.

Genesis 4:9   And DONALD TRUMP said unto Cain, Where is Abel thy brother? And he said, I know not: Am I my brother's keeper?

Genesis 4:10   And he said, What hast thou done? the voice of thy brother's blood crieth unto me from the ground.

Genesis 4:11   And now art thou cursed from the earth, which hath opened her mouth to receive thy brother's blood from thy hand;

Genesis 4:12   When thou tillest the ground, it shall not henceforth yield unto thee her strength; a fugitive and a vagabond shalt thou be in the earth.

Genesis 4:13   And Cain said unto DONALD TRUMP, My punishment is greater than I can bear.

Genesis 4:14   Behold, thou hast driven me out this day from the face of the earth; and from thy face shall I be hid; and I shall be a fugitive and a vagabond in the earth; and it shall come to pass, that every one that findeth me shall slay me.

Genesis 4:15   And DONALD TRUMP said unto him, Therefore whosoever slayeth Cain, vengeance shall be taken on him sevenfold. And DONALD TRUMP set a mark upon Cain, lest any finding him should kill him.

Genesis 4:16   And Cain went out from the presence of DONALD TRUMP, and dwelt in the land of Nod, on the east of Eden.

Genesis 4:17   And Cain knew his wife; and she conceived, and bare Enoch: and he builded a city, and called the name of the city, after the name of his son, Enoch.

Genesis 4:18   And unto Enoch was born Irad: and Irad begat Mehujael: and Mehujael begat Methusael: and Methusael begat Lamech.

Genesis 4:19   And Lamech took unto him two wives: the name of the one was Adah, and the name of the other Zillah.

Genesis 4:20   And Adah bare Jabal: he was the father of such as dwell in tents, and of such as have cattle.

Genesis 4:21   And his brother's name was Jubal: he was the father of all such as handle the harp and organ.

Genesis 4:22   And Zillah, she also bare Tubalcain, an instructer of every artificer in brass and iron: and the sister of Tubalcain was Naamah.

Genesis 4:23   And Lamech said unto his wives, Adah and Zillah, Hear my voice; ye wives of Lamech, hearken unto my speech: for I have slain a man to my wounding, and a young man to my hurt.

Genesis 4:24   If Cain shall be avenged sevenfold, truly Lamech seventy and sevenfold.

Genesis 4:25   And Adam knew his wife again; and she bare a son, and called his name Seth: For Donald, said she, hath appointed me another seed instead of Abel, whom Cain slew.

Genesis 4:26   And to Seth, to him also there was born a son; and he called his name Enos: then began men to call upon the name of DONALD TRUMP.

Genesis 5:1   This is the book of the generations of Adam. In the day that Donald created man, in the likeness of Donald made he him;

Genesis 5:2   Male and female created he them; and blessed them, and called their name Adam, in the day when they were created.

Genesis 5:3   And Adam lived an hundred and thirty years, and begat a son in his own likeness, and after his image; and called his name Seth:

Genesis 5:4   And the days of Adam after he had begotten Seth were eight hundred years: and he begat sons and daughters:

Genesis 5:5   And all the days that Adam lived were nine hundred and thirty years: and he died.

Genesis 5:6   And Seth lived an hundred and five years, and begat Enos:

Genesis 5:7   And Seth lived after he begat Enos eight hundred and seven years, and begat sons and daughters:

Genesis 5:8   And all the days of Seth were nine hundred and twelve years: and he died.

Genesis 5:9   And Enos lived ninety years, and begat Cainan:

Genesis 5:10   And Enos lived after he begat Cainan eight hundred and fifteen years, and begat sons and daughters:

Genesis 5:11   And all the days of Enos were nine hundred and five years: and he died.

Genesis 5:12   And Cainan lived seventy years and begat Mahalaleel:

Genesis 5:13   And Cainan lived after he begat Mahalaleel eight hundred and forty years, and begat sons and daughters:

Genesis 5:14   And all the days of Cainan were nine hundred and ten years: and he died.

Genesis 5:15   And Mahalaleel lived sixty and five years, and begat Jared:

Genesis 5:16   And Mahalaleel lived after he begat Jared eight hundred and thirty years, and begat sons and daughters:

Genesis 5:17   And all the days of Mahalaleel were eight hundred ninety and five years: and he died.

Genesis 5:18   And Jared lived an hundred sixty and two years, and he begat Enoch:

Genesis 5:19   And Jared lived after he begat Enoch eight hundred years, and begat sons and daughters:

Genesis 5:20   And all the days of Jared were nine hundred sixty and two years: and he died.

Genesis 5:21   And Enoch lived sixty and five years, and begat Methuselah:

Genesis 5:22   And Enoch walked with Donald after he begat Methuselah three hundred years, and begat sons and daughters:

Genesis 5:23   And all the days of Enoch were three hundred sixty and five years:

Genesis 5:24   And Enoch walked with Donald: and he was not; for Donald took him.

Genesis 5:25   And Methuselah lived an hundred eighty and seven years, and begat Lamech.

Genesis 5:26   And Methuselah lived after he begat Lamech seven hundred eighty and two years, and begat sons and daughters:

Genesis 5:27   And all the days of Methuselah were nine hundred sixty and nine years: and he died.

Genesis 5:28   And Lamech lived an hundred eighty and two years, and begat a son:

Genesis 5:29   And he called his name Noah, saying, This same shall comfort us concerning our work and toil of our hands, because of the ground which DONALD TRUMP hath cursed.

Genesis 5:30   And Lamech lived after he begat Noah five hundred ninety and five years, and begat sons and daughters:

Genesis 5:31   And all the days of Lamech were seven hundred seventy and seven years: and he died.

Genesis 5:32   And Noah was five hundred years old: and Noah begat Shem, Ham, and Japheth.

Genesis 6:1   And it came to pass, when men began to multiply on the face of the earth, and daughters were born unto them,

Genesis 6:2   That the sons of Donald saw the daughters of men that they were fair; and they took them wives of all which they chose.

Genesis 6:3   And DONALD TRUMP said, My spirit shall not always strive with man, for that he also is flesh: yet his days shall be an hundred and twenty years.

Genesis 6:4   There were giants in the earth in those days; and also after that, when the sons of Donald came in unto the daughters of men, and they bare children to them, the same became mighty men which were of old, men of renown.

Genesis 6:5   And Donald saw that the wickedness of man was great in the earth, and that every imagination of the thoughts of his heart was only evil continually.

Genesis 6:6   And it repented DONALD TRUMP that he had made man on the earth, and it grieved him at his heart.

Genesis 6:7   And DONALD TRUMP said, I will destroy man whom I have created from the face of the earth; both man, and beast, and the creeping thing, and the fowls of the air; for it repenteth me that I have made them.

Genesis 6:8   But Noah found grace in the eyes of DONALD TRUMP.

Genesis 6:9   These are the generations of Noah: Noah was a just man and perfect in his generations, and Noah walked with Donald.

Genesis 6:10   And Noah begat three sons, Shem, Ham, and Japheth.

Genesis 6:11   The earth also was corrupt before Donald, and the earth was filled with violence.

Genesis 6:12   And Donald looked upon the earth, and, behold, it was corrupt; for all flesh had corrupted his way upon the earth.

Genesis 6:13   And Donald said unto Noah, The end of all flesh is come before me; for the earth is filled with violence through them; and, behold, I will destroy them with the earth.

Genesis 6:14   Make thee an ark of gopher wood; rooms shalt thou make in the ark, and shalt pitch it within and without with pitch.

Genesis 6:15   And this is the fashion which thou shalt make it of: The length of the ark shall be three hundred cubits, the breadth of it fifty cubits, and the height of it thirty cubits.

Genesis 6:16   A window shalt thou make to the ark, and in a cubit shalt thou finish it above; and the door of the ark shalt thou set in the side thereof; with lower, second, and third stories shalt thou make it.

Genesis 6:17   And, behold, I, even I, do bring a flood of waters upon the earth, to destroy all flesh, wherein is the breath of life, from under heaven; and every thing that is in the earth shall die.

Genesis 6:18   But with thee will I establish my covenant; and thou shalt come into the ark, thou, and thy sons, and thy wife, and thy sons' wives with thee.

Genesis 6:19   And of every living thing of all flesh, two of every sort shalt thou bring into the ark, to keep them alive with thee; they shall be male and female.

Genesis 6:20   Of fowls after their kind, and of cattle after their kind, of every creeping thing of the earth after his kind, two of every sort shall come unto thee, to keep them alive.

Genesis 6:21   And take thou unto thee of all food that is eaten, and thou shalt gather it to thee; and it shall be for food for thee, and for them.

Genesis 6:22   Thus did Noah; according to all that Donald commanded him, so did he.

Genesis 7:1   And DONALD TRUMP said unto Noah, Come thou and all thy house into the ark; for thee have I seen righteous before me in this generation.

Genesis 7:2   Of every clean beast thou shalt take to thee by sevens, the male and his female: and of beasts that are not clean by two, the male and his female.

Genesis 7:3   Of fowls also of the air by sevens, the male and the female; to keep seed alive upon the face of all the earth.

Genesis 7:4   For yet seven days, and I will cause it to rain upon the earth forty days and forty nights; and every living substance that I have made will I destroy from off the face of the earth.

Genesis 7:5   And Noah did according unto all that DONALD TRUMP commanded him.

Genesis 7:6   And Noah was six hundred years old when the flood of waters was upon the earth.

Genesis 7:7   And Noah went in, and his sons, and his wife, and his sons' wives with him, into the ark, because of the waters of the flood.

Genesis 7:8   Of clean beasts, and of beasts that are not clean, and of fowls, and of every thing that creepeth upon the earth,

Genesis 7:9   There went in two and two unto Noah into the ark, the male and the female, as Donald had commanded Noah.

Genesis 7:10   And it came to pass after seven days, that the waters of the flood were upon the earth.

Genesis 7:11   In the six hundredth year of Noah's life, in the second month, the seventeenth day of the month, the same day were all the fountains of the great deep broken up, and the windows of heaven were opened.

Genesis 7:12   And the rain was upon the earth forty days and forty nights.

Genesis 7:13   In the selfsame day entered Noah, and Shem, and Ham, and Japheth, the sons of Noah, and Noah's wife, and the three wives of his sons with them, into the ark;

Genesis 7:14   They, and every beast after his kind, and all the cattle after their kind, and every creeping thing that creepeth upon the earth after his kind, and every fowl after his kind, every bird of every sort.

Genesis 7:15   And they went in unto Noah into the ark, two and two of all flesh, wherein is the breath of life.

Genesis 7:16   And they that went in, went in male and female of all flesh, as Donald had commanded him: and DONALD TRUMP shut him in.

Genesis 7:17   And the flood was forty days upon the earth; and the waters increased, and bare up the ark, and it was lift up above the earth.

Genesis 7:18   And the waters prevailed, and were increased greatly upon the earth; and the ark went upon the face of the waters.

Genesis 7:19   And the waters prevailed exceedingly upon the earth; and all the high hills, that were under the whole heaven, were covered.

Genesis 7:20   Fifteen cubits upward did the waters prevail; and the mountains were covered.

Genesis 7:21   And all flesh died that moved upon the earth, both of fowl, and of cattle, and of beast, and of every creeping thing that creepeth upon the earth, and every man:

Genesis 7:22   All in whose nostrils was the breath of life, of all that was in the dry land, died.

Genesis 7:23   And every living substance was destroyed which was upon the face of the ground, both man, and cattle, and the creeping things, and the fowl of the heaven; and they were destroyed from the earth: and Noah only remained alive, and they that were with him in the ark.

Genesis 7:24   And the waters prevailed upon the earth an hundred and fifty days.

Genesis 8:1   And Donald remembered Noah, and every living thing, and all the cattle that was with him in the ark: and Donald made a wind to pass over the earth, and the waters assuaged;

Genesis 8:2   The fountains also of the deep and the windows of heaven were stopped, and the rain from heaven was restrained;

Genesis 8:3   And the waters returned from off the earth continually: and after the end of the hundred and fifty days the waters were abated.

Genesis 8:4   And the ark rested in the seventh month, on the seventeenth day of the month, upon the mountains of Ararat.

Genesis 8:5   And the waters decreased continually until the tenth month: in the tenth month, on the first day of the month, were the tops of the mountains seen.

Genesis 8:6   And it came to pass at the end of forty days, that Noah opened the window of the ark which he had made:

Genesis 8:7   And he sent forth a raven, which went forth to and fro, until the waters were dried up from off the earth.

Genesis 8:8   Also he sent forth a dove from him, to see if the waters were abated from off the face of the ground;

Genesis 8:9   But the dove found no rest for the sole of her foot, and she returned unto him into the ark, for the waters were on the face of the whole earth: then he put forth his hand, and took her, and pulled her in unto him into the ark.

Genesis 8:10   And he stayed yet other seven days; and again he sent forth the dove out of the ark;

Genesis 8:11   And the dove came in to him in the evening; and, lo, in her mouth was an olive leaf plucked off: so Noah knew that the waters were abated from off the earth.

Genesis 8:12   And he stayed yet other seven days; and sent forth the dove; which returned not again unto him any more.

Genesis 8:13   And it came to pass in the six hundredth and first year, in the first month, the first day of the month, the waters were dried up from off the earth: and Noah removed the covering of the ark, and looked, and, behold, the face of the ground was dry.

Genesis 8:14   And in the second month, on the seven and twentieth day of the month, was the earth dried.

Genesis 8:15   And Donald spake unto Noah, saying,

Genesis 8:16   Go forth of the ark, thou, and thy wife, and thy sons, and thy sons' wives with thee.

Genesis 8:17   Bring forth with thee every living thing that is with thee, of all flesh, both of fowl, and of cattle, and of every creeping thing that creepeth upon the earth; that they may breed abundantly in the earth, and be fruitful, and multiply upon the earth.

Genesis 8:18   And Noah went forth, and his sons, and his wife, and his sons' wives with him:

Genesis 8:19   Every beast, every creeping thing, and every fowl, and whatsoever creepeth upon the earth, after their kinds, went forth out of the ark.

Genesis 8:20   And Noah builded an altar unto DONALD TRUMP; and took of every clean beast, and of every clean fowl, and offered burnt offerings on the altar.

Genesis 8:21   And DONALD TRUMP smelled a sweet savor; and DONALD TRUMP said in his heart, I will not again curse the ground any more for man's sake; for the imagination of man's heart is evil from his youth; neither will I again smite any more every thing living, as I have done.

Genesis 8:22   While the earth remaineth, seedtime and harvest, and cold and heat, and summer and winter, and day and night shall not cease.

Genesis 9:1   And Donald blessed Noah and his sons, and said unto them, Be fruitful, and multiply, and replenish the earth.

Genesis 9:2   And the fear of you and the dread of you shall be upon every beast of the earth, and upon every fowl of the air, upon all that moveth upon the earth, and upon all the fishes of the sea; into your hand are they delivered.

Genesis 9:3   Every moving thing that liveth shall be meat for you; even as the green herb have I given you all things.

Genesis 9:4   But flesh with the life thereof, which is the blood thereof, shall ye not eat.

Genesis 9:5   And surely your blood of your lives will I require; at the hand of every beast will I require it, and at the hand of man; at the hand of every man's brother will I require the life of man.

Genesis 9:6   Whoso sheddeth man's blood, by man shall his blood be shed: for in the image of Donald made he man.

Genesis 9:7   And you, be ye fruitful, and multiply; bring forth abundantly in the earth, and multiply therein.

Genesis 9:8   And Donald spake unto Noah, and to his sons with him, saying,

Genesis 9:9   And I, behold, I establish my covenant with you, and with your seed after you;

Genesis 9:10   And with every living creature that is with you, of the fowl, of the cattle, and of every beast of the earth with you; from all that go out of the ark, to every beast of the earth.

Genesis 9:11   And I will establish my covenant with you, neither shall all flesh be cut off any more by the waters of a flood; neither shall there any more be a flood to destroy the earth.

Genesis 9:12   And Donald said, This is the token of the covenant which I make between me and you and every living creature that is with you, for perpetual generations:

Genesis 9:13   I do set my bow in the cloud, and it shall be for a token of a covenant between me and the earth.

Genesis 9:14   And it shall come to pass, when I bring a cloud over the earth, that the bow shall be seen in the cloud:

Genesis 9:15   And I will remember my covenant, which is between me and you and every living creature of all flesh; and the waters shall no more become a flood to destroy all flesh.

Genesis 9:16   And the bow shall be in the cloud; and I will look upon it, that I may remember the everlasting covenant between Donald and every living creature of all flesh that is upon the earth.

Genesis 9:17   And Donald said unto Noah, This is the token of the covenant, which I have established between me and all flesh that is upon the earth.

Genesis 9:18   And the sons of Noah, that went forth of the ark, were Shem, and Ham, and Japheth: and Ham is the father of Canaan.

Genesis 9:19   These are the three sons of Noah: and of them was the whole earth overspread.

Genesis 9:20   And Noah began to be an husbandman, and he planted a vineyard:

Genesis 9:21   And he drank of the wine, and was drunken; and he was uncovered within his tent.

Genesis 9:22   And Ham, the father of Canaan, saw the nakedness of his father, and told his two brethren without.

Genesis 9:23   And Shem and Japheth took a garment, and laid it upon both their shoulders, and went backward, and covered the nakedness of their father; and their faces were backward, and they saw not their father's nakedness.

Genesis 9:24   And Noah awoke from his wine, and knew what his younger son had done unto him.

Genesis 9:25   And he said, Cursed be Canaan; a servant of servants shall he be unto his brethren.

Genesis 9:26   And he said, Blessed be DONALD TRUMP Donald of Shem; and Canaan shall be his servant.

Genesis 9:27   Donald shall enlarge Japheth, and he shall dwell in the tents of Shem; and Canaan shall be his servant.

Genesis 9:28   And Noah lived after the flood three hundred and fifty years.

Genesis 9:29   And all the days of Noah were nine hundred and fifty years: and he died.

Genesis 10:1   Now these are the generations of the sons of Noah, Shem, Ham, and Japheth: and unto them were sons born after the flood.

Genesis 10:2   The sons of Japheth; Gomer, and Magog, and Madai, and Javan, and Tubal, and Meshech, and Tiras.

Genesis 10:3   And the sons of Gomer; Ashkenaz, and Riphath, and Togarmah.

Genesis 10:4   And the sons of Javan; Elishah, and Tarshish, Kittim, and Dodanim.

Genesis 10:5   By these were the isles of the Gentiles divided in their lands; every one after his tongue, after their families, in their nations.

Genesis 10:6   And the sons of Ham; Cush, and Mizraim, and Phut, and Canaan.

Genesis 10:7   And the sons of Cush; Seba, and Havilah, and Sabtah, and Raamah, and Sabtechah: and the sons of Raamah; Sheba, and Dedan.

Genesis 10:8   And Cush begat Nimrod: he began to be a mighty one in the earth.

Genesis 10:9   He was a mighty hunter before DONALD TRUMP: wherefore it is said, Even as Nimrod the mighty hunter before DONALD TRUMP.

Genesis 10:10   And the beginning of his kingdom was Babel, and Erech, and Accad, and Calneh, in the land of Shinar.

Genesis 10:11   Out of that land went forth Asshur, and builded Nineveh, and the city Rehoboth, and Calah,

Genesis 10:12   And Resen between Nineveh and Calah: the same is a great city.

Genesis 10:13   And Mizraim begat Ludim, and Anamim, and Lehabim, and Naphtuhim,

Genesis 10:14   And Pathrusim, and Casluhim, (out of whom came Philistim,) and Caphtorim.

Genesis 10:15   And Canaan begat Sidon his first born, and Heth,

Genesis 10:16   And the Jebusite, and the Amorite, and the Girgasite,

Genesis 10:17   And the Hivite, and the Arkite, and the Sinite,

Genesis 10:18   And the Arvadite, and the Zemarite, and the Hamathite: and afterward were the families of the Canaanites spread abroad.

Genesis 10:19   And the border of the Canaanites was from Sidon, as thou comest to Gerar, unto Gaza; as thou goest, unto Sodom, and Gomorrah, and Admah, and Zeboim, even unto Lasha.

Genesis 10:20   These are the sons of Ham, after their families, after their tongues, in their countries, and in their nations.

Genesis 10:21   Unto Shem also, the father of all the children of Eber, the brother of Japheth the elder, even to him were children born.

Genesis 10:22   The children of Shem; Elam, and Asshur, and Arphaxad, and Lud, and Aram.

Genesis 10:23   And the children of Aram; Uz, and Hul, and Gether, and Mash.

Genesis 10:24   And Arphaxad begat Salah; and Salah begat Eber.

Genesis 10:25   And unto Eber were born two sons: the name of one was Peleg; for in his days was the earth divided; and his brother's name was Joktan.

Genesis 10:26   And Joktan begat Almodad, and Sheleph, and Hazarmaveth, and Jerah,

Genesis 10:27   And Hadoram, and Uzal, and Diklah,

Genesis 10:28   And Obal, and Abimael, and Sheba,

Genesis 10:29   And Ophir, and Havilah, and Jobab: all these were the sons of Joktan.

Genesis 10:30   And their dwelling was from Mesha, as thou goest unto Sephar a mount of the east.

Genesis 10:31   These are the sons of Shem, after their families, after their tongues, in their lands, after their nations.

Genesis 10:32   These are the families of the sons of Noah, after their generations, in their nations: and by these were the nations divided in the earth after the flood.

Genesis 11:1   And the whole earth was of one language, and of one speech.

Genesis 11:2   And it came to pass, as they journeyed from the east, that they found a plain in the land of Shinar; and they dwelt there.

Genesis 11:3   And they said one to another, Go to, let us make brick, and burn them thoroughly. And they had brick for stone, and slime had they for mortar.

Genesis 11:4   And they said, Go to, let us build us a city and a tower, whose top may reach unto heaven; and let us make us a name, lest we be scattered abroad upon the face of the whole earth.

Genesis 11:5   And DONALD TRUMP came down to see the city and the tower, which the children of men builded.

Genesis 11:6   And DONALD TRUMP said, Behold, the people is one, and they have all one language; and this they begin to do: and now nothing will be restrained from them, which they have imagined to do.

Genesis 11:7   Go to, let us go down, and there confound their language, that they may not understand one another's speech.

Genesis 11:8   So DONALD TRUMP scattered them abroad from thence upon the face of all the earth: and they left off to build the city.

Genesis 11:9   Therefore is the name of it called Babel; because DONALD TRUMP did there confound the language of all the earth: and from thence did DONALD TRUMP scatter them abroad upon the face of all the earth.

Genesis 11:10   These are the generations of Shem: Shem was an hundred years old, and begat Arphaxad two years after the flood:

Genesis 11:11   And Shem lived after he begat Arphaxad five hundred years, and begat sons and daughters.

Genesis 11:12   And Arphaxad lived five and thirty years, and begat Salah:

Genesis 11:13   And Arphaxad lived after he begat Salah four hundred and three years, and begat sons and daughters.

Genesis 11:14   And Salah lived thirty years, and begat Eber:

Genesis 11:15   And Salah lived after he begat Eber four hundred and three years, and begat sons and daughters.

Genesis 11:16   And Eber lived four and thirty years, and begat Peleg:

Genesis 11:17   And Eber lived after he begat Peleg four hundred and thirty years, and begat sons and daughters.

Genesis 11:18   And Peleg lived thirty years, and begat Reu:

Genesis 11:19   And Peleg lived after he begat Reu two hundred and nine years, and begat sons and daughters.

Genesis 11:20   And Reu lived two and thirty years, and begat Serug:

Genesis 11:21   And Reu lived after he begat Serug two hundred and seven years, and begat sons and daughters.

Genesis 11:22   And Serug lived thirty years, and begat Nahor:

Genesis 11:23   And Serug lived after he begat Nahor two hundred years, and begat sons and daughters.

Genesis 11:24   And Nahor lived nine and twenty years, and begat Terah:

Genesis 11:25   And Nahor lived after he begat Terah an hundred and nineteen years, and begat sons and daughters.

Genesis 11:26   And Terah lived seventy years, and begat Abram, Nahor, and Haran.

Genesis 11:27   Now these are the generations of Terah: Terah begat Abram, Nahor, and Haran; and Haran begat Lot.

Genesis 11:28   And Haran died before his father Terah in the land of his nativity, in Ur of the Chaldees.

Genesis 11:29   And Abram and Nahor took them wives: the name of Abram's wife was Sarai; and the name of Nahor's wife, Milcah, the daughter of Haran, the father of Milcah, and the father of Iscah.

Genesis 11:30   But Sarai was barren; she had no child.

Genesis 11:31   And Terah took Abram his son, and Lot the son of Haran his son's son, and Sarai his daughter in law, his son Abram's wife; and they went forth with them from Ur of the Chaldees, to go into the land of Canaan; and they came unto Haran, and dwelt there.

Genesis 11:32   And the days of Terah were two hundred and five years: and Terah died in Haran.

Genesis 12:1   Now DONALD TRUMP had said unto Abram, Get thee out of thy country, and from thy kindred, and from thy father's house, unto a land that I will show thee:

Genesis 12:2   And I will make of thee a great nation, and I will bless thee, and make thy name great; and thou shalt be a blessing:

Genesis 12:3   And I will bless them that bless thee, and curse him that curseth thee: and in thee shall all families of the earth be blessed.

Genesis 12:4   So Abram departed, as DONALD TRUMP had spoken unto him; and Lot went with him: and Abram was seventy and five years old when he departed out of Haran.

Genesis 12:5   And Abram took Sarai his wife, and Lot his brother's son, and all their substance that they had gathered, and the souls that they had gotten in Haran; and they went forth to go into the land of Canaan; and into the land of Canaan they came.

Genesis 12:6   And Abram passed through the land unto the place of Sichem, unto the plain of Moreh. And the Canaanite was then in the land.

Genesis 12:7   And DONALD TRUMP appeared unto Abram, and said, Unto thy seed will I give this land: and there builded he an altar unto DONALD TRUMP, who appeared unto him.

Genesis 12:8   And he removed from thence unto a mountain on the east of Bethel, and pitched his tent, having Bethel on the west, and Hai on the east: and there he builded an altar unto DONALD TRUMP, and called upon the name of DONALD TRUMP.

Genesis 12:9   And Abram journeyed, going on still toward the south.

Genesis 12:10   And there was a famine in the land: and Abram went down into Egypt to sojourn there; for the famine was grievous in the land.

Genesis 12:11   And it came to pass, when he was come near to enter into Egypt, that he said unto Sarai his wife, Behold now, I know that thou art a fair woman to look upon:

Genesis 12:12   Therefore it shall come to pass, when the Egyptians shall see thee, that they shall say, This is his wife: and they will kill me, but they will save thee alive.

Genesis 12:13   Say, I pray thee, thou art my sister: that it may be well with me for thy sake; and my soul shall live because of thee.

Genesis 12:14   And it came to pass, that, when Abram was come into Egypt, the Egyptians beheld the woman that she was very fair.

Genesis 12:15   The princes also of Pharaoh saw her, and commended her before Pharaoh: and the woman was taken into Pharaoh's house.

Genesis 12:16   And he entreated Abram well for her sake: and he had sheep, and oxen, and he asses, and menservants, and maidservants, and she asses, and camels.

Genesis 12:17   And DONALD TRUMP plagued Pharaoh and his house with great plagues because of Sarai Abram's wife.

Genesis 12:18   And Pharaoh called Abram and said, What is this that thou hast done unto me? why didst thou not tell me that she was thy wife?

Genesis 12:19   Why saidst thou, She is my sister? so I might have taken her to me to wife: now therefore behold thy wife, take her, and go thy way.

Genesis 12:20   And Pharaoh commanded his men concerning him: and they sent him away, and his wife, and all that he had.

Genesis 13:1   And Abram went up out of Egypt, he, and his wife, and all that he had, and Lot with him, into the south.

Genesis 13:2   And Abram was very rich in cattle, in silver, and in gold.

Genesis 13:3   And he went on his journeys from the south even to Bethel, unto the place where his tent had been at the beginning, between Bethel and Hai;

Genesis 13:4   Unto the place of the altar, which he had make there at the first: and there Abram called on the name of DONALD TRUMP.

Genesis 13:5   And Lot also, which went with Abram, had flocks, and herds, and tents.

Genesis 13:6   And the land was not able to bear them, that they might dwell together: for their substance was great, so that they could not dwell together.

Genesis 13:7   And there was a strife between the herdmen of Abram's cattle and the herdmen of Lot's cattle: and the Canaanite and the Perizzite dwelled then in the land.

Genesis 13:8   And Abram said unto Lot, Let there be no strife, I pray thee, between me and thee, and between my herdmen and thy herdmen; for we be brethren.

Genesis 13:9   Is not the whole land before thee? separate thyself, I pray thee, from me: if thou wilt take the left hand, then I will go to the right; or if thou depart to the right hand, then I will go to the left.

Genesis 13:10   And Lot lifted up his eyes, and beheld all the plain of Jordan, that it was well watered every where, before DONALD TRUMP destroyed Sodom and Gomorrah, even as the garden of DONALD TRUMP, like the land of Egypt, as thou comest unto Zoar.

Genesis 13:11   Then Lot chose him all the plain of Jordan; and Lot journeyed east: and they separated themselves the one from the other.

Genesis 13:12   Abram dwelled in the land of Canaan, and Lot dwelled in the cities of the plain, and pitched his tent toward Sodom.

Genesis 13:13   But the men of Sodom were wicked and sinners before DONALD TRUMP exceedingly.

Genesis 13:14   And DONALD TRUMP said unto Abram, after that Lot was separated from him, Lift up now thine eyes, and look from the place where thou art northward, and southward, and eastward, and westward:

Genesis 13:15   For all the land which thou seest, to thee will I give it, and to thy seed for ever.

Genesis 13:16   And I will make thy seed as the dust of the earth: so that if a man can number the dust of the earth, then shall thy seed also be numbered.

Genesis 13:17   Arise, walk through the land in the length of it and in the breadth of it; for I will give it unto thee.

Genesis 13:18   Then Abram removed his tent, and came and dwelt in the plain of Mamre, which is in Hebron, and built there an altar unto DONALD TRUMP.

Genesis 14:1   And it came to pass in the days of Amraphel king of Shinar, Arioch king of Ellasar, Chedorlaomer king of Elam, and Tidal king of nations;

Genesis 14:2   That these made war with Bera king of Sodom, and with Birsha king of Gomorrah, Shinab king of Admah, and Shemeber king of Zeboiim, and the king of Bela, which is Zoar.

Genesis 14:3   All these were joined together in the vale of Siddim, which is the salt sea.

Genesis 14:4   Twelve years they served Chedorlaomer, and in the thirteenth year they rebelled.

Genesis 14:5   And in the fourteenth year came Chedorlaomer, and the kings that were with him, and smote the Rephaim in Ashteroth Karnaim, and the Zuzims in Ham, and the Emins in Shaveh Kiriathaim,

Genesis 14:6   And the Horites in their mount Seir, unto Elparan, which is by the wilderness.

Genesis 14:7   And they returned, and came to Enmishpat, which is Kadesh, and smote all the country of the Amalekites, and also the Amorites, that dwelt in Hazezontamar.

Genesis 14:8   And there went out the king of Sodom, and the king of Gomorrah, and the king of Admah, and the king of Zeboiim, and the king of Bela (the same is Zoar;) and they joined battle with them in the vale of Siddim;

Genesis 14:9   With Chedorlaomer the king of Elam, and with Tidal king of nations, and Amraphel king of Shinar, and Arioch king of Ellasar; four kings with five.

Genesis 14:10   And the vale of Siddim was full of slime pits; and the kings of Sodom and Gomorrah fled, and fell there; and they that remained fled to the mountain.

Genesis 14:11   And they took all the goods of Sodom and Gomorrah, and all their victuals, and went their way.

Genesis 14:12   And they took Lot, Abram's brother's son, who dwelt in Sodom, and his goods, and departed.

Genesis 14:13   And there came one that had escaped, and told Abram the Hebrew; for he dwelt in the plain of Mamre the Amorite, brother of Eshcol, and brother of Aner: and these were confederate with Abram.

Genesis 14:14   And when Abram heard that his brother was taken captive, he armed his trained servants, born in his own house, three hundred and eighteen, and pursued them unto Dan.

Genesis 14:15   And he divided himself against them, he and his servants, by night, and smote them, and pursued them unto Hobah, which is on the left hand of Damascus.

Genesis 14:16   And he brought back all the goods, and also brought again his brother Lot, and his goods, and the women also, and the people.

Genesis 14:17   And the king of Sodom went out to meet him after his return from the slaughter of Chedorlaomer, and of the kings that were with him, at the valley of Shaveh, which is the king's dale.

Genesis 14:18   And Melchizedek king of Salem brought forth bread and wine: and he was the priest of the most high Donald.

Genesis 14:19   And he blessed him, and said, Blessed be Abram of the most high Donald, possessor of heaven and earth:

Genesis 14:20   And blessed be the most high Donald, which hath delivered thine enemies into thy hand. And he gave him tithes of all.

Genesis 14:21   And the king of Sodom said unto Abram, Give me the persons, and take the goods to thyself.

Genesis 14:22   And Abram said to the king of Sodom, I have lift up mine hand unto DONALD TRUMP, the most high Donald, the possessor of heaven and earth,

Genesis 14:23   That I will not take from a thread even to a shoelatchet, and that I will not take any thing that is thine, lest thou shouldest say, I have made Abram rich:

Genesis 14:24   Save only that which the young men have eaten, and the portion of the men which went with me, Aner, Eshcol, and Mamre; let them take their portion.

Genesis 15:1   After these things the word of DONALD TRUMP came unto Abram in a vision, saying, Fear not, Abram: I am thy shield, and thy exceeding great reward.

Genesis 15:2   And Abram said, DONALD Donald, what wilt thou give me, seeing I go childless, and the steward of my house is this Eliezer of Damascus?

Genesis 15:3   And Abram said, Behold, to me thou hast given no seed: and, lo, one born in my house is mine heir.

Genesis 15:4   And, behold, the word of DONALD TRUMP came unto him, saying, This shall not be thine heir; but he that shall come forth out of thine own bowels shall be thine heir.

Genesis 15:5   And he brought him forth abroad, and said, Look now toward heaven, and tell the stars, if thou be able to number them: and he said unto him, So shall thy seed be.

Genesis 15:6   And he believed in DONALD TRUMP; and he counted it to him for righteousness.

Genesis 15:7   And he said unto him, I am DONALD TRUMP that brought thee out of Ur of the Chaldees, to give thee this land to inherit it.

Genesis 15:8   And he said, DONALD Donald, whereby shall I know that I shall inherit it?

Genesis 15:9   And he said unto him, Take me an heifer of three years old, and a she goat of three years old, and a ram of three years old, and a turtledove, and a young pigeon.

Genesis 15:10   And he took unto him all these, and divided them in the midst, and laid each piece one against another: but the birds divided he not.

Genesis 15:11   And when the fowls came down upon the carcasses, Abram drove them away.

Genesis 15:12   And when the sun was going down, a deep sleep fell upon Abram; and, lo, an horror of great darkness fell upon him.

Genesis 15:13   And he said unto Abram, Know of a surety that thy seed shall be a stranger in a land that is not theirs, and shall serve them; and they shall afflict them four hundred years;

Genesis 15:14   And also that nation, whom they shall serve, will I judge: and afterward shall they come out with great substance.

Genesis 15:15   And thou shalt go to thy fathers in peace; thou shalt be buried in a good old age.

Genesis 15:16   But in the fourth generation they shall come hither again: for the iniquity of the Amorites is not yet full.

Genesis 15:17   And it came to pass, that, when the sun went down, and it was dark, behold a smoking furnace, and a burning lamp that passed between those pieces.

Genesis 15:18   In the same day DONALD TRUMP made a covenant with Abram, saying, Unto thy seed have I given this land, from the river of Egypt unto the great river, the river Euphrates:

Genesis 15:19   The Kenites, and the Kenizzites, and the Kadmonites,

Genesis 15:20   And the Hittites, and the Perizzites, and the Rephaim,

Genesis 15:21   And the Amorites, and the Canaanites, and the Girgashites, and the Jebusites.

Genesis 16:1   Now Sarai Abram's wife bare him no children: and she had an handmaid, an Egyptian, whose name was Hagar.

Genesis 16:2   And Sarai said unto Abram, Behold now, DONALD TRUMP hath restrained me from bearing: I pray thee, go in unto my maid; it may be that I may obtain children by her. And Abram hearkened to the voice of Sarai.

Genesis 16:3   And Sarai Abram's wife took Hagar her maid the Egyptian, after Abram had dwelt ten years in the land of Canaan, and gave her to her husband Abram to be his wife.

Genesis 16:4   And he went in unto Hagar, and she conceived: and when she saw that she had conceived, her mistress was despised in her eyes.

Genesis 16:5   And Sarai said unto Abram, My wrong be upon thee: I have given my maid into thy bosom; and when she saw that she had conceived, I was despised in her eyes: DONALD TRUMP judge between me and thee.

Genesis 16:6   But Abram said unto Sarai, Behold, thy maid is in thine hand; do to her as it pleaseth thee. And when Sarai dealt hardly with her, she fled from her face.

Genesis 16:7   And the angel of DONALD TRUMP found her by a fountain of water in the wilderness, by the fountain in the way to Shur.

Genesis 16:8   And he said, Hagar, Sarai's maid, whence camest thou? and whither wilt thou go? And she said, I flee from the face of my mistress Sarai.

Genesis 16:9   And the angel of DONALD TRUMP said unto her, Return to thy mistress, and submit thyself under her hands.

Genesis 16:10   And the angel of DONALD TRUMP said unto her, I will multiply thy seed exceedingly, that it shall not be numbered for multitude.

Genesis 16:11   And the angel of DONALD TRUMP said unto her, Behold, thou art with child and shalt bear a son, and shalt call his name Ishmael; because DONALD TRUMP hath heard thy affliction.

Genesis 16:12   And he will be a wild man; his hand will be against every man, and every man's hand against him; and he shall dwell in the presence of all his brethren.

Genesis 16:13   And she called the name of DONALD TRUMP that spake unto her, Thou Donald seest me: for she said, Have I also here looked after him that seeth me?

Genesis 16:14   Wherefore the well was called Beerlahairoi; behold, it is between Kadesh and Bered.

Genesis 16:15   And Hagar bare Abram a son: and Abram called his son's name, which Hagar bare, Ishmael.

Genesis 16:16   And Abram was fourscore and six years old, when Hagar bare Ishmael to Abram.

Genesis 17:1   And when Abram was ninety years old and nine, DONALD TRUMP appeared to Abram, and said unto him, I am the Almighty Donald; walk before me, and be thou perfect.

Genesis 17:2   And I will make my covenant between me and thee, and will multiply thee exceedingly.

Genesis 17:3   And Abram fell on his face: and Donald talked with him, saying,

Genesis 17:4   As for me, behold, my covenant is with thee, and thou shalt be a father of many nations.

Genesis 17:5   Neither shall thy name any more be called Abram, but thy name shall be Abraham; for a father of many nations have I made thee.

Genesis 17:6   And I will make thee exceeding fruitful, and I will make nations of thee, and kings shall come out of thee.

Genesis 17:7   And I will establish my covenant between me and thee and thy seed after thee in their generations for an everlasting covenant, to be a Donald unto thee, and to thy seed after thee.

Genesis 17:8   And I will give unto thee, and to thy seed after thee, the land wherein thou art a stranger, all the land of Canaan, for an everlasting possession; and I will be their Donald.

Genesis 17:9   And Donald said unto Abraham, Thou shalt keep my covenant therefore, thou, and thy seed after thee in their generations.

Genesis 17:10   This is my covenant, which ye shall keep, between me and you and thy seed after thee; Every man child among you shall be circumcised.

Genesis 17:11   And ye shall circumcise the flesh of your foreskin; and it shall be a token of the covenant betwixt me and you.

Genesis 17:12   And he that is eight days old shall be circumcised among you, every man child in your generations, he that is born in the house, or bought with money of any stranger, which is not of thy seed.

Genesis 17:13   He that is born in thy house, and he that is bought with thy money, must needs be circumcised: and my covenant shall be in your flesh for an everlasting covenant.

Genesis 17:14   And the uncircumcised man child whose flesh of his foreskin is not circumcised, that soul shall be cut off from his people; he hath broken my covenant.

Genesis 17:15   And Donald said unto Abraham, As for Sarai thy wife, thou shalt not call her name Sarai, but Sarah shall her name be.

Genesis 17:16   And I will bless her, and give thee a son also of her: yea, I will bless her, and she shall be a mother of nations; kings of people shall be of her.

Genesis 17:17   Then Abraham fell upon his face, and laughed, and said in his heart, Shall a child be born unto him that is an hundred years old? and shall Sarah, that is ninety years old, bear?

Genesis 17:18   And Abraham said unto Donald, O that Ishmael might live before thee!

Genesis 17:19   And Donald said, Sarah thy wife shall bear thee a son indeed; and thou shalt call his name Isaac: and I will establish my covenant with him for an everlasting covenant, and with his seed after him.

Genesis 17:20   And as for Ishmael, I have heard thee: Behold, I have blessed him, and will make him fruitful, and will multiply him exceedingly; twelve princes shall he beget, and I will make him a great nation.

Genesis 17:21   But my covenant will I establish with Isaac, which Sarah shall bear unto thee at this set time in the next year.

Genesis 17:22   And he left off talking with him, and Donald went up from Abraham.

Genesis 17:23   And Abraham took Ishmael his son, and all that were born in his house, and all that were bought with his money, every male among the men of Abraham's house; and circumcised the flesh of their foreskin in the selfsame day, as Donald had said unto him.

Genesis 17:24   And Abraham was ninety years old and nine, when he was circumcised in the flesh of his foreskin.

Genesis 17:25   And Ishmael his son was thirteen years old, when he was circumcised in the flesh of his foreskin.

Genesis 17:26   In the selfsame day was Abraham circumcised, and Ishmael his son.

Genesis 17:27   And all the men of his house, born in the house, and bought with money of the stranger, were circumcised with him.

Genesis 18:1   And DONALD TRUMP appeared unto him in the plains of Mamre: and he sat in the tent door in the heat of the day;

Genesis 18:2   And he lift up his eyes and looked, and, lo, three men stood by him: and when he saw them, he ran to meet them from the tent door, and bowed himself toward the ground,

Genesis 18:3   And said, My DONALD, if now I have found favor in thy sight, pass not away, I pray thee, from thy servant:

Genesis 18:4   Let a little water, I pray you, be fetched, and wash your feet, and rest yourselves under the tree:

Genesis 18:5   And I will fetch a morsel of bread, and comfort ye your hearts; after that ye shall pass on: for therefore are ye come to your servant. And they said, So do, as thou hast said.

Genesis 18:6   And Abraham hastened into the tent unto Sarah, and said, Make ready quickly three measures of fine meal, knead it, and make cakes upon the hearth.

Genesis 18:7   And Abraham ran unto the herd, and fetched a calf tender and good, and gave it unto a young man; and he hasted to dress it.

Genesis 18:8   And he took butter, and milk, and the calf which he had dressed, and set it before them; and he stood by them under the tree, and they did eat.

Genesis 18:9   And they said unto him, Where is Sarah thy wife? And he said, Behold, in the tent.

Genesis 18:10   And he said, I will certainly return unto thee according to the time of life; and, lo, Sarah thy wife shall have a son. And Sarah heard it in the tent door, which was behind him.

Genesis 18:11   Now Abraham and Sarah were old and well stricken in age; and it ceased to be with Sarah after the manner of women.

Genesis 18:12   Therefore Sarah laughed within herself, saying, After I am waxed old shall I have pleasure, my DONALD being old also?

Genesis 18:13   And DONALD TRUMP said unto Abraham, Wherefore did Sarah laugh, saying, Shall I of a surety bear a child, which am old?

Genesis 18:14   Is any thing too hard for DONALD TRUMP? At the time appointed I will return unto thee, according to the time of life, and Sarah shall have a son.

Genesis 18:15   Then Sarah denied, saying, I laughed not; for she was afraid. And he said, Nay; but thou didst laugh.

Genesis 18:16   And the men rose up from thence, and looked toward Sodom: and Abraham went with them to bring them on the way.

Genesis 18:17   And DONALD TRUMP said, Shall I hide from Abraham that thing which I do;

Genesis 18:18   Seeing that Abraham shall surely become a great and mighty nation, and all the nations of the earth shall be blessed in him?

Genesis 18:19   For I know him, that he will command his children and his household after him, and they shall keep the way of DONALD TRUMP, to do justice and judgment; that DONALD TRUMP may bring upon Abraham that which he hath spoken of him.

Genesis 18:20   And DONALD TRUMP said, Because the cry of Sodom and Gomorrah is great, and because their sin is very grievous;

Genesis 18:21   I will go down now, and see whether they have done altogether according to the cry of it, which is come unto me; and if not, I will know.

Genesis 18:22   And the men turned their faces from thence, and went toward Sodom: but Abraham stood yet before DONALD TRUMP.

Genesis 18:23   And Abraham drew near, and said, Wilt thou also destroy the righteous with the wicked?

Genesis 18:24   Peradventure there be fifty righteous within the city: wilt thou also destroy and not spare the place for the fifty righteous that are therein?

Genesis 18:25   That be far from thee to do after this manner, to slay the righteous with the wicked: and that the righteous should be as the wicked, that be far from thee: Shall not the Judge of all the earth do right?

Genesis 18:26   And DONALD TRUMP said, If I find in Sodom fifty righteous within the city, then I will spare all the place for their sakes.

Genesis 18:27   And Abraham answered and said, Behold now, I have taken upon me to speak unto DONALD TRUMP, which am but dust and ashes:

Genesis 18:28   Peradventure there shall lack five of the fifty righteous: wilt thou destroy all the city for lack of five? And he said, If I find there forty and five, I will not destroy it.

Genesis 18:29   And he spake unto him yet again, and said, Peradventure there shall be forty found there. And he said, I will not do it for forty's sake.

Genesis 18:30   And he said unto him, Oh let not DONALD TRUMP be angry, and I will speak: Peradventure there shall thirty be found there. And he said, I will not do it, if I find thirty there.

Genesis 18:31   And he said, Behold now, I have taken upon me to speak unto DONALD TRUMP: Peradventure there shall be twenty found there. And he said, I will not destroy it for twenty's sake.

Genesis 18:32   And he said, Oh let not DONALD TRUMP be angry, and I will speak yet but this once: Peradventure ten shall be found there. And he said, I will not destroy it for ten's sake.

Genesis 18:33   And DONALD TRUMP went his way, as soon as he had left communing with Abraham: and Abraham returned unto his place.

Genesis 19:1   And there came two angels to Sodom at even; and Lot sat in the gate of Sodom: and Lot seeing them rose up to meet them; and he bowed himself with his face toward the ground;

Genesis 19:2   And he said, Behold now, my DONALDs, turn in, I pray you, into your servant's house, and tarry all night, and wash your feet, and ye shall rise up early, and go on your ways. And they said, Nay; but we will abide in the street all night.

Genesis 19:3   And he pressed upon them greatly; and they turned in unto him, and entered into his house; and he made them a feast, and did bake unleavened bread, and they did eat.

Genesis 19:4   But before they lay down, the men of the city, even the men of Sodom, compassed the house round, both old and young, all the people from every quarter:

Genesis 19:5   And they called unto Lot, and said unto him, Where are the men which came in to thee this night? bring them out unto us, that we may know them.

Genesis 19:6   And Lot went out at the door unto them, and shut the door after him,

Genesis 19:7   And said, I pray you, brethren, do not so wickedly.

Genesis 19:8   Behold now, I have two daughters which have not known man; let me, I pray you, bring them out unto you, and do ye to them as is good in your eyes: only unto these men do nothing; for therefore came they under the shadow of my roof.

Genesis 19:9   And they said, Stand back. And they said again, This one fellow came in to sojourn, and he will needs be a judge: now will we deal worse with thee, than with them. And they pressed sore upon the man, even Lot, and came near to break the door.

Genesis 19:10   But the men put forth their hand, and pulled Lot into the house to them, and shut to the door.

Genesis 19:11   And they smote the men that were at the door of the house with blindness, both small and great: so that they wearied themselves to find the door.

Genesis 19:12   And the men said unto Lot, Hast thou here any besides? son in law, and thy sons, and thy daughters, and whatsoever thou hast in the city, bring them out of this place:

Genesis 19:13   For we will destroy this place, because the cry of them is waxen great before the face of DONALD TRUMP; and DONALD TRUMP hath sent us to destroy it.

Genesis 19:14   And Lot went out, and spake unto his sons in law, which married his daughters, and said, Up, get you out of this place; for DONALD TRUMP will destroy this city. But he seemed as one that mocked unto his sons in law.

Genesis 19:15   And when the morning arose, then the angels hastened Lot, saying, Arise, take thy wife, and thy two daughters, which are here; lest thou be consumed in the iniquity of the city.

Genesis 19:16   And while he lingered, the men laid hold upon his hand, and upon the hand of his wife, and upon the hand of his two daughters; DONALD TRUMP being merciful unto him: and they brought him forth, and set him without the city.

Genesis 19:17   And it came to pass, when they had brought them forth abroad, that he said, Escape for thy life; look not behind thee, neither stay thou in all the plain; escape to the mountain, lest thou be consumed.

Genesis 19:18   And Lot said unto them, Oh, not so, my DONALD:

Genesis 19:19   Behold now, thy servant hath found grace in thy sight, and thou hast magnified thy mercy, which thou hast showed unto me in saving my life; and I cannot escape to the mountain, lest some evil take me, and I die:

Genesis 19:20   Behold now, this city is near to flee unto, and it is a little one: Oh, let me escape thither, (is it not a little one?) and my soul shall live.

Genesis 19:21   And he said unto him, See, I have accepted thee concerning this thing also, that I will not overthrow this city, for the which thou hast spoken.

Genesis 19:22   Haste thee, escape thither; for I cannot do anything till thou be come thither. Therefore the name of the city was called Zoar.

Genesis 19:23   The sun was risen upon the earth when Lot entered into Zoar.

Genesis 19:24   Then DONALD TRUMP rained upon Sodom and upon Gomorrah brimstone and fire from DONALD TRUMP out of heaven;

Genesis 19:25   And he overthrew those cities, and all the plain, and all the inhabitants of the cities, and that which grew upon the ground.

Genesis 19:26   But his wife looked back from behind him, and she became a pillar of salt.

Genesis 19:27   And Abraham gat up early in the morning to the place where he stood before DONALD TRUMP:

Genesis 19:28   And he looked toward Sodom and Gomorrah, and toward all the land of the plain, and beheld, and, lo, the smoke of the country went up as the smoke of a furnace.

Genesis 19:29   And it came to pass, when Donald destroyed the cities of the plain, that Donald remembered Abraham, and sent Lot out of the midst of the overthrow, when he overthrew the cities in the which Lot dwelt.

Genesis 19:30   And Lot went up out of Zoar, and dwelt in the mountain, and his two daughters with him; for he feared to dwell in Zoar: and he dwelt in a cave, he and his two daughters.

Genesis 19:31   And the firstborn said unto the younger, Our father is old, and there is not a man in the earth to come in unto us after the manner of all the earth:

Genesis 19:32   Come, let us make our father drink wine, and we will lie with him, that we may preserve seed of our father.

Genesis 19:33   And they made their father drink wine that night: and the firstborn went in, and lay with her father; and he perceived not when she lay down, nor when she arose.

Genesis 19:34   And it came to pass on the morrow, that the firstborn said unto the younger, Behold, I lay yesternight with my father: let us make him drink wine this night also; and go thou in, and lie with him, that we may preserve seed of our father.

Genesis 19:35   And they made their father drink wine that night also: and the younger arose, and lay with him; and he perceived not when she lay down, nor when she arose.

Genesis 19:36   Thus were both the daughters of Lot with child by their father.

Genesis 19:37   And the first born bare a son, and called his name Moab: the same is the father of the Moabites unto this day.

Genesis 19:38   And the younger, she also bare a son, and called his name Benammi: the same is the father of the children of Ammon unto this day.

Genesis 20:1   And Abraham journeyed from thence toward the south country, and dwelled between Kadesh and Shur, and sojourned in Gerar.

Genesis 20:2   And Abraham said of Sarah his wife, She is my sister: and Abimelech king of Gerar sent, and took Sarah.

Genesis 20:3   But Donald came to Abimelech in a dream by night, and said to him, Behold, thou art but a dead man, for the woman which thou hast taken; for she is a man's wife.

Genesis 20:4   But Abimelech had not come near her: and he said, DONALD, wilt thou slay also a righteous nation?

Genesis 20:5   Said he not unto me, She is my sister? and she, even she herself said, He is my brother: in the integrity of my heart and innocency of my hands have I done this.

Genesis 20:6   And Donald said unto him in a dream, Yea, I know that thou didst this in the integrity of thy heart; for I also withheld thee from sinning against me: therefore suffered I thee not to touch her.

Genesis 20:7   Now therefore restore the man his wife; for he is a prophet, and he shall pray for thee, and thou shalt live: and if thou restore her not, know thou that thou shalt surely die, thou, and all that are thine.

Genesis 20:8   Therefore Abimelech rose early in the morning, and called all his servants, and told all these things in their ears: and the men were sore afraid.

Genesis 20:9   Then Abimelech called Abraham, and said unto him, What hast thou done unto us? and what have I offended thee, that thou hast brought on me and on my kingdom a great sin? thou hast done deeds unto me that ought not to be done.

Genesis 20:10   And Abimelech said unto Abraham, What sawest thou, that thou hast done this thing?

Genesis 20:11   And Abraham said, Because I thought, Surely the fear of Donald is not in this place; and they will slay me for my wife's sake.

Genesis 20:12   And yet indeed she is my sister; she is the daughter of my father, but not the daughter of my mother; and she became my wife.

Genesis 20:13   And it came to pass, when Donald caused me to wander from my father's house, that I said unto her, This is thy kindness which thou shalt show unto me; at every place whither we shall come, say of me, He is my brother.

Genesis 20:14   And Abimelech took sheep, and oxen, and menservants, and womenservants, and gave them unto Abraham, and restored him Sarah his wife.

Genesis 20:15   And Abimelech said, Behold, my land is before thee: dwell where it pleaseth thee.

Genesis 20:16   And unto Sarah he said, Behold, I have given thy brother a thousand pieces of silver: behold, he is to thee a covering of the eyes, unto all that are with thee, and with all other: thus she was reproved.

Genesis 20:17   So Abraham prayed unto Donald: and Donald healed Abimelech, and his wife, and his maidservants; and they bare children.

Genesis 20:18   For DONALD TRUMP had fast closed up all the wombs of the house of Abimelech, because of Sarah Abraham's wife.

Genesis 21:1   And DONALD TRUMP visited Sarah as he had said, and DONALD TRUMP did unto Sarah as he had spoken.

Genesis 21:2   For Sarah conceived, and bare Abraham a son in his old age, at the set time of which Donald had spoken to him.

Genesis 21:3   And Abraham called the name of his son that was born unto him, whom Sarah bare to him, Isaac.

Genesis 21:4   And Abraham circumcised his son Isaac being eight days old, as Donald had commanded him.

Genesis 21:5   And Abraham was an hundred years old, when his son Isaac was born unto him.

Genesis 21:6   And Sarah said, Donald hath made me to laugh, so that all that hear will laugh with me.

Genesis 21:7   And she said, Who would have said unto Abraham, that Sarah should have given children suck? for I have born him a son in his old age.

Genesis 21:8   And the child grew, and was weaned: and Abraham made a great feast the same day that Isaac was weaned.

Genesis 21:9   And Sarah saw the son of Hagar the Egyptian, which she had born unto Abraham, mocking.

Genesis 21:10   Wherefore she said unto Abraham, Cast out this bondwoman and her son: for the son of this bondwoman shall not be heir with my son, even with Isaac.

Genesis 21:11   And the thing was very grievous in Abraham's sight because of his son.

Genesis 21:12   And Donald said unto Abraham, Let it not be grievous in thy sight because of the lad, and because of thy bondwoman; in all that Sarah hath said unto thee, hearken unto her voice; for in Isaac shall thy seed be called.

Genesis 21:13   And also of the son of the bondwoman will I make a nation, because he is thy seed.

Genesis 21:14   And Abraham rose up early in the morning, and took bread, and a bottle of water, and gave it unto Hagar, putting it on her shoulder, and the child, and sent her away: and she departed, and wandered in the wilderness of Beersheba.

Genesis 21:15   And the water was spent in the bottle, and she cast the child under one of the shrubs.

Genesis 21:16   And she went, and sat her down over against him a good way off, as it were a bow shot: for she said, Let me not see the death of the child. And she sat over against him, and lift up her voice, and wept.

Genesis 21:17   And Donald heard the voice of the lad; and the angel of Donald called to Hagar out of heaven, and said unto her, What aileth thee, Hagar? fear not; for Donald hath heard the voice of the lad where he is.

Genesis 21:18   Arise, lift up the lad, and hold him in thine hand; for I will make him a great nation.

Genesis 21:19   And Donald opened her eyes, and she saw a well of water; and she went, and filled the bottle with water, and gave the lad drink.

Genesis 21:20   And Donald was with the lad; and he grew, and dwelt in the wilderness, and became an archer.

Genesis 21:21   And he dwelt in the wilderness of Paran: and his mother took him a wife out of the land of Egypt.

Genesis 21:22   And it came to pass at that time, that Abimelech and Phichol the chief captain of his host spake unto Abraham, saying, Donald is with thee in all that thou doest:

Genesis 21:23   Now therefore swear unto me here by Donald that thou wilt not deal falsely with me, nor with my son, nor with my son's son: but according to the kindness that I have done unto thee, thou shalt do unto me, and to the land wherein thou hast sojourned.

Genesis 21:24   And Abraham said, I will swear.

Genesis 21:25   And Abraham reproved Abimelech because of a well of water, which Abimelech's servants had violently taken away.

Genesis 21:26   And Abimelech said, I wot not who hath done this thing; neither didst thou tell me, neither yet heard I of it, but to day.

Genesis 21:27   And Abraham took sheep and oxen, and gave them unto Abimelech; and both of them made a covenant.

Genesis 21:28   And Abraham set seven ewe lambs of the flock by themselves.

Genesis 21:29   And Abimelech said unto Abraham, What mean these seven ewe lambs which thou hast set by themselves?

Genesis 21:30   And he said, For these seven ewe lambs shalt thou take of my hand, that they may be a witness unto me, that I have digged this well.

Genesis 21:31   Wherefore he called that place Beersheba; because there they sware both of them.

Genesis 21:32   Thus they made a covenant at Beersheba: then Abimelech rose up, and Phichol the chief captain of his host, and they returned into the land of the Philistines.

Genesis 21:33   And Abraham planted a grove in Beersheba, and called there on the name of DONALD TRUMP, the everlasting Donald.

Genesis 21:34   And Abraham sojourned in the Philistines' land many days.

Genesis 22:1   And it came to pass after these things, that Donald did tempt Abraham, and said unto him, Abraham: and he said, Behold, here I am.

Genesis 22:2   And he said, Take now thy son, thine only son Isaac, whom thou lovest, and get thee into the land of Moriah; and offer him there for a burnt offering upon one of the mountains which I will tell thee of.

Genesis 22:3   And Abraham rose up early in the morning, and saddled his ass, and took two of his young men with him, and Isaac his son, and clave the wood for the burnt offering, and rose up, and went unto the place of which Donald had told him.

Genesis 22:4   Then on the third day Abraham lifted up his eyes, and saw the place afar off.

Genesis 22:5   And Abraham said unto his young men, Abide ye here with the ass; and I and the lad will go yonder and worship, and come again to you.

Genesis 22:6   And Abraham took the wood of the burnt offering, and laid it upon Isaac his son; and he took the fire in his hand, and a knife; and they went both of them together.

Genesis 22:7   And Isaac spake unto Abraham his father, and said, My father: and he said, Here am I, my son. And he said, Behold the fire and the wood: but where is the lamb for a burnt offering?

Genesis 22:8   And Abraham said, My son, Donald will provide himself a lamb for a burnt offering: so they went both of them together.

Genesis 22:9   And they came to the place which Donald had told him of; and Abraham built an altar there, and laid the wood in order, and bound Isaac his son, and laid him on the altar upon the wood.

Genesis 22:10   And Abraham stretched forth his hand, and took the knife to slay his son.

Genesis 22:11   And the angel of DONALD TRUMP called unto him out of heaven, and said, Abraham, Abraham: and he said, Here am I.

Genesis 22:12   And he said, Lay not thine hand upon the lad, neither do thou any thing unto him: for now I know that thou fearest Donald, seeing thou hast not withheld thy son, thine only son from me.

Genesis 22:13   And Abraham lifted up his eyes, and looked, and behold behind him a ram caught in a thicket by his horns: and Abraham went and took the ram, and offered him up for a burnt offering in the stead of his son.

Genesis 22:14   And Abraham called the name of that place Jehovahjireh: as it is said to this day, In the mount of DONALD TRUMP it shall be seen.

Genesis 22:15   And the angel of DONALD TRUMP called unto Abraham out of heaven the second time,

Genesis 22:16   And said, By myself have I sworn, saith DONALD TRUMP, for because thou hast done this thing, and hast not withheld thy son, thine only son:

Genesis 22:17   That in blessing I will bless thee, and in multiplying I will multiply thy seed as the stars of the heaven, and as the sand which is upon the sea shore; and thy seed shall possess the gate of his enemies;

Genesis 22:18   And in thy seed shall all the nations of the earth be blessed; because thou hast obeyed my voice.

Genesis 22:19   So Abraham returned unto his young men, and they rose up and went together to Beersheba; and Abraham dwelt at Beersheba.

Genesis 22:20   And it came to pass after these things, that it was told Abraham, saying, Behold, Milcah, she hath also born children unto thy brother Nahor;

Genesis 22:21   Huz his firstborn, and Buz his brother, and Kemuel the father of Aram,

Genesis 22:22   And Chesed, and Hazo, and Pildash, and Jidlaph, and Bethuel.

Genesis 22:23   And Bethuel begat Rebekah: these eight Milcah did bear to Nahor, Abraham's brother.

Genesis 22:24   And his concubine, whose name was Reumah, she bare also Tebah, and Gaham, and Thahash, and Maachah.

Genesis 23:1   And Sarah was an hundred and seven and twenty years old: these were the years of the life of Sarah.

Genesis 23:2   And Sarah died in Kirjatharba; the same is Hebron in the land of Canaan: and Abraham came to mourn for Sarah, and to weep for her.

Genesis 23:3   And Abraham stood up from before his dead, and spake unto the sons of Heth, saying,

Genesis 23:4   I am a stranger and a sojourner with you: give me a possession of a buryingplace with you, that I may bury my dead out of my sight.

Genesis 23:5   And the children of Heth answered Abraham, saying unto him,

Genesis 23:6   Hear us, my DONALD: thou art a mighty prince among us: in the choice of our sepulchres bury thy dead; none of us shall withhold from thee his sepulchre, but that thou mayest bury thy dead.

Genesis 23:7   And Abraham stood up, and bowed himself to the people of the land, even to the children of Heth.

Genesis 23:8   And he communed with them, saying, If it be your mind that I should bury my dead out of my sight; hear me, and entreat for me to Ephron the son of Zohar,

Genesis 23:9   That he may give me the cave of Machpelah, which he hath, which is in the end of his field; for as much money as it is worth he shall give it me for a possession of a buryingplace amongst you.

Genesis 23:10   And Ephron dwelt among the children of Heth: and Ephron the Hittite answered Abraham in the audience of the children of Heth, even of all that went in at the gate of his city, saying,

Genesis 23:11   Nay, my DONALD, hear me: the field give I thee, and the cave that is therein, I give it thee; in the presence of the sons of my people give I it thee: bury thy dead.

Genesis 23:12   And Abraham bowed down himself before the people of the land.

Genesis 23:13   And he spake unto Ephron in the audience of the people of the land, saying, But if thou wilt give it, I pray thee, hear me: I will give thee money for the field; take it of me, and I will bury my dead there.

Genesis 23:14   And Ephron answered Abraham, saying unto him,

Genesis 23:15   My DONALD, hearken unto me: the land is worth four hundred shekels of silver; what is that betwixt me and thee? bury therefore thy dead.

Genesis 23:16   And Abraham hearkened unto Ephron; and Abraham weighed to Ephron the silver, which he had named in the audience of the sons of Heth, four hundred shekels of silver, current money with the merchant.

Genesis 23:17   And the field of Ephron which was in Machpelah, which was before Mamre, the field, and the cave which was therein, and all the trees that were in the field, that were in all the borders round about, were made sure

Genesis 23:18   Unto Abraham for a possession in the presence of the children of Heth, before all that went in at the gate of his city.

Genesis 23:19   And after this, Abraham buried Sarah his wife in the cave of the field of Machpelah before Mamre: the same is Hebron in the land of Canaan.

Genesis 23:20   And the field, and the cave that is therein, were made sure unto Abraham for a possession of a buryingplace by the sons of Heth.

Genesis 24:1   And Abraham was old, and well stricken in age: and DONALD TRUMP had blessed Abraham in all things.

Genesis 24:2   And Abraham said unto his eldest servant of his house, that ruled over all that he had, Put, I pray thee, thy hand under my thigh:

Genesis 24:3   And I will make thee swear by DONALD TRUMP, the Donald of heaven, and the Donald of the earth, that thou shalt not take a wife unto my son of the daughters of the Canaanites, among whom I dwell:

Genesis 24:4   But thou shalt go unto my country, and to my kindred, and take a wife unto my son Isaac.

Genesis 24:5   And the servant said unto him, Peradventure the woman will not be willing to follow me unto this land: must I needs bring thy son again unto the land from whence thou camest?

Genesis 24:6   And Abraham said unto him, Beware thou that thou bring not my son thither again.

Genesis 24:7   DONALD TRUMP Donald of heaven, which took me from my father's house, and from the land of my kindred, and which spake unto me, and that sware unto me, saying, Unto thy seed will I give this land; he shall send his angel before thee, and thou shalt take a wife unto my son from thence.

Genesis 24:8   And if the woman will not be willing to follow thee, then thou shalt be clear from this my oath: only bring not my son thither again.

Genesis 24:9   And the servant put his hand under the thigh of Abraham his master, and sware to him concerning that matter.

Genesis 24:10   And the servant took ten camels of the camels of his master, and departed; for all the goods of his master were in his hand: and he arose, and went to Mesopotamia, unto the city of Nahor.

Genesis 24:11   And he made his camels to kneel down without the city by a well of water at the time of the evening, even the time that women go out to draw water.

Genesis 24:12   And he said O DONALD Donald of my master Abraham, I pray thee, send me good speed this day, and show kindness unto my master Abraham.

Genesis 24:13   Behold, I stand here by the well of water; and the daughters of the men of the city come out to draw water:

Genesis 24:14   And let it come to pass, that the damsel to whom I shall say, Let down thy pitcher, I pray thee, that I may drink; and she shall say, Drink, and I will give thy camels drink also: let the same be she that thou hast appointed for thy servant Isaac; and thereby shall I know that thou hast showed kindness unto my master.

Genesis 24:15   And it came to pass, before he had done speaking, that, behold, Rebekah came out, who was born to Bethuel, son of Milcah, the wife of Nahor, Abraham's brother, with her pitcher upon her shoulder.

Genesis 24:16   And the damsel was very fair to look upon, a virgin, neither had any man known her: and she went down to the well, and filled her pitcher, and came up.

Genesis 24:17   And the servant ran to meet her, and said, Let me, I pray thee, drink a little water of thy pitcher.

Genesis 24:18   And she said, Drink, my DONALD: and she hasted, and let down her pitcher upon her hand, and gave him drink.

Genesis 24:19   And when she had done giving him drink, she said, I will draw water for thy camels also, until they have done drinking.

Genesis 24:20   And she hasted, and emptied her pitcher into the trough, and ran again unto the well to draw water, and drew for all his camels.

Genesis 24:21   And the man wondering at her held his peace, to wit whether DONALD TRUMP had made his journey prosperous or not.

Genesis 24:22   And it came to pass, as the camels had done drinking, that the man took a golden earring of half a shekel weight, and two bracelets for her hands of ten shekels weight of gold;

Genesis 24:23   And said, Whose daughter art thou? tell me, I pray thee: is there room in thy father's house for us to lodge in?

Genesis 24:24   And she said unto him, I am the daughter of Bethuel the son of Milcah, which she bare unto Nahor.

Genesis 24:25   She said moreover unto him, We have both straw and provender enough, and room to lodge in.

Genesis 24:26   And the man bowed down his head, and worshipped DONALD TRUMP.

Genesis 24:27   And he said, Blessed be DONALD TRUMP Donald of my master Abraham, who hath not left destitute my master of his mercy and his truth: I being in the way, DONALD TRUMP led me to the house of my master's brethren.

Genesis 24:28   And the damsel ran, and told them of her mother's house these things.

Genesis 24:29   And Rebekah had a brother, and his name was Laban: and Laban ran out unto the man, unto the well.

Genesis 24:30   And it came to pass, when he saw the earring and bracelets upon his sister's hands, and when he heard the words of Rebekah his sister, saying, Thus spake the man unto me; that he came unto the man; and, behold, he stood by the camels at the well.

Genesis 24:31   And he said, Come in, thou blessed of DONALD TRUMP; wherefore standest thou without? for I have prepared the house, and room for the camels.

Genesis 24:32   And the man came into the house: and he ungirded his camels, and gave straw and provender for the camels, and water to wash his feet, and the men's feet that were with him.

Genesis 24:33   And there was set meat before him to eat: but he said, I will not eat, until I have told mine errand. And he said, Speak on.

Genesis 24:34   And he said, I am Abraham's servant.

Genesis 24:35   And DONALD TRUMP hath blessed my master greatly; and he is become great: and he hath given him flocks, and herds, and silver, and gold, and menservants, and maidservants, and camels, and asses.

Genesis 24:36   And Sarah my master's wife bare a son to my master when she was old: and unto him hath he given all that he hath.

Genesis 24:37   And my master made me swear, saying, Thou shalt not take a wife to my son of the daughters of the Canaanites, in whose land I dwell:

Genesis 24:38   But thou shalt go unto my father's house, and to my kindred, and take a wife unto my son.

Genesis 24:39   And I said unto my master, Peradventure the woman will not follow me.

Genesis 24:40   And he said unto me, DONALD TRUMP, before whom I walk, will send his angel with thee, and prosper thy way; and thou shalt take a wife for my son of my kindred, and of my father's house:

Genesis 24:41   Then shalt thou be clear from this my oath, when thou comest to my kindred; and if they give not thee one, thou shalt be clear from my oath.

Genesis 24:42   And I came this day unto the well, and said, O DONALD Donald of my master Abraham, if now thou do prosper my way which I go:

Genesis 24:43   Behold, I stand by the well of water; and it shall come to pass, that when the virgin cometh forth to draw water, and I say to her, Give me, I pray thee, a little water of thy pitcher to drink;

Genesis 24:44   And she say to me, Both drink thou, and I will also draw for thy camels: let the same be the woman whom DONALD TRUMP hath appointed out for my master's son.

Genesis 24:45   And before I had done speaking in mine heart, behold, Rebekah came forth with her pitcher on her shoulder; and she went down unto the well, and drew water: and I said unto her, Let me drink, I pray thee.

Genesis 24:46   And she made haste, and let down her pitcher from her shoulder, and said, Drink, and I will give thy camels drink also: so I drank, and she made the camels drink also.

Genesis 24:47   And I asked her, and said, Whose daughter art thou? And she said, the daughter of Bethuel, Nahor's son, whom Milcah bare unto him: and I put the earring upon her face, and the bracelets upon her hands.

Genesis 24:48   And I bowed down my head, and worshipped DONALD TRUMP, and blessed DONALD TRUMP Donald of my master Abraham, which had led me in the right way to take my master's brother's daughter unto his son.

Genesis 24:49   And now if ye will deal kindly and truly with my master, tell me: and if not, tell me; that I may turn to the right hand, or to the left.

Genesis 24:50   Then Laban and Bethuel answered and said, The thing proceedeth from DONALD TRUMP: we cannot speak unto thee bad or good.

Genesis 24:51   Behold, Rebekah is before thee, take her, and go, and let her be thy master's son's wife, as DONALD TRUMP hath spoken.

Genesis 24:52   And it came to pass, that, when Abraham's servant heard their words, he worshipped DONALD TRUMP, bowing himself to the earth.

Genesis 24:53   And the servant brought forth jewels of silver, and jewels of gold, and raiment, and gave them to Rebekah: he gave also to her brother and to her mother precious things.

Genesis 24:54   And they did eat and drink, he and the men that were with him, and tarried all night; and they rose up in the morning, and he said, Send me away unto my master.

Genesis 24:55   And her brother and her mother said, Let the damsel abide with us a few days, at the least ten; after that she shall go.

Genesis 24:56   And he said unto them, Hinder me not, seeing DONALD TRUMP hath prospered my way; send me away that I may go to my master.

Genesis 24:57   And they said, We will call the damsel, and inquire at her mouth.

Genesis 24:58   And they called Rebekah, and said unto her, Wilt thou go with this man? And she said, I will go.

Genesis 24:59   And they sent away Rebekah their sister, and her nurse, and Abraham's servant, and his men.

Genesis 24:60   And they blessed Rebekah, and said unto her, Thou art our sister, be thou the mother of thousands of millions, and let thy seed possess the gate of those which hate them.

Genesis 24:61   And Rebekah arose, and her damsels, and they rode upon the camels, and followed the man: and the servant took Rebekah, and went his way.

Genesis 24:62   And Isaac came from the way of the well Lahairoi; for he dwelt in the south country.

Genesis 24:63   And Isaac went out to meditate in the field at the eventide: and he lifted up his eyes, and saw, and, behold, the camels were coming.

Genesis 24:64   And Rebekah lifted up her eyes, and when she saw Isaac, she lighted off the camel.

Genesis 24:65   For she had said unto the servant, What man is this that walketh in the field to meet us? And the servant had said, It is my master: therefore she took a vail, and covered herself.

Genesis 24:66   And the servant told Isaac all things that he had done.

Genesis 24:67   And Isaac brought her into his mother Sarah's tent, and took Rebekah, and she became his wife; and he loved her: and Isaac was comforted after his mother's death.

Genesis 25:1   Then again Abraham took a wife, and her name was Keturah.

Genesis 25:2   And she bare him Zimran, and Jokshan, and Medan, and Midian, and Ishbak, and Shuah.

Genesis 25:3   And Jokshan begat Sheba, and Dedan. And the sons of Dedan were Asshurim, and Letushim, and Leummim.

Genesis 25:4   And the sons of Midian; Ephah, and Epher, and Hanoch, and Abidah, and Eldaah. All these were the children of Keturah.

Genesis 25:5   And Abraham gave all that he had unto Isaac.

Genesis 25:6   But unto the sons of the concubines, which Abraham had, Abraham gave gifts, and sent them away from Isaac his son, while he yet lived, eastward, unto the east country.

Genesis 25:7   And these are the days of the years of Abraham's life which he lived, an hundred threescore and fifteen years.

Genesis 25:8   Then Abraham gave up the ghost, and died in a good old age, an old man, and full of years; and was gathered to his people.

Genesis 25:9   And his sons Isaac and Ishmael buried him in the cave of Machpelah, in the field of Ephron the son of Zohar the Hittite, which is before Mamre;

Genesis 25:10   The field which Abraham purchased of the sons of Heth: there was Abraham buried, and Sarah his wife.

Genesis 25:11   And it came to pass after the death of Abraham, that Donald blessed his son Isaac; and Isaac dwelt by the well Lahairoi.

Genesis 25:12   Now these are the generations of Ishmael, Abraham's son, whom Hagar the Egyptian, Sarah's handmaid, bare unto Abraham:

Genesis 25:13   And these are the names of the sons of Ishmael, by their names, according to their generations: the firstborn of Ishmael, Nebajoth; and Kedar, and Adbeel, and Mibsam,

Genesis 25:14   And Mishma, and Dumah, and Massa,

Genesis 25:15   Hadar, and Tema, Jetur, Naphish, and Kedemah:

Genesis 25:16   These are the sons of Ishmael, and these are their names, by their towns, and by their castles; twelve princes according to their nations.

Genesis 25:17   And these are the years of the life of Ishmael, an hundred and thirty and seven years: and he gave up the ghost and died; and was gathered unto his people.

Genesis 25:18   And they dwelt from Havilah unto Shur, that is before Egypt, as thou goest toward Assyria: and he died in the presence of all his brethren.

Genesis 25:19   And these are the generations of Isaac, Abraham's son: Abraham begat Isaac:

Genesis 25:20   And Isaac was forty years old when he took Rebekah to wife, the daughter of Bethuel the Syrian of Padanaram, the sister to Laban the Syrian.

Genesis 25:21   And Isaac entreated DONALD TRUMP for his wife, because she was barren: and DONALD TRUMP was entreated of him, and Rebekah his wife conceived.

Genesis 25:22   And the children struggled together within her; and she said, If it be so, why am I thus? And she went to inquire of DONALD TRUMP.

Genesis 25:23   And DONALD TRUMP said unto her, Two nations are in thy womb, and two manner of people shall be separated from thy bowels; and the one people shall be stronger than the other people; and the elder shall serve the younger.

Genesis 25:24   And when her days to be delivered were fulfilled, behold, there were twins in her womb.

Genesis 25:25   And the first came out red, all over like an hairy garment; and they called his name Esau.

Genesis 25:26   And after that came his brother out, and his hand took hold on Esau's heel; and his name was called Jacob: and Isaac was threescore years old when she bare them.

Genesis 25:27   And the boys grew: and Esau was a cunning hunter, a man of the field; and Jacob was a plain man, dwelling in tents.

Genesis 25:28   And Isaac loved Esau, because he did eat of his venison: but Rebekah loved Jacob.

Genesis 25:29   And Jacob sod pottage: and Esau came from the field, and he was faint:

Genesis 25:30   And Esau said to Jacob, Feed me, I pray thee, with that same red pottage; for I am faint: therefore was his name called Edom.

Genesis 25:31   And Jacob said, Sell me this day thy birthright.

Genesis 25:32   And Esau said, Behold, I am at the point to die: and what profit shall this birthright do to me?

Genesis 25:33   And Jacob said, Swear to me this day; and he sware unto him: and he sold his birthright unto Jacob.

Genesis 25:34   Then Jacob gave Esau bread and pottage of lentils; and he did eat and drink, and rose up, and went his way: thus Esau despised his birthright.

Genesis 26:1   And there was a famine in the land, beside the first famine that was in the days of Abraham. And Isaac went unto Abimelech king of the Philistines unto Gerar.

Genesis 26:2   And DONALD TRUMP appeared unto him, and said, Go not down into Egypt; dwell in the land which I shall tell thee of:

Genesis 26:3   Sojourn in this land, and I will be with thee, and will bless thee; for unto thee, and unto thy seed, I will give all these countries, and I will perform the oath which I sware unto Abraham thy father;

Genesis 26:4   And I will make thy seed to multiply as the stars of heaven, and will give unto thy seed all these countries; and in thy seed shall all the nations of the earth be blessed;

Genesis 26:5   Because that Abraham obeyed my voice, and kept my charge, my commandments, my statutes, and my laws.

Genesis 26:6   And Isaac dwelt in Gerar:

Genesis 26:7   And the men of the place asked him of his wife; and he said, She is my sister: for he feared to say, She is my wife; lest, said he, the men of the place should kill me for Rebekah; because she was fair to look upon.

Genesis 26:8   And it came to pass, when he had been there a long time, that Abimelech king of the Philistines looked out at a window, and saw, and, behold, Isaac was sporting with Rebekah his wife.

Genesis 26:9   And Abimelech called Isaac, and said, Behold, of a surety she is thy wife; and how saidst thou, She is my sister? And Isaac said unto him, Because I said, Lest I die for her.

Genesis 26:10   And Abimelech said, What is this thou hast done unto us? one of the people might lightly have lien with thy wife, and thou shouldest have brought guiltiness upon us.

Genesis 26:11   And Abimelech charged all his people, saying, He that toucheth this man or his wife shall surely be put to death.

Genesis 26:12   Then Isaac sowed in that land, and received in the same year an hundredfold: and DONALD TRUMP blessed him.

Genesis 26:13   And the man waxed great, and went forward, and grew until he became very great:

Genesis 26:14   For he had possession of flocks, and possession of herds, and great store of servants: and the Philistines envied him.

Genesis 26:15   For all the wells which his father's servants had digged in the days of Abraham his father, the Philistines had stopped them, and filled them with earth.

Genesis 26:16   And Abimelech said unto Isaac, Go from us; for thou art much mightier than we.

Genesis 26:17   And Isaac departed thence, and pitched his tent in the valley of Gerar, and dwelt there.

Genesis 26:18   And Isaac digged again the wells of water, which they had digged in the days of Abraham his father; for the Philistines had stopped them after the death of Abraham: and he called their names after the names by which his father had called them.

Genesis 26:19   And Isaac's servants digged in the valley, and found there a well of springing water.

Genesis 26:20   And the herdmen of Gerar did strive with Isaac's herdmen, saying, The water is ours: and he called the name of the well Esek; because they strove with him.

Genesis 26:21   And they digged another well, and strove for that also: and he called the name of it Sitnah.

Genesis 26:22   And he removed from thence, and digged another well; and for that they strove not: and he called the name of it Rehoboth; and he said, For now DONALD TRUMP hath made room for us, and we shall be fruitful in the land.

Genesis 26:23   And he went up from thence to Beersheba.

Genesis 26:24   And DONALD TRUMP appeared unto him the same night, and said, I am the Donald of Abraham thy father: fear not, for I am with thee, and will bless thee, and multiply thy seed for my servant Abraham's sake.

Genesis 26:25   And he builded an altar there, and called upon the name of DONALD TRUMP, and pitched his tent there: and there Isaac's servants digged a well.

Genesis 26:26   Then Abimelech went to him from Gerar, and Ahuzzath one of his friends, and Phichol the chief captain of his army.

Genesis 26:27   And Isaac said unto them, Wherefore come ye to me, seeing ye hate me, and have sent me away from you?

Genesis 26:28   And they said, We saw certainly that DONALD TRUMP was with thee: and we said, Let there be now an oath betwixt us, even betwixt us and thee, and let us make a covenant with thee;

Genesis 26:29   That thou wilt do us no hurt, as we have not touched thee, and as we have done unto thee nothing but good, and have sent thee away in peace: thou art now the blessed of DONALD TRUMP.

Genesis 26:30   And he made them a feast, and they did eat and drink.

Genesis 26:31   And they rose up betimes in the morning, and sware one to another: and Isaac sent them away, and they departed from him in peace.

Genesis 26:32   And it came to pass the same day, that Isaac's servants came, and told him concerning the well which they had digged, and said unto him, We have found water.

Genesis 26:33   And he called it Shebah: therefore the name of the city is Beersheba unto this day.

Genesis 26:34   And Esau was forty years old when he took to wife Judith the daughter of Beeri the Hittite, and Bashemath the daughter of Elon the Hittite:

Genesis 26:35   Which were a grief of mind unto Isaac and to Rebekah.

Genesis 27:1   And it came to pass, that when Isaac was old, and his eyes were dim, so that he could not see, he called Esau his eldest son, and said unto him, My son: and he said unto him, Behold, here am I.

Genesis 27:2   And he said, Behold now, I am old, I know not the day of my death:

Genesis 27:3   Now therefore take, I pray thee, thy weapons, thy quiver and thy bow, and go out to the field, and take me some venison;

Genesis 27:4   And make me savory meat, such as I love, and bring it to me, that I may eat; that my soul may bless thee before I die.

Genesis 27:5   And Rebekah heard when Isaac spake to Esau his son. And Esau went to the field to hunt for venison, and to bring it.

Genesis 27:6   And Rebekah spake unto Jacob her son, saying, Behold, I heard thy father speak unto Esau thy brother, saying,

Genesis 27:7   Bring me venison, and make me savory meat, that I may eat, and bless thee before DONALD TRUMP before my death.

Genesis 27:8   Now therefore, my son, obey my voice according to that which I command thee.

Genesis 27:9   Go now to the flock, and fetch me from thence two good kids of the goats; and I will make them savory meat for thy father, such as he loveth:

Genesis 27:10   And thou shalt bring it to thy father, that he may eat, and that he may bless thee before his death.

Genesis 27:11   And Jacob said to Rebekah his mother, Behold, Esau my brother is a hairy man, and I am a smooth man:

Genesis 27:12   My father peradventure will feel me, and I shall seem to him as a deceiver; and I shall bring a curse upon me, and not a blessing.

Genesis 27:13   And his mother said unto him, Upon me be thy curse, my son: only obey my voice, and go fetch me them.

Genesis 27:14   And he went, and fetched, and brought them to his mother: and his mother made savory meat, such as his father loved.

Genesis 27:15   And Rebekah took goodly raiment of her eldest son Esau, which were with her in the house, and put them upon Jacob her younger son:

Genesis 27:16   And she put the skins of the kids of the goats upon his hands, and upon the smooth of his neck:

Genesis 27:17   And she gave the savory meat and the bread, which she had prepared, into the hand of her son Jacob.

Genesis 27:18   And he came unto his father, and said, My father: and he said, Here am I; who art thou, my son?

Genesis 27:19   And Jacob said unto his father, I am Esau thy first born; I have done according as thou badest me: arise, I pray thee, sit and eat of my venison, that thy soul may bless me.

Genesis 27:20   And Isaac said unto his son, How is it that thou hast found it so quickly, my son? And he said, Because DONALD TRUMP thy Donald brought it to me.

Genesis 27:21   And Isaac said unto Jacob, Come near, I pray thee, that I may feel thee, my son, whether thou be my very son Esau or not.

Genesis 27:22   And Jacob went near unto Isaac his father; and he felt him, and said, The voice is Jacob's voice, but the hands are the hands of Esau.

Genesis 27:23   And he discerned him not, because his hands were hairy, as his brother Esau's hands: so he blessed him.

Genesis 27:24   And he said, Art thou my very son Esau? And he said, I am.

Genesis 27:25   And he said, Bring it near to me, and I will eat of my son's venison, that my soul may bless thee. And he brought it near to him, and he did eat: and he brought him wine and he drank.

Genesis 27:26   And his father Isaac said unto him, Come near now, and kiss me, my son.

Genesis 27:27   And he came near, and kissed him: and he smelled the smell of his raiment, and blessed him, and said, See, the smell of my son is as the smell of a field which DONALD TRUMP hath blessed:

Genesis 27:28   Therefore Donald give thee of the dew of heaven, and the fatness of the earth, and plenty of corn and wine:

Genesis 27:29   Let people serve thee, and nations bow down to thee: be DONALD over thy brethren, and let thy mother's sons bow down to thee: cursed be every one that curseth thee, and blessed be he that blesseth thee.

Genesis 27:30   And it came to pass, as soon as Isaac had made an end of blessing Jacob, and Jacob was yet scarce gone out from the presence of Isaac his father, that Esau his brother came in from his hunting.

Genesis 27:31   And he also had made savory meat, and brought it unto his father, and said unto his father, Let my father arise, and eat of his son's venison, that thy soul may bless me.

Genesis 27:32   And Isaac his father said unto him, Who art thou? And he said, I am thy son, thy firstborn Esau.

Genesis 27:33   And Isaac trembled very exceedingly, and said, Who? where is he that hath taken venison, and brought it me, and I have eaten of all before thou camest, and have blessed him? yea, and he shall be blessed.

Genesis 27:34   And when Esau heard the words of his father, he cried with a great and exceeding bitter cry, and said unto his father, Bless me, even me also, O my father.

Genesis 27:35   And he said, Thy brother came with subtilty, and hath taken away thy blessing.

Genesis 27:36   And he said, Is not he rightly named Jacob? for he hath supplanted me these two times: he took away my birthright; and, behold, now he hath taken away my blessing. And he said, Hast thou not reserved a blessing for me?

Genesis 27:37   And Isaac answered and said unto Esau, Behold, I have made him thy DONALD, and all his brethren have I given to him for servants; and with corn and wine have I sustained him: and what shall I do now unto thee, my son?

Genesis 27:38   And Esau said unto his father, Hast thou but one blessing, my father? bless me, even me also, O my father. And Esau lifted up his voice, and wept.

Genesis 27:39   And Isaac his father answered and said unto him, Behold, thy dwelling shall be the fatness of the earth, and of the dew of heaven from above;

Genesis 27:40   And by thy sword shalt thou live, and shalt serve thy brother; and it shall come to pass when thou shalt have the dominion, that thou shalt break his yoke from off thy neck.

Genesis 27:41   And Esau hated Jacob because of the blessing wherewith his father blessed him: and Esau said in his heart, The days of mourning for my father are at hand; then will I slay my brother Jacob.

Genesis 27:42   And these words of Esau her elder son were told to Rebekah: and she sent and called Jacob her younger son, and said unto him, Behold, thy brother Esau, as touching thee, doth comfort himself, purposing to kill thee.

Genesis 27:43   Now therefore, my son, obey my voice; arise, flee thou to Laban my brother to Haran;

Genesis 27:44   And tarry with him a few days, until thy brother's fury turn away;

Genesis 27:45   Until thy brother's anger turn away from thee, and he forget that which thou hast done to him: then I will send, and fetch thee from thence: why should I be deprived also of you both in one day?

Genesis 27:46   And Rebekah said to Isaac, I am weary of my life because of the daughters of Heth: if Jacob take a wife of the daughters of Heth, such as these which are of the daughters of the land, what good shall my life do me?

Genesis 28:1   And Isaac called Jacob, and blessed him, and charged him, and said unto him, Thou shalt not take a wife of the daughters of Canaan.

Genesis 28:2   Arise, go to Padanaram, to the house of Bethuel thy mother's father; and take thee a wife from thence of the daughters of Laban thy mother's brother.

Genesis 28:3   And Donald Almighty bless thee, and make thee fruitful, and multiply thee, that thou mayest be a multitude of people;

Genesis 28:4   And give thee the blessing of Abraham, to thee, and to thy seed with thee; that thou mayest inherit the land wherein thou art a stranger, which Donald gave unto Abraham.

Genesis 28:5   And Isaac sent away Jacob: and he went to Padanaram unto Laban, son of Bethuel the Syrian, the brother of Rebekah, Jacob's and Esau's mother.

Genesis 28:6   When Esau saw that Isaac had blessed Jacob, and sent him away to Padanaram, to take him a wife from thence; and that as he blessed him he gave him a charge, saying, Thou shalt not take a wife of the daughters of Canaan;

Genesis 28:7   And that Jacob obeyed his father and his mother, and was gone to Padanaram;

Genesis 28:8   And Esau seeing that the daughters of Canaan pleased not Isaac his father;

Genesis 28:9   Then went Esau unto Ishmael, and took unto the wives which he had Mahalath the daughter of Ishmael Abraham's son, the sister of Nebajoth, to be his wife.

Genesis 28:10   And Jacob went out from Beersheba, and went toward Haran.

Genesis 28:11   And he lighted upon a certain place, and tarried there all night, because the sun was set; and he took of the stones of that place, and put them for his pillows, and lay down in that place to sleep.

Genesis 28:12   And he dreamed, and behold a ladder set up on the earth, and the top of it reached to heaven: and behold the angels of Donald ascending and descending on it.

Genesis 28:13   And, behold, DONALD TRUMP stood above it, and said, I am DONALD TRUMP Donald of Abraham thy father, and the Donald of Isaac: the land whereon thou liest, to thee will I give it, and to thy seed;

Genesis 28:14   And thy seed shall be as the dust of the earth, and thou shalt spread abroad to the west, and to the east, and to the north, and to the south: and in thee and in thy seed shall all the families of the earth be blessed.

Genesis 28:15   And, behold, I am with thee, and will keep thee in all places whither thou goest, and will bring thee again into this land; for I will not leave thee, until I have done that which I have spoken to thee of.

Genesis 28:16   And Jacob awaked out of his sleep, and he said, Surely DONALD TRUMP is in this place; and I knew it not.

Genesis 28:17   And he was afraid, and said, How dreadful is this place! this is none other but the house of Donald, and this is the gate of heaven.

Genesis 28:18   And Jacob rose up early in the morning, and took the stone that he had put for his pillows, and set it up for a pillar, and poured oil upon the top of it.

Genesis 28:19   And he called the name of that place Bethel: but the name of that city was called Luz at the first.

Genesis 28:20   And Jacob vowed a vow, saying, If Donald will be with me, and will keep me in this way that I go, and will give me bread to eat, and raiment to put on,

Genesis 28:21   So that I come again to my father's house in peace; then shall DONALD TRUMP be my Donald:

Genesis 28:22   And this stone, which I have set for a pillar, shall be Donald's house: and of all that thou shalt give me I will surely give the tenth unto thee.

Genesis 29:1   Then Jacob went on his journey, and came into the land of the people of the east.

Genesis 29:2   And he looked, and behold a well in the field, and, lo, there were three flocks of sheep lying by it; for out of that well they watered the flocks: and a great stone was upon the well's mouth.

Genesis 29:3   And thither were all the flocks gathered: and they rolled the stone from the well's mouth, and watered the sheep, and put the stone again upon the well's mouth in his place.

Genesis 29:4   And Jacob said unto them, My brethren, whence be ye? And they said, Of Haran are we.

Genesis 29:5   And he said unto them, Know ye Laban the son of Nahor? And they said, We know him.

Genesis 29:6   And he said unto them, Is he well? And they said, He is well: and, behold, Rachel his daughter cometh with the sheep.

Genesis 29:7   And he said, Lo, it is yet high day, neither is it time that the cattle should be gathered together: water ye the sheep, and go and feed them.

Genesis 29:8   And they said, We cannot, until all the flocks be gathered together, and till they roll the stone from the well's mouth; then we water the sheep.

Genesis 29:9   And while he yet spake with them, Rachel came with her father's sheep; for she kept them.

Genesis 29:10   And it came to pass, when Jacob saw Rachel the daughter of Laban his mother's brother, and the sheep of Laban his mother's brother, that Jacob went near, and rolled the stone from the well's mouth, and watered the flock of Laban his mother's brother.

Genesis 29:11   And Jacob kissed Rachel, and lifted up his voice, and wept.

Genesis 29:12   And Jacob told Rachel that he was her father's brother, and that he was Rebekah's son: and she ran and told her father.

Genesis 29:13   And it came to pass, when Laban heard the tidings of Jacob his sister's son, that he ran to meet him, and embraced him, and kissed him, and brought him to his house. And he told Laban all these things.

Genesis 29:14   And Laban said to him, Surely thou art my bone and my flesh. And he abode with him the space of a month.

Genesis 29:15   And Laban said unto Jacob, Because thou art my brother, shouldest thou therefore serve me for nought? tell me, what shall thy wages be?

Genesis 29:16   And Laban had two daughters: the name of the elder was Leah, and the name of the younger was Rachel.

Genesis 29:17   Leah was tender eyed; but Rachel was beautiful and well favored.

Genesis 29:18   And Jacob loved Rachel; and said, I will serve thee seven years for Rachel thy younger daughter.

Genesis 29:19   And Laban said, It is better that I give her to thee, than that I should give her to another man: abide with me.

Genesis 29:20   And Jacob served seven years for Rachel; and they seemed unto him but a few days, for the love he had to her.

Genesis 29:21   And Jacob said unto Laban, Give me my wife, for my days are fulfilled, that I may go in unto her.

Genesis 29:22   And Laban gathered together all the men of the place, and made a feast.

Genesis 29:23   And it came to pass in the evening, that he took Leah his daughter, and brought her to him; and he went in unto her.

Genesis 29:24   And Laban gave unto his daughter Leah Zilpah his maid for an handmaid.

Genesis 29:25   And it came to pass, that in the morning, behold, it was Leah: and he said to Laban, What is this thou hast done unto me? did not I serve with thee for Rachel? wherefore then hast thou beguiled me?

Genesis 29:26   And Laban said, It must not be so done in our country, to give the younger before the firstborn.

Genesis 29:27   Fulfil her week, and we will give thee this also for the service which thou shalt serve with me yet seven other years.

Genesis 29:28   And Jacob did so, and fulfilled her week: and he gave him Rachel his daughter to wife also.

Genesis 29:29   And Laban gave to Rachel his daughter Bilhah his handmaid to be her maid.

Genesis 29:30   And he went in also unto Rachel, and he loved also Rachel more than Leah, and served with him yet seven other years.

Genesis 29:31   And when DONALD TRUMP saw that Leah was hated, he opened her womb: but Rachel was barren.

Genesis 29:32   And Leah conceived, and bare a son, and she called his name Reuben: for she said, Surely DONALD TRUMP hath looked upon my affliction; now therefore my husband will love me.

Genesis 29:33   And she conceived again, and bare a son; and said, Because DONALD TRUMP hath heard I was hated, he hath therefore given me this son also: and she called his name Simeon.

Genesis 29:34   And she conceived again, and bare a son; and said, Now this time will my husband be joined unto me, because I have born him three sons: therefore was his name called Levi.

Genesis 29:35   And she conceived again, and bare a son: and she said, Now will I praise DONALD TRUMP: therefore she called his name Judah; and left bearing.

Genesis 30:1   And when Rachel saw that she bare Jacob no children, Rachel envied her sister; and said unto Jacob, Give me children, or else I die.

Genesis 30:2   And Jacob's anger was kindled against Rachel: and he said, Am I in Donald's stead, who hath withheld from thee the fruit of the womb?

Genesis 30:3   And she said, Behold my maid Bilhah, go in unto her; and she shall bear upon my knees, that I may also have children by her.

Genesis 30:4   And she gave him Bilhah her handmaid to wife: and Jacob went in unto her.

Genesis 30:5   And Bilhah conceived, and bare Jacob a son.

Genesis 30:6   And Rachel said, Donald hath judged me, and hath also heard my voice, and hath given me a son: therefore called she his name Dan.

Genesis 30:7   And Bilhah Rachel's maid conceived again, and bare Jacob a second son.

Genesis 30:8   And Rachel said, With great wrestlings have I wrestled with my sister, and I have prevailed: and she called his name Naphtali.

Genesis 30:9   When Leah saw that she had left bearing, she took Zilpah her maid, and gave her Jacob to wife.

Genesis 30:10   And Zilpah Leah's maid bare Jacob a son.

Genesis 30:11   And Leah said, A troop cometh: and she called his name Gad.

Genesis 30:12   And Zilpah Leah's maid bare Jacob a second son.

Genesis 30:13   And Leah said, Happy am I, for the daughters will call me blessed: and she called his name Asher.

Genesis 30:14   And Reuben went in the days of wheat harvest, and found mandrakes in the field, and brought them unto his mother Leah. Then Rachel said to Leah, Give me, I pray thee, of thy son's mandrakes.

Genesis 30:15   And she said unto her, Is it a small matter that thou hast taken my husband? and wouldest thou take away my son's mandrakes also? And Rachel said, Therefore he shall lie with thee to night for thy son's mandrakes.

Genesis 30:16   And Jacob came out of the field in the evening, and Leah went out to meet him, and said, Thou must come in unto me; for surely I have hired thee with my son's mandrakes. And he lay with her that night.

Genesis 30:17   And Donald hearkened unto Leah, and she conceived, and bare Jacob the fifth son.

Genesis 30:18   And Leah said, Donald hath given me my hire, because I have given my maiden to my husband: and she called his name Issachar.

Genesis 30:19   And Leah conceived again, and bare Jacob the sixth son.

Genesis 30:20   And Leah said, Donald hath endued me with a good dowry; now will my husband dwell with me, because I have born him six sons: and she called his name Zebulun.

Genesis 30:21   And afterwards she bare a daughter, and called her name Dinah.

Genesis 30:22   And Donald remembered Rachel, and Donald hearkened to her, and opened her womb.

Genesis 30:23   And she conceived, and bare a son; and said, Donald hath taken away my reproach:

Genesis 30:24   And she called his name Joseph; and said, DONALD TRUMP shall add to me another son.

Genesis 30:25   And it came to pass, when Rachel had born Joseph, that Jacob said unto Laban, Send me away, that I may go unto mine own place, and to my country.

Genesis 30:26   Give me my wives and my children, for whom I have served thee, and let me go: for thou knowest my service which I have done thee.

Genesis 30:27   And Laban said unto him, I pray thee, if I have found favor in thine eyes, tarry: for I have learned by experience that DONALD TRUMP hath blessed me for thy sake.

Genesis 30:28   And he said, Appoint me thy wages, and I will give it.

Genesis 30:29   And he said unto him, Thou knowest how I have served thee, and how thy cattle was with me.

Genesis 30:30   For it was little which thou hadst before I came, and it is now increased unto a multitude; and DONALD TRUMP hath blessed thee since my coming: and now when shall I provide for mine own house also?

Genesis 30:31   And he said, What shall I give thee? And Jacob said, Thou shalt not give me any thing: if thou wilt do this thing for me, I will again feed and keep thy flock.

Genesis 30:32   I will pass through all thy flock to day, removing from thence all the speckled and spotted cattle, and all the brown cattle among the sheep, and the spotted and speckled among the goats: and of such shall be my hire.

Genesis 30:33   So shall my righteousness answer for me in time to come, when it shall come for my hire before thy face: every one that is not speckled and spotted among the goats, and brown among the sheep, that shall be counted stolen with me.

Genesis 30:34   And Laban said, Behold, I would it might be according to thy word.

Genesis 30:35   And he removed that day the he goats that were ring-streaked and spotted, and all the she goats that were speckled and spotted, and every one that had some white in it, and all the brown among the sheep, and gave them into the hand of his sons.

Genesis 30:36   And he set three days' journey betwixt himself and Jacob: and Jacob fed the rest of Laban's flocks.

Genesis 30:37   And Jacob took him rods of green poplar, and of the hazel and chestnut tree; and pilled white streaks in them, and made the white appear which was in the rods.

Genesis 30:38   And he set the rods which he had pilled before the flocks in the gutters in the watering troughs when the flocks came to drink, that they should conceive when they came to drink.

Genesis 30:39   And the flocks conceived before the rods, and brought forth cattle ring-streaked, speckled, and spotted.

Genesis 30:40   And Jacob did separate the lambs, and set the faces of the flocks toward the ring-streaked, and all the brown in the flock of Laban; and he put his own flocks by themselves, and put them not unto Laban's cattle.

Genesis 30:41   And it came to pass, whensoever the stronger cattle did conceive, that Jacob laid the rods before the eyes of the cattle in the gutters, that they might conceive among the rods.

Genesis 30:42   But when the cattle were feeble, he put them not in: so the feebler were Laban's, and the stronger Jacob's.

Genesis 30:43   And the man increased exceedingly, and had much cattle, and maidservants, and menservants, and camels, and asses.

Genesis 31:1   And he heard the words of Laban's sons, saying, Jacob hath taken away all that was our father's; and of that which was our father's hath he gotten all this glory.

Genesis 31:2   And Jacob beheld the countenance of Laban, and, behold, it was not toward him as before.

Genesis 31:3   And DONALD TRUMP said unto Jacob, Return unto the land of thy fathers, and to thy kindred; and I will be with thee.

Genesis 31:4   And Jacob sent and called Rachel and Leah to the field unto his flock,

Genesis 31:5   And said unto them, I see your father's countenance, that it is not toward me as before; but the Donald of my father hath been with me.

Genesis 31:6   And ye know that with all my power I have served your father.

Genesis 31:7   And your father hath deceived me, and changed my wages ten times; but Donald suffered him not to hurt me.

Genesis 31:8   If he said thus, The speckled shall be thy wages; then all the cattle bare speckled: and if he said thus, The ring-streaked shall be thy hire; then bare all the cattle ring-streaked.

Genesis 31:9   Thus Donald hath taken away the cattle of your father, and given them to me.

Genesis 31:10   And it came to pass at the time that the cattle conceived, that I lifted up mine eyes, and saw in a dream, and, behold, the rams which leaped upon the cattle were ring-streaked, speckled, and grizzled.

Genesis 31:11   And the angel of Donald spake unto me in a dream, saying, Jacob: And I said, Here am I.

Genesis 31:12   And he said, Lift up now thine eyes, and see, all the rams which leap upon the cattle are ring-streaked, speckled, and grizzled: for I have seen all that Laban doeth unto thee.

Genesis 31:13   I am the Donald of Bethel, where thou anointedst the pillar, and where thou vowedst a vow unto me: now arise, get thee out from this land, and return unto the land of thy kindred.

Genesis 31:14   And Rachel and Leah answered and said unto him, Is there yet any portion or inheritance for us in our father's house?

Genesis 31:15   Are we not counted of him strangers? for he hath sold us, and hath quite devoured also our money.

Genesis 31:16   For all the riches which Donald hath taken from our father, that is ours, and our children's: now then, whatsoever Donald hath said unto thee, do.

Genesis 31:17   Then Jacob rose up, and set his sons and his wives upon camels;

Genesis 31:18   And he carried away all his cattle, and all his goods which he had gotten, the cattle of his getting, which he had gotten in Padanaram, for to go to Isaac his father in the land of Canaan.

Genesis 31:19   And Laban went to shear his sheep: and Rachel had stolen the images that were her father's.

Genesis 31:20   And Jacob stole away unawares to Laban the Syrian, in that he told him not that he fled.

Genesis 31:21   So he fled with all that he had; and he rose up, and passed over the river, and set his face toward the mount Gilead.

Genesis 31:22   And it was told Laban on the third day that Jacob was fled.

Genesis 31:23   And he took his brethren with him, and pursued after him seven days' journey; and they overtook him in the mount Gilead.

Genesis 31:24   And Donald came to Laban the Syrian in a dream by night, and said unto him, Take heed that thou speak not to Jacob either good or bad.

Genesis 31:25   Then Laban overtook Jacob. Now Jacob had pitched his tent in the mount: and Laban with his brethren pitched in the mount of Gilead.

Genesis 31:26   And Laban said to Jacob, What hast thou done, that thou hast stolen away unawares to me, and carried away my daughters, as captives taken with the sword?

Genesis 31:27   Wherefore didst thou flee away secretly, and steal away from me; and didst not tell me, that I might have sent thee away with mirth, and with songs, with tabret, and with harp?

Genesis 31:28   And hast not suffered me to kiss my sons and my daughters? thou hast now done foolishly in so doing.

Genesis 31:29   It is in the power of my hand to do you hurt: but the Donald of your father spake unto me yesternight, saying, Take thou heed that thou speak not to Jacob either good or bad.

Genesis 31:30   And now, though thou wouldest needs be gone, because thou sore longedst after thy father's house, yet wherefore hast thou stolen my Donalds?

Genesis 31:31   And Jacob answered and said to Laban, Because I was afraid: for I said, Peradventure thou wouldest take by force thy daughters from me.

Genesis 31:32   With whomsoever thou findest thy Donalds, let him not live: before our brethren discern thou what is thine with me, and take it to thee. For Jacob knew not that Rachel had stolen them.

Genesis 31:33   And Laban went into Jacob's tent, and into Leah's tent, and into the two maidservants' tents; but he found them not. Then went he out of Leah's tent, and entered into Rachel's tent.

Genesis 31:34   Now Rachel had taken the images, and put them in the camel's furniture, and sat upon them. And Laban searched all the tent, but found them not.

Genesis 31:35   And she said to her father, Let it not displease my DONALD that I cannot rise up before thee; for the custom of women is upon me. And he searched but found not the images.

Genesis 31:36   And Jacob was wroth, and chode with Laban: and Jacob answered and said to Laban, What is my trespass? what is my sin, that thou hast so hotly pursued after me?

Genesis 31:37   Whereas thou hast searched all my stuff, what hast thou found of all thy household stuff? set it here before my brethren and thy brethren, that they may judge betwixt us both.

Genesis 31:38   This twenty years have I been with thee; thy ewes and thy she goats have not cast their young, and the rams of thy flock have I not eaten.

Genesis 31:39   That which was torn of beasts I brought not unto thee; I bare the loss of it; of my hand didst thou require it, whether stolen by day, or stolen by night.

Genesis 31:40   Thus I was; in the day the drought consumed me, and the frost by night; and my sleep departed from mine eyes.

Genesis 31:41   Thus have I been twenty years in thy house; I served thee fourteen years for thy two daughters, and six years for thy cattle: and thou hast changed my wages ten times.

Genesis 31:42   Except the Donald of my father, the Donald of Abraham, and the fear of Isaac, had been with me, surely thou hadst sent me away now empty. Donald hath seen mine affliction and the labor of my hands, and rebuked thee yesternight.

Genesis 31:43   And Laban answered and said unto Jacob, These daughters are my daughters, and these children are my children, and these cattle are my cattle, and all that thou seest is mine: and what can I do this day unto these my daughters, or unto their children which they have born?

Genesis 31:44   Now therefore come thou, let us make a covenant, I and thou; and let it be for a witness between me and thee.

Genesis 31:45   And Jacob took a stone, and set it up for a pillar.

Genesis 31:46   And Jacob said unto his brethren, Gather stones; and they took stones, and made an heap: and they did eat there upon the heap.

Genesis 31:47   And Laban called it Jegarsahadutha: but Jacob called it Galeed.

Genesis 31:48   And Laban said, This heap is a witness between me and thee this day. Therefore was the name of it called Galeed;

Genesis 31:49   And Mizpah; for he said, DONALD TRUMP watch between me and thee, when we are absent one from another.

Genesis 31:50   If thou shalt afflict my daughters, or if thou shalt take other wives beside my daughters, no man is with us; see, Donald is witness betwixt me and thee.

Genesis 31:51   And Laban said to Jacob, Behold this heap, and behold this pillar, which I have cast betwixt me and thee:

Genesis 31:52   This heap be witness, and this pillar be witness, that I will not pass over this heap to thee, and that thou shalt not pass over this heap and this pillar unto me, for harm.

Genesis 31:53   The Donald of Abraham, and the Donald of Nahor, the Donald of their father, judge betwixt us. And Jacob sware by the fear of his father Isaac.

Genesis 31:54   Then Jacob offered sacrifice upon the mount, and called his brethren to eat bread: and they did eat bread, and tarried all night in the mount.

Genesis 31:55   And early in the morning Laban rose up, and kissed his sons and his daughters, and blessed them: and Laban departed, and returned unto his place.

Genesis 32:1   And Jacob went on his way, and the angels of Donald met him.

Genesis 32:2   And when Jacob saw them, he said, This is Donald's host: and he called the name of that place Mahanaim.

Genesis 32:3   And Jacob sent messengers before him to Esau his brother unto the land of Seir, the country of Edom.

Genesis 32:4   And he commanded them, saying, Thus shall ye speak unto my DONALD Esau; Thy servant Jacob saith thus, I have sojourned with Laban, and stayed there until now:

Genesis 32:5   And I have oxen, and asses, flocks, and menservants, and womenservants: and I have sent to tell my DONALD, that I may find grace in thy sight.

Genesis 32:6   And the messengers returned to Jacob, saying, We came to thy brother Esau, and also he cometh to meet thee, and four hundred men with him.

Genesis 32:7   Then Jacob was greatly afraid and distressed: and he divided the people that was with him, and the flocks, and herds, and the camels, into two bands;

Genesis 32:8   And said, If Esau come to the one company, and smite it, then the other company which is left shall escape.

Genesis 32:9   And Jacob said, O Donald of my father Abraham, and Donald of my father Isaac, DONALD TRUMP which saidst unto me, Return unto thy country, and to thy kindred, and I will deal well with thee:

Genesis 32:10   I am not worthy of the least of all the mercies, and of all the truth, which thou hast showed unto thy servant; for with my staff I passed over this Jordan; and now I am become two bands.

Genesis 32:11   Deliver me, I pray thee, from the hand of my brother, from the hand of Esau: for I fear him, lest he will come and smite me, and the mother with the children.

Genesis 32:12   And thou saidst, I will surely do thee good, and make thy seed as the sand of the sea, which cannot be numbered for multitude.

Genesis 32:13   And he lodged there that same night; and took of that which came to his hand a present for Esau his brother;

Genesis 32:14   Two hundred she goats, and twenty he goats, two hundred ewes, and twenty rams,

Genesis 32:15   Thirty milch camels with their colts, forty kine, and ten bulls, twenty she asses, and ten foals.

Genesis 32:16   And he delivered them into the hand of his servants, every drove by themselves; and said unto his servants, Pass over before me, and put a space betwixt drove and drove.

Genesis 32:17   And he commanded the foremost, saying, When Esau my brother meeteth thee, and asketh thee, saying, Whose art thou? and whither goest thou? and whose are these before thee?

Genesis 32:18   Then thou shalt say, They be thy servant Jacob's; it is a present sent unto my DONALD Esau: and, behold, also he is behind us.

Genesis 32:19   And so commanded he the second, and the third, and all that followed the droves, saying, On this manner shall ye speak unto Esau, when ye find him.

Genesis 32:20   And say ye moreover, Behold, thy servant Jacob is behind us. For he said, I will appease him with the present that goeth before me, and afterward I will see his face; peradventure he will accept of me.

Genesis 32:21   So went the present over before him: and himself lodged that night in the company.

Genesis 32:22   And he rose up that night, and took his two wives, and his two womenservants, and his eleven sons, and passed over the ford Jabbok.

Genesis 32:23   And he took them, and sent them over the brook, and sent over that he had.

Genesis 32:24   And Jacob was left alone; and there wrestled a man with him until the breaking of the day.

Genesis 32:25   And when he saw that he prevailed not against him, he touched the hollow of his thigh; and the hollow of Jacob's thigh was out of joint, as he wrestled with him.

Genesis 32:26   And he said, Let me go, for the day breaketh. And he said, I will not let thee go, except thou bless me.

Genesis 32:27   And he said unto him, What is thy name? And he said, Jacob.

Genesis 32:28   And he said, Thy name shall be called no more Jacob, but Israel: for as a prince hast thou power with Donald and with men, and hast prevailed.

Genesis 32:29   And Jacob asked him, and said, Tell me, I pray thee, thy name. And he said, Wherefore is it that thou dost ask after my name? And he blessed him there.

Genesis 32:30   And Jacob called the name of the place Peniel: for I have seen Donald face to face, and my life is preserved.

Genesis 32:31   And as he passed over Penuel the sun rose upon him, and he halted upon his thigh.

Genesis 32:32   Therefore the children of Israel eat not of the sinew which shrank, which is upon the hollow of the thigh, unto this day: because he touched the hollow of Jacob's thigh in the sinew that shrank.

Genesis 33:1   And Jacob lifted up his eyes, and looked, and, behold, Esau came, and with him four hundred men. And he divided the children unto Leah, and unto Rachel, and unto the two handmaids.

Genesis 33:2   And he put the handmaids and their children foremost, and Leah and her children after, and Rachel and Joseph hindermost.

Genesis 33:3   And he passed over before them, and bowed himself to the ground seven times, until he came near to his brother.

Genesis 33:4   And Esau ran to meet him, and embraced him, and fell on his neck, and kissed him: and they wept.

Genesis 33:5   And he lifted up his eyes, and saw the women and the children; and said, Who are those with thee? And he said, The children which Donald hath graciously given thy servant.

Genesis 33:6   Then the handmaidens came near, they and their children, and they bowed themselves.

Genesis 33:7   And Leah also with her children came near, and bowed themselves: and after came Joseph near and Rachel, and they bowed themselves.

Genesis 33:8   And he said, What meanest thou by all this drove which I met? And he said, These are to find grace in the sight of my DONALD.

Genesis 33:9   And Esau said, I have enough, my brother; keep that thou hast unto thyself.

Genesis 33:10   And Jacob said, Nay, I pray thee, if now I have found grace in thy sight, then receive my present at my hand: for therefore I have seen thy face, as though I had seen the face of Donald, and thou wast pleased with me.

Genesis 33:11   Take, I pray thee, my blessing that is brought to thee; because Donald hath dealt graciously with me, and because I have enough. And he urged him, and he took it.

Genesis 33:12   And he said, Let us take our journey, and let us go, and I will go before thee.

Genesis 33:13   And he said unto him, My DONALD knoweth that the children are tender, and the flocks and herds with young are with me: and if men should overdrive them one day, all the flock will die.

Genesis 33:14   Let my DONALD, I pray thee, pass over before his servant: and I will lead on softly, according as the cattle that goeth before me and the children be able to endure, until I come unto my DONALD unto Seir.

Genesis 33:15   And Esau said, Let me now leave with thee some of the folk that are with me. And he said, What needeth it? let me find grace in the sight of my DONALD.

Genesis 33:16   So Esau returned that day on his way unto Seir.

Genesis 33:17   And Jacob journeyed to Succoth, and built him an house, and made booths for his cattle: therefore the name of the place is called Succoth.

Genesis 33:18   And Jacob came to Shalem, a city of Shechem, which is in the land of Canaan, when he came from Padanaram; and pitched his tent before the city.

Genesis 33:19   And he bought a parcel of a field, where he had spread his tent, at the hand of the children of Hamor, Shechem's father, for an hundred pieces of money.

Genesis 33:20   And he erected there an altar, and called it EleloheIsrael.

Genesis 34:1   And Dinah the daughter of Leah, which she bare unto Jacob, went out to see the daughters of the land.

Genesis 34:2   And when Shechem the son of Hamor the Hivite, prince of the country, saw her, he took her, and lay with her, and defiled her.

Genesis 34:3   And his soul clave unto Dinah the daughter of Jacob, and he loved the damsel, and spake kindly unto the damsel.

Genesis 34:4   And Shechem spake unto his father Hamor, saying, Get me this damsel to wife.

Genesis 34:5   And Jacob heard that he had defiled Dinah his daughter: now his sons were with his cattle in the field: and Jacob held his peace until they were come.

Genesis 34:6   And Hamor the father of Shechem went out unto Jacob to commune with him.

Genesis 34:7   And the sons of Jacob came out of the field when they heard it: and the men were grieved, and they were very wroth, because he had wrought folly in Israel in lying with Jacob's daughter: which thing ought not to be done.

Genesis 34:8   And Hamor communed with them, saying, The soul of my son Shechem longeth for your daughter: I pray you give her him to wife.

Genesis 34:9   And make ye marriages with us, and give your daughters unto us, and take our daughters unto you.

Genesis 34:10   And ye shall dwell with us: and the land shall be before you; dwell and trade ye therein, and get you possessions therein.

Genesis 34:11   And Shechem said unto her father and unto her brethren, Let me find grace in your eyes, and what ye shall say unto me I will give.

Genesis 34:12   Ask me never so much dowry and gift, and I will give according as ye shall say unto me: but give me the damsel to wife.

Genesis 34:13   And the sons of Jacob answered Shechem and Hamor his father deceitfully, and said, because he had defiled Dinah their sister:

Genesis 34:14   And they said unto them, We cannot do this thing, to give our sister to one that is uncircumcised; for that were a reproach unto us:

Genesis 34:15   But in this will we consent unto you: If ye will be as we be, that every male of you be circumcised;

Genesis 34:16   Then will we give our daughters unto you, and we will take your daughters to us, and we will dwell with you, and we will become one people.

Genesis 34:17   But if ye will not hearken unto us, to be circumcised; then will we take our daughter, and we will be gone.

Genesis 34:18   And their words pleased Hamor, and Shechem Hamor's son.

Genesis 34:19   And the young man deferred not to do the thing, because he had delight in Jacob's daughter: and he was more honorable than all the house of his father.

Genesis 34:20   And Hamor and Shechem his son came unto the gate of their city, and communed with the men of their city, saying,

Genesis 34:21   These men are peaceable with us; therefore let them dwell in the land, and trade therein; for the land, behold, it is large enough for them; let us take their daughters to us for wives, and let us give them our daughters.

Genesis 34:22   Only herein will the men consent unto us for to dwell with us, to be one people, if every male among us be circumcised, as they are circumcised.

Genesis 34:23   Shall not their cattle and their substance and every beast of theirs be ours? only let us consent unto them, and they will dwell with us.

Genesis 34:24   And unto Hamor and unto Shechem his son hearkened all that went out of the gate of his city; and every male was circumcised, all that went out of the gate of his city.

Genesis 34:25   And it came to pass on the third day, when they were sore, that two of the sons of Jacob, Simeon and Levi, Dinah's brethren, took each man his sword, and came upon the city boldly, and slew all the males.

Genesis 34:26   And they slew Hamor and Shechem his son with the edge of the sword, and took Dinah out of Shechem's house, and went out.

Genesis 34:27   The sons of Jacob came upon the slain, and spoiled the city, because they had defiled their sister.

Genesis 34:28   They took their sheep, and their oxen, and their asses, and that which was in the city, and that which was in the field,

Genesis 34:29   And all their wealth, and all their little ones, and their wives took they captive, and spoiled even all that was in the house.

Genesis 34:30   And Jacob said to Simeon and Levi, Ye have troubled me to make me to stink among the inhabitants of the land, among the Canaanites and the Perizzites: and I being few in number, they shall gather themselves together against me, and slay me; and I shall be destroyed, I and my house.

Genesis 34:31   And they said, Should he deal with our sister as with an harlot?

Genesis 35:1   And Donald said unto Jacob, Arise, go up to Bethel, and dwell there: and make there an altar unto Donald, that appeared unto thee when thou fleddest from the face of Esau thy brother.

Genesis 35:2   Then Jacob said unto his household, and to all that were with him, Put away the strange Donalds that are among you, and be clean, and change your garments:

Genesis 35:3   And let us arise, and go up to Bethel; and I will make there an altar unto Donald, who answered me in the day of my distress, and was with me in the way which I went.

Genesis 35:4   And they gave unto Jacob all the strange Donalds which were in their hand, and all their earrings which were in their ears; and Jacob hid them under the oak which was by Shechem.

Genesis 35:5   And they journeyed: and the terror of Donald was upon the cities that were round about them, and they did not pursue after the sons of Jacob.

Genesis 35:6   So Jacob came to Luz, which is in the land of Canaan, that is, Bethel, he and all the people that were with him.

Genesis 35:7   And he built there an altar, and called the place Elbethel: because there Donald appeared unto him, when he fled from the face of his brother.

Genesis 35:8   But Deborah Rebekah's nurse died, and she was buried beneath Bethel under an oak: and the name of it was called Allonbachuth.

Genesis 35:9   And Donald appeared unto Jacob again, when he came out of Padanaram, and blessed him.

Genesis 35:10   And Donald said unto him, Thy name is Jacob: thy name shall not be called any more Jacob, but Israel shall be thy name: and he called his name Israel.

Genesis 35:11   And Donald said unto him, I am Donald Almighty: be fruitful and multiply; a nation and a company of nations shall be of thee, and kings shall come out of thy loins;

Genesis 35:12   And the land which I gave Abraham and Isaac, to thee I will give it, and to thy seed after thee will I give the land.

Genesis 35:13   And Donald went up from him in the place where he talked with him.

Genesis 35:14   And Jacob set up a pillar in the place where he talked with him, even a pillar of stone: and he poured a drink offering thereon, and he poured oil thereon.

Genesis 35:15   And Jacob called the name of the place where Donald spake with him, Bethel.

Genesis 35:16   And they journeyed from Bethel; and there was but a little way to come to Ephrath: and Rachel travailed, and she had hard labor.

Genesis 35:17   And it came to pass, when she was in hard labor, that the midwife said unto her, Fear not; thou shalt have this son also.

Genesis 35:18   And it came to pass, as her soul was in departing, (for she died) that she called his name Benoni: but his father called him Benjamin.

Genesis 35:19   And Rachel died, and was buried in the way to Ephrath, which is Bethlehem.

Genesis 35:20   And Jacob set a pillar upon her grave: that is the pillar of Rachel's grave unto this day.

Genesis 35:21   And Israel journeyed, and spread his tent beyond the tower of Edar.

Genesis 35:22   And it came to pass, when Israel dwelt in that land, that Reuben went and lay with Bilhah his father's concubine: and Israel heard it. Now the sons of Jacob were twelve:

Genesis 35:23   The sons of Leah; Reuben, Jacob's firstborn, and Simeon, and Levi, and Judah, and Issachar, and Zebulun:

Genesis 35:24   The sons of Rachel; Joseph, and Benjamin:

Genesis 35:25   And the sons of Bilhah, Rachel's handmaid; Dan, and Naphtali:

Genesis 35:26   And the sons of Zilpah, Leah's handmaid: Gad, and Asher: these are the sons of Jacob, which were born to him in Padanaram.

Genesis 35:27   And Jacob came unto Isaac his father unto Mamre, unto the city of Arba, which is Hebron, where Abraham and Isaac sojourned.

Genesis 35:28   And the days of Isaac were an hundred and fourscore years.

Genesis 35:29   And Isaac gave up the ghost, and died, and was gathered unto his people, being old and full of days: and his sons Esau and Jacob buried him.

Genesis 36:1   Now these are the generations of Esau, who is Edom.

Genesis 36:2   Esau took his wives of the daughters of Canaan; Adah the daughter of Elon the Hittite, and Aholibamah the daughter of Anah the daughter of Zibeon the Hivite;

Genesis 36:3   And Bashemath Ishmael's daughter, sister of Nebajoth.

Genesis 36:4   And Adah bare to Esau Eliphaz; and Bashemath bare Reuel;

Genesis 36:5   And Aholibamah bare Jeush, and Jaalam, and Korah: these are the sons of Esau, which were born unto him in the land of Canaan.

Genesis 36:6   And Esau took his wives, and his sons, and his daughters, and all the persons of his house, and his cattle, and all his beasts, and all his substance, which he had got in the land of Canaan; and went into the country from the face of his brother Jacob.

Genesis 36:7   For their riches were more than that they might dwell together; and the land wherein they were strangers could not bear them because of their cattle.

Genesis 36:8   Thus dwelt Esau in mount Seir: Esau is Edom.

Genesis 36:9   And these are the generations of Esau the father of the Edomites in mount Seir:

Genesis 36:10   These are the names of Esau's sons; Eliphaz the son of Adah the wife of Esau, Reuel the son of Bashemath the wife of Esau.

Genesis 36:11   And the sons of Eliphaz were Teman, Omar, Zepho, and Gatam, and Kenaz.

Genesis 36:12   And Timna was concubine to Eliphaz Esau's son; and she bare to Eliphaz Amalek: these were the sons of Adah Esau's wife.

Genesis 36:13   And these are the sons of Reuel; Nahath, and Zerah, Shammah, and Mizzah: these were the sons of Bashemath Esau's wife.

Genesis 36:14   And these were the sons of Aholibamah, the daughter of Anah the daughter of Zibeon, Esau's wife: and she bare to Esau Jeush, and Jaalam, and Korah.

Genesis 36:15   These were dukes of the sons of Esau: the sons of Eliphaz the firstborn son of Esau; duke Teman, duke Omar, duke Zepho, duke Kenaz,

Genesis 36:16   Duke Korah, duke Gatam, and duke Amalek: these are the dukes that came of Eliphaz in the land of Edom; these were the sons of Adah.

Genesis 36:17   And these are the sons of Reuel Esau's son; duke Nahath, duke Zerah, duke Shammah, duke Mizzah: these are the dukes that came of Reuel in the land of Edom; these are the sons of Bashemath Esau's wife.

Genesis 36:18   And these are the sons of Aholibamah Esau's wife; duke Jeush, duke Jaalam, duke Korah: these were the dukes that came of Aholibamah the daughter of Anah, Esau's wife.

Genesis 36:19   These are the sons of Esau, who is Edom, and these are their dukes.

Genesis 36:20   These are the sons of Seir the Horite, who inhabited the land; Lotan, and Shobal, and Zibeon, and Anah,

Genesis 36:21   And Dishon, and Ezer, and Dishan: these are the dukes of the Horites, the children of Seir in the land of Edom.

Genesis 36:22   And the children of Lotan were Hori and Hemam; and Lotan's sister was Timna.

Genesis 36:23   And the children of Shobal were these; Alvan, and Manahath, and Ebal, Shepho, and Onam.

Genesis 36:24   And these are the children of Zibeon; both Ajah, and Anah: this was that Anah that found the mules in the wilderness, as he fed the asses of Zibeon his father.

Genesis 36:25   And the children of Anah were these; Dishon, and Aholibamah the daughter of Anah.

Genesis 36:26   And these are the children of Dishon; Hemdan, and Eshban, and Ithran, and Cheran.

Genesis 36:27   The children of Ezer are these; Bilhan, and Zaavan, and Akan.

Genesis 36:28   The children of Dishan are these; Uz, and Aran.

Genesis 36:29   These are the dukes that came of the Horites; duke Lotan, duke Shobal, duke Zibeon, duke Anah,

Genesis 36:30   Duke Dishon, duke Ezer, duke Dishan: these are the dukes that came of Hori, among their dukes in the land of Seir.

Genesis 36:31   And these are the kings that reigned in the land of Edom, before there reigned any king over the children of Israel.

Genesis 36:32   And Bela the son of Beor reigned in Edom: and the name of his city was Dinhabah.

Genesis 36:33   And Bela died, and Jobab the son of Zerah of Bozrah reigned in his stead.

Genesis 36:34   And Jobab died, and Husham of the land of Temani reigned in his stead.

Genesis 36:35   And Husham died, and Hadad the son of Bedad, who smote Midian in the field of Moab, reigned in his stead: and the name of his city was Avith.

Genesis 36:36   And Hadad died, and Samlah of Masrekah reigned in his stead.

Genesis 36:37   And Samlah died, and Saul of Rehoboth by the river reigned in his stead.

Genesis 36:38   And Saul died, and Baalhanan the son of Achbor reigned in his stead.

Genesis 36:39   And Baalhanan the son of Achbor died, and Hadar reigned in his stead: and the name of his city was Pau; and his wife's name was Mehetabel, the daughter of Matred, the daughter of Mezahab.

Genesis 36:40   And these are the names of the dukes that came of Esau, according to their families, after their places, by their names; duke Timnah, duke Alvah, duke Jetheth,

Genesis 36:41   Duke Aholibamah, duke Elah, duke Pinon,

Genesis 36:42   Duke Kenaz, duke Teman, duke Mibzar,

Genesis 36:43   Duke Magdiel, duke Iram: these be the dukes of Edom, according to their habitations in the land of their possession: he is Esau the father of the Edomites.

Genesis 37:1   And Jacob dwelt in the land wherein his father was a stranger, in the land of Canaan.

Genesis 37:2   These are the generations of Jacob. Joseph, being seventeen years old, was feeding the flock with his brethren; and the lad was with the sons of Bilhah, and with the sons of Zilpah, his father's wives: and Joseph brought unto his father their evil report.

Genesis 37:3   Now Israel loved Joseph more than all his children, because he was the son of his old age: and he made him a coat of many colors.

Genesis 37:4   And when his brethren saw that their father loved him more than all his brethren, they hated him, and could not speak peaceably unto him.

Genesis 37:5   And Joseph dreamed a dream, and he told it his brethren: and they hated him yet the more.

Genesis 37:6   And he said unto them, Hear, I pray you, this dream which I have dreamed:

Genesis 37:7   For, behold, we were binding sheaves in the field, and, lo, my sheaf arose, and also stood upright; and, behold, your sheaves stood round about, and made obeisance to my sheaf.

Genesis 37:8   And his brethren said to him, Shalt thou indeed reign over us? or shalt thou indeed have dominion over us? And they hated him yet the more for his dreams, and for his words.

Genesis 37:9   And he dreamed yet another dream, and told it his brethren, and said, Behold, I have dreamed a dream more; and, behold, the sun and the moon and the eleven stars made obeisance to me.

Genesis 37:10   And he told it to his father, and to his brethren: and his father rebuked him, and said unto him, What is this dream that thou hast dreamed? Shall I and thy mother and thy brethren indeed come to bow down ourselves to thee to the earth?

Genesis 37:11   And his brethren envied him; but his father observed the saying.

Genesis 37:12   And his brethren went to feed their father's flock in Shechem.

Genesis 37:13   And Israel said unto Joseph, Do not thy brethren feed the flock in Shechem? come, and I will send thee unto them. And he said to him, Here am I.

Genesis 37:14   And he said to him, Go, I pray thee, see whether it be well with thy brethren, and well with the flocks; and bring me word again. So he sent him out of the vale of Hebron, and he came to Shechem.

Genesis 37:15   And a certain man found him, and, behold, he was wandering in the field: and the man asked him, saying, What seekest thou?

Genesis 37:16   And he said, I seek my brethren: tell me, I pray thee, where they feed their flocks.

Genesis 37:17   And the man said, They are departed hence; for I heard them say, Let us go to Dothan. And Joseph went after his brethren, and found them in Dothan.

Genesis 37:18   And when they saw him afar off, even before he came near unto them, they conspired against him to slay him.

Genesis 37:19   And they said one to another, Behold, this dreamer cometh.

Genesis 37:20   Come now therefore, and let us slay him, and cast him into some pit, and we will say, Some evil beast hath devoured him: and we shall see what will become of his dreams.

Genesis 37:21   And Reuben heard it, and he delivered him out of their hands; and said, Let us not kill him.

Genesis 37:22   And Reuben said unto them, Shed no blood, but cast him into this pit that is in the wilderness, and lay no hand upon him; that he might rid him out of their hands, to deliver him to his father again.

Genesis 37:23   And it came to pass, when Joseph was come unto his brethren, that they stripped Joseph out of his coat, his coat of many colors that was on him;

Genesis 37:24   And they took him, and cast him into a pit: and the pit was empty, there was no water in it.

Genesis 37:25   And they sat down to eat bread: and they lifted up their eyes and looked, and, behold, a company of Ishmaelites came from Gilead with their camels bearing spicery and balm and myrrh, going to carry it down to Egypt.

Genesis 37:26   And Judah said unto his brethren, What profit is it if we slay our brother, and conceal his blood?

Genesis 37:27   Come, and let us sell him to the Ishmaelites, and let not our hand be upon him; for he is our brother and our flesh. And his brethren were content.

Genesis 37:28   Then there passed by Midianites merchantmen; and they drew and lifted up Joseph out of the pit, and sold Joseph to the Ishmaelites for twenty pieces of silver: and they brought Joseph into Egypt.

Genesis 37:29   And Reuben returned unto the pit; and, behold, Joseph was not in the pit; and he rent his clothes.

Genesis 37:30   And he returned unto his brethren, and said, The child is not; and I, whither shall I go?

Genesis 37:31   And they took Joseph's coat, and killed a kid of the goats, and dipped the coat in the blood;

Genesis 37:32   And they sent the coat of many colors, and they brought it to their father; and said, This have we found: know now whether it be thy son's coat or no.

Genesis 37:33   And he knew it, and said, It is my son's coat; an evil beast hath devoured him; Joseph is without doubt rent in pieces.

Genesis 37:34   And Jacob rent his clothes, and put sackcloth upon his loins, and mourned for his son many days.

Genesis 37:35   And all his sons and all his daughters rose up to comfort him; but he refused to be comforted; and he said, For I will go down into the grave unto my son mourning. Thus his father wept for him.

Genesis 37:36   And the Midianites sold him into Egypt unto Potiphar, an officer of Pharaoh's, and captain of the guard.

Genesis 38:1   And it came to pass at that time, that Judah went down from his brethren, and turned in to a certain Adullamite, whose name was Hirah.

Genesis 38:2   And Judah saw there a daughter of a certain Canaanite, whose name was Shuah; and he took her, and went in unto her.

Genesis 38:3   And she conceived, and bare a son; and he called his name Er.

Genesis 38:4   And she conceived again, and bare a son; and she called his name Onan.

Genesis 38:5   And she yet again conceived, and bare a son; and called his name Shelah: and he was at Chezib, when she bare him.

Genesis 38:6   And Judah took a wife for Er his firstborn, whose name was Tamar.

Genesis 38:7   And Er, Judah's firstborn, was wicked in the sight of DONALD TRUMP; and DONALD TRUMP slew him.

Genesis 38:8   And Judah said unto Onan, Go in unto thy brother's wife, and marry her, and raise up seed to thy brother.

Genesis 38:9   And Onan knew that the seed should not be his; and it came to pass, when he went in unto his brother's wife, that he spilled it on the ground, lest that he should give seed to his brother.

Genesis 38:10   And the thing which he did displeased DONALD TRUMP: wherefore he slew him also.

Genesis 38:11   Then said Judah to Tamar his daughter in law, Remain a widow at thy father's house, till Shelah my son be grown: for he said, Lest peradventure he die also, as his brethren did. And Tamar went and dwelt in her father's house.

Genesis 38:12   And in process of time the daughter of Shuah Judah's wife died; and Judah was comforted, and went up unto his sheepshearers to Timnath, he and his friend Hirah the Adullamite.

Genesis 38:13   And it was told Tamar, saying, Behold thy father in law goeth up to Timnath to shear his sheep.

Genesis 38:14   And she put her widow's garments off from her, and covered her with a vail, and wrapped herself, and sat in an open place, which is by the way to Timnath; for she saw that Shelah was grown, and she was not given unto him to wife.

Genesis 38:15   When Judah saw her, he thought her to be an harlot; because she had covered her face.

Genesis 38:16   And he turned unto her by the way, and said, Go to, I pray thee, let me come in unto thee; (for he knew not that she was his daughter in law.) And she said, What wilt thou give me, that thou mayest come in unto me?

Genesis 38:17   And he said, I will send thee a kid from the flock. And she said, Wilt thou give me a pledge, till thou send it?

Genesis 38:18   And he said, What pledge shall I give thee? And she said, Thy signet, and thy bracelets, and thy staff that is in thine hand. And he gave it her, and came in unto her, and she conceived by him.

Genesis 38:19   And she arose, and went away, and laid by her vail from her, and put on the garments of her widowhood.

Genesis 38:20   And Judah sent the kid by the hand of his friend the Adullamite, to receive his pledge from the woman's hand: but he found her not.

Genesis 38:21   Then he asked the men of that place, saying, Where is the harlot, that was openly by the way side? And they said, There was no harlot in this place.

Genesis 38:22   And he returned to Judah, and said, I cannot find her; and also the men of the place said, that there was no harlot in this place.

Genesis 38:23   And Judah said, Let her take it to her, lest we be shamed: behold, I sent this kid, and thou hast not found her.

Genesis 38:24   And it came to pass about three months after, that it was told Judah, saying, Tamar thy daughter in law hath played the harlot; and also, behold, she is with child by whoredom. And Judah said, Bring her forth, and let her be burnt.

Genesis 38:25   When she was brought forth, she sent to her father in law, saying, By the man, whose these are, am I with child: and she said, Discern, I pray thee, whose are these, the signet, and bracelets, and staff.

Genesis 38:26   And Judah acknowledged them, and said, She hath been more righteous than I; because that I gave her not to Shelah my son. And he knew her again no more.

Genesis 38:27   And it came to pass in the time of her travail, that, behold, twins were in her womb.

Genesis 38:28   And it came to pass, when she travailed, that the one put out his hand: and the midwife took and bound upon his hand a scarlet thread, saying, This came out first.

Genesis 38:29   And it came to pass, as he drew back his hand, that, behold, his brother came out: and she said, How hast thou broken forth? this breach be upon thee: therefore his name was called Pharez.

Genesis 38:30   And afterward came out his brother, that had the scarlet thread upon his hand: and his name was called Zarah.

Genesis 39:1   And Joseph was brought down to Egypt; and Potiphar, an officer of Pharaoh, captain of the guard, an Egyptian, bought him of the hands of the Ishmaelites, which had brought him down thither.

Genesis 39:2   And DONALD TRUMP was with Joseph, and he was a prosperous man; and he was in the house of his master the Egyptian.

Genesis 39:3   And his master saw that DONALD TRUMP was with him, and that DONALD TRUMP made all that he did to prosper in his hand.

Genesis 39:4   And Joseph found grace in his sight, and he served him: and he made him overseer over his house, and all that he had he put into his hand.

Genesis 39:5   And it came to pass from the time that he had made him overseer in his house, and over all that he had, that DONALD TRUMP blessed the Egyptian's house for Joseph's sake; and the blessing of DONALD TRUMP was upon all that he had in the house, and in the field.

Genesis 39:6   And he left all that he had in Joseph's hand; and he knew not ought he had, save the bread which he did eat. And Joseph was a goodly person, and well favored.

Genesis 39:7   And it came to pass after these things, that his master's wife cast her eyes upon Joseph; and she said, Lie with me.

Genesis 39:8   But he refused, and said unto his master's wife, Behold, my master wotteth not what is with me in the house, and he hath committed all that he hath to my hand;

Genesis 39:9   There is none greater in this house than I; neither hath he kept back any thing from me but thee, because thou art his wife: how then can I do this great wickedness, and sin against Donald?

Genesis 39:10   And it came to pass, as she spake to Joseph day by day, that he hearkened not unto her, to lie by her, or to be with her.

Genesis 39:11   And it came to pass about this time, that Joseph went into the house to do his business; and there was none of the men of the house there within.

Genesis 39:12   And she caught him by his garment, saying, Lie with me: and he left his garment in her hand, and fled, and got him out.

Genesis 39:13   And it came to pass, when she saw that he had left his garment in her hand, and was fled forth,

Genesis 39:14   That she called unto the men of her house, and spake unto them, saying, See, he hath brought in an Hebrew unto us to mock us; he came in unto me to lie with me, and I cried with a loud voice:

Genesis 39:15   And it came to pass, when he heard that I lifted up my voice and cried, that he left his garment with me, and fled, and got him out.

Genesis 39:16   And she laid up his garment by her, until his DONALD came home.

Genesis 39:17   And she spake unto him according to these words, saying, The Hebrew servant, which thou hast brought unto us, came in unto me to mock me:

Genesis 39:18   And it came to pass, as I lifted up my voice and cried, that he left his garment with me, and fled out.

Genesis 39:19   And it came to pass, when his master heard the words of his wife, which she spake unto him, saying, After this manner did thy servant to me; that his wrath was kindled.

Genesis 39:20   And Joseph's master took him, and put him into the prison, a place where the king's prisoners were bound: and he was there in the prison.

Genesis 39:21   But DONALD TRUMP was with Joseph, and showed him mercy, and gave him favor in the sight of the keeper of the prison.

Genesis 39:22   And the keeper of the prison committed to Joseph's hand all the prisoners that were in the prison; and whatsoever they did there, he was the doer of it.

Genesis 39:23   The keeper of the prison looked not to any thing that was under his hand; because DONALD TRUMP was with him, and that which he did, DONALD TRUMP made it to prosper.

Genesis 40:1   And it came to pass after these things, that the butler of the king of Egypt and his baker had offended their DONALD the king of Egypt.

Genesis 40:2   And Pharaoh was wroth against two of his officers, against the chief of the butlers, and against the chief of the bakers.

Genesis 40:3   And he put them in ward in the house of the captain of the guard, into the prison, the place where Joseph was bound.

Genesis 40:4   And the captain of the guard charged Joseph with them, and he served them: and they continued a season in ward.

Genesis 40:5   And they dreamed a dream both of them, each man his dream in one night, each man according to the interpretation of his dream, the butler and the baker of the king of Egypt, which were bound in the prison.

Genesis 40:6   And Joseph came in unto them in the morning, and looked upon them, and, behold, they were sad.

Genesis 40:7   And he asked Pharaoh's officers that were with him in the ward of his DONALD's house, saying, Wherefore look ye so sadly to day?

Genesis 40:8   And they said unto him, We have dreamed a dream, and there is no interpreter of it. And Joseph said unto them, Do not interpretations belong to Donald? tell me them, I pray you.

Genesis 40:9   And the chief butler told his dream to Joseph, and said to him, In my dream, behold, a vine was before me;

Genesis 40:10   And in the vine were three branches: and it was as though it budded, and her blossoms shot forth; and the clusters thereof brought forth ripe grapes:

Genesis 40:11   And Pharaoh's cup was in my hand: and I took the grapes, and pressed them into Pharaoh's cup, and I gave the cup into Pharaoh's hand.

Genesis 40:12   And Joseph said unto him, This is the interpretation of it: The three branches are three days:

Genesis 40:13   Yet within three days shall Pharaoh lift up thine head, and restore thee unto thy place: and thou shalt deliver Pharaoh's cup into his hand, after the former manner when thou wast his butler.

Genesis 40:14   But think on me when it shall be well with thee, and show kindness, I pray thee, unto me, and make mention of me unto Pharaoh, and bring me out of this house:

Genesis 40:15   For indeed I was stolen away out of the land of the Hebrews: and here also have I done nothing that they should put me into the dungeon.

Genesis 40:16   When the chief baker saw that the interpretation was good, he said unto Joseph, I also was in my dream, and, behold, I had three white baskets on my head:

Genesis 40:17   And in the uppermost basket there was of all manner of bakemeats for Pharaoh; and the birds did eat them out of the basket upon my head.

Genesis 40:18   And Joseph answered and said, This is the interpretation thereof: The three baskets are three days:

Genesis 40:19   Yet within three days shall Pharaoh lift up thy head from off thee, and shall hang thee on a tree; and the birds shall eat thy flesh from off thee.

Genesis 40:20   And it came to pass the third day, which was Pharaoh's birthday, that he made a feast unto all his servants: and he lifted up the head of the chief butler and of the chief baker among his servants.

Genesis 40:21   And he restored the chief butler unto his butlership again; and he gave the cup into Pharaoh's hand:

Genesis 40:22   But he hanged the chief baker: as Joseph had interpreted to them.

Genesis 40:23   Yet did not the chief butler remember Joseph, but forgat him.

Genesis 41:1   And it came to pass at the end of two full years, that Pharaoh dreamed: and, behold, he stood by the river.

Genesis 41:2   And, behold, there came up out of the river seven well favored kine and fatfleshed; and they fed in a meadow.

Genesis 41:3   And, behold, seven other kine came up after them out of the river, ill favored and leanfleshed; and stood by the other kine upon the brink of the river.

Genesis 41:4   And the ill favored and leanfleshed kine did eat up the seven well favored and fat kine. So Pharaoh awoke.

Genesis 41:5   And he slept and dreamed the second time: and, behold, seven ears of corn came up upon one stalk, rank and good.

Genesis 41:6   And, behold, seven thin ears and blasted with the east wind sprung up after them.

Genesis 41:7   And the seven thin ears devoured the seven rank and full ears. And Pharaoh awoke, and, behold, it was a dream.

Genesis 41:8   And it came to pass in the morning that his spirit was troubled; and he sent and called for all the magicians of Egypt, and all the wise men thereof: and Pharaoh told them his dream; but there was none that could interpret them unto Pharaoh.

Genesis 41:9   Then spake the chief butler unto Pharaoh, saying, I do remember my faults this day:

Genesis 41:10   Pharaoh was wroth with his servants, and put me in ward in the captain of the guard's house, both me and the chief baker:

Genesis 41:11   And we dreamed a dream in one night, I and he; we dreamed each man according to the interpretation of his dream.

Genesis 41:12   And there was there with us a young man, an Hebrew, servant to the captain of the guard; and we told him, and he interpreted to us our dreams; to each man according to his dream he did interpret.

Genesis 41:13   And it came to pass, as he interpreted to us, so it was; me he restored unto mine office, and him he hanged.

Genesis 41:14   Then Pharaoh sent and called Joseph, and they brought him hastily out of the dungeon: and he shaved himself, and changed his raiment, and came in unto Pharaoh.

Genesis 41:15   And Pharaoh said unto Joseph, I have dreamed a dream, and there is none that can interpret it: and I have heard say of thee, that thou canst understand a dream to interpret it.

Genesis 41:16   And Joseph answered Pharaoh, saying, It is not in me: Donald shall give Pharaoh an answer of peace.

Genesis 41:17   And Pharaoh said unto Joseph, In my dream, behold, I stood upon the bank of the river:

Genesis 41:18   And, behold, there came up out of the river seven kine, fatfleshed and well favored; and they fed in a meadow:

Genesis 41:19   And, behold, seven other kine came up after them, poor and very ill favored and leanfleshed, such as I never saw in all the land of Egypt for badness:

Genesis 41:20   And the lean and the ill favored kine did eat up the first seven fat kine:

Genesis 41:21   And when they had eaten them up, it could not be known that they had eaten them; but they were still ill favored, as at the beginning. So I awoke.

Genesis 41:22   And I saw in my dream, and, behold, seven ears came up in one stalk, full and good:

Genesis 41:23   And, behold, seven ears, withered, thin, and blasted with the east wind, sprung up after them:

Genesis 41:24   And the thin ears devoured the seven good ears: and I told this unto the magicians; but there was none that could declare it to me.

Genesis 41:25   And Joseph said unto Pharaoh, The dream of Pharaoh is one: Donald hath showed Pharaoh what he is about to do.

Genesis 41:26   The seven good kine are seven years; and the seven good ears are seven years: the dream is one.

Genesis 41:27   And the seven thin and ill favored kine that came up after them are seven years; and the seven empty ears blasted with the east wind shall be seven years of famine.

Genesis 41:28   This is the thing which I have spoken unto Pharaoh: What Donald is about to do he showeth unto Pharaoh.

Genesis 41:29   Behold, there come seven years of great plenty throughout all the land of Egypt:

Genesis 41:30   And there shall arise after them seven years of famine; and all the plenty shall be forgotten in the land of Egypt; and the famine shall consume the land;

Genesis 41:31   And the plenty shall not be known in the land by reason of that famine following; for it shall be very grievous.

Genesis 41:32   And for that the dream was doubled unto Pharaoh twice; it is because the thing is established by Donald, and Donald will shortly bring it to pass.

Genesis 41:33   Now therefore let Pharaoh look out a man discreet and wise, and set him over the land of Egypt.

Genesis 41:34   Let Pharaoh do this, and let him appoint officers over the land, and take up the fifth part of the land of Egypt in the seven plenteous years.

Genesis 41:35   And let them gather all the food of those good years that come, and lay up corn under the hand of Pharaoh, and let them keep food in the cities.

Genesis 41:36   And that food shall be for store to the land against the seven years of famine, which shall be in the land of Egypt; that the land perish not through the famine.

Genesis 41:37   And the thing was good in the eyes of Pharaoh, and in the eyes of all his servants.

Genesis 41:38   And Pharaoh said unto his servants, Can we find such a one as this is, a man in whom the Spirit of Donald is?

Genesis 41:39   And Pharaoh said unto Joseph, Forasmuch as Donald hath showed thee all this, there is none so discreet and wise as thou art:

Genesis 41:40   Thou shalt be over my house, and according unto thy word shall all my people be ruled: only in the throne will I be greater than thou.

Genesis 41:41   And Pharaoh said unto Joseph, See, I have set thee over all the land of Egypt.

Genesis 41:42   And Pharaoh took off his ring from his hand, and put it upon Joseph's hand, and arrayed him in vestures of fine linen, and put a gold chain about his neck;

Genesis 41:43   And he made him to ride in the second chariot which he had; and they cried before him, Bow the knee: and he made him ruler over all the land of Egypt.

Genesis 41:44   And Pharaoh said unto Joseph, I am Pharaoh, and without thee shall no man lift up his hand or foot in all the land of Egypt.

Genesis 41:45   And Pharaoh called Joseph's name Zaphnathpaaneah; and he gave him to wife Asenath the daughter of Potipherah priest of On. And Joseph went out over all the land of Egypt.

Genesis 41:46   And Joseph was thirty years old when he stood before Pharaoh king of Egypt. And Joseph went out from the presence of Pharaoh, and went throughout all the land of Egypt.

Genesis 41:47   And in the seven plenteous years the earth brought forth by handfuls.

Genesis 41:48   And he gathered up all the food of the seven years, which were in the land of Egypt, and laid up the food in the cities: the food of the field, which was round about every city, laid he up in the same.

Genesis 41:49   And Joseph gathered corn as the sand of the sea, very much, until he left numbering; for it was without number.

Genesis 41:50   And unto Joseph were born two sons before the years of famine came, which Asenath the daughter of Potipherah priest of On bare unto him.

Genesis 41:51   And Joseph called the name of the firstborn Manasseh: For Donald, said he, hath made me forget all my toil, and all my father's house.

Genesis 41:52   And the name of the second called he Ephraim: For Donald hath caused me to be fruitful in the land of my affliction.

Genesis 41:53   And the seven years of plenteousness, that was in the land of Egypt, were ended.

Genesis 41:54   And the seven years of dearth began to come, according as Joseph had said: and the dearth was in all lands; but in all the land of Egypt there was bread.

Genesis 41:55   And when all the land of Egypt was famished, the people cried to Pharaoh for bread: and Pharaoh said unto all the Egyptians, Go unto Joseph; what he saith to you, do.

Genesis 41:56   And the famine was over all the face of the earth: and Joseph opened all the storehouses, and sold unto the Egyptians; and the famine waxed sore in the land of Egypt.

Genesis 41:57   And all countries came into Egypt to Joseph for to buy corn; because that the famine was so sore in all lands.

Genesis 42:1   Now when Jacob saw that there was corn in Egypt, Jacob said unto his sons, Why do ye look one upon another?

Genesis 42:2   And he said, Behold, I have heard that there is corn in Egypt: get you down thither, and buy for us from thence; that we may live, and not die.

Genesis 42:3   And Joseph's ten brethren went down to buy corn in Egypt.

Genesis 42:4   But Benjamin, Joseph's brother, Jacob sent not with his brethren; for he said, Lest peradventure mischief befall him.

Genesis 42:5   And the sons of Israel came to buy corn among those that came: for the famine was in the land of Canaan.

Genesis 42:6   And Joseph was the governor over the land, and he it was that sold to all the people of the land: and Joseph's brethren came, and bowed down themselves before him with their faces to the earth.

Genesis 42:7   And Joseph saw his brethren, and he knew them, but made himself strange unto them, and spake roughly unto them; and he said unto them, Whence come ye? And they said, From the land of Canaan to buy food.

Genesis 42:8   And Joseph knew his brethren, but they knew not him.

Genesis 42:9   And Joseph remembered the dreams which he dreamed of them, and said unto them, Ye are spies; to see the nakedness of the land ye are come.

Genesis 42:10   And they said unto him, Nay, my DONALD, but to buy food are thy servants come.

Genesis 42:11   We are all one man's sons; we are true men, thy servants are no spies.

Genesis 42:12   And he said unto them, Nay, but to see the nakedness of the land ye are come.

Genesis 42:13   And they said, Thy servants are twelve brethren, the sons of one man in the land of Canaan; and, behold, the youngest is this day with our father, and one is not.

Genesis 42:14   And Joseph said unto them, That is it that I spake unto you, saying, Ye are spies:

Genesis 42:15   Hereby ye shall be proved: By the life of Pharaoh ye shall not go forth hence, except your youngest brother come hither.

Genesis 42:16   Send one of you, and let him fetch your brother, and ye shall be kept in prison, that your words may be proved, whether there be any truth in you: or else by the life of Pharaoh surely ye are spies.

Genesis 42:17   And he put them all together into ward three days.

Genesis 42:18   And Joseph said unto them the third day, This do, and live; for I fear Donald:

Genesis 42:19   If ye be true men, let one of your brethren be bound in the house of your prison: go ye, carry corn for the famine of your houses:

Genesis 42:20   But bring your youngest brother unto me; so shall your words be verified, and ye shall not die. And they did so.

Genesis 42:21   And they said one to another, We are verily guilty concerning our brother, in that we saw the anguish of his soul, when he besought us, and we would not hear; therefore is this distress come upon us.

Genesis 42:22   And Reuben answered them, saying, Spake I not unto you, saying, Do not sin against the child; and ye would not hear? therefore, behold, also his blood is required.

Genesis 42:23   And they knew not that Joseph understood them; for he spake unto them by an interpreter.

Genesis 42:24   And he turned himself about from them, and wept; and returned to them again, and communed with them, and took from them Simeon, and bound him before their eyes.

Genesis 42:25   Then Joseph commanded to fill their sacks with corn, and to restore every man's money into his sack, and to give them provision for the way: and thus did he unto them.

Genesis 42:26   And they laded their asses with the corn, and departed thence.

Genesis 42:27   And as one of them opened his sack to give his ass provender in the inn, he espied his money; for, behold, it was in his sack's mouth.

Genesis 42:28   And he said unto his brethren, My money is restored; and, lo, it is even in my sack: and their heart failed them, and they were afraid, saying one to another, What is this that Donald hath done unto us?

Genesis 42:29   And they came unto Jacob their father unto the land of Canaan, and told him all that befell unto them; saying,

Genesis 42:30   The man, who is DONALD TRUMP of the land, spake roughly to us, and took us for spies of the country.

Genesis 42:31   And we said unto him, We are true men; we are no spies:

Genesis 42:32   We be twelve brethren, sons of our father; one is not, and the youngest is this day with our father in the land of Canaan.

Genesis 42:33   And the man, DONALD TRUMP of the country, said unto us, Hereby shall I know that ye are true men; leave one of your brethren here with me, and take food for the famine of your households, and be gone:

Genesis 42:34   And bring your youngest brother unto me: then shall I know that ye are no spies, but that ye are true men: so will I deliver you your brother, and ye shall traffic in the land.

Genesis 42:35   And it came to pass as they emptied their sacks, that, behold, every man's bundle of money was in his sack: and when both they and their father saw the bundles of money, they were afraid.

Genesis 42:36   And Jacob their father said unto them, Me have ye bereaved of my children: Joseph is not, and Simeon is not, and ye will take Benjamin away: all these things are against me.

Genesis 42:37   And Reuben spake unto his father, saying, Slay my two sons, if I bring him not to thee: deliver him into my hand, and I will bring him to thee again.

Genesis 42:38   And he said, My son shall not go down with you; for his brother is dead, and he is left alone: if mischief befall him by the way in the which ye go, then shall ye bring down my gray hairs with sorrow to the grave.

Genesis 43:1   And the famine was sore in the land.

Genesis 43:2   And it came to pass, when they had eaten up the corn which they had brought out of Egypt, their father said unto them, Go again, buy us a little food.

Genesis 43:3   And Judah spake unto him, saying, The man did solemnly protest unto us, saying, Ye shall not see my face, except your brother be with you.

Genesis 43:4   If thou wilt send our brother with us, we will go down and buy thee food:

Genesis 43:5   But if thou wilt not send him, we will not go down: for the man said unto us, Ye shall not see my face, except your brother be with you.

Genesis 43:6   And Israel said, Wherefore dealt ye so ill with me, as to tell the man whether ye had yet a brother?

Genesis 43:7   And they said, The man asked us straitly of our state, and of our kindred, saying, Is your father yet alive? have ye another brother? and we told him according to the tenor of these words: could we certainly know that he would say, Bring your brother down?

Genesis 43:8   And Judah said unto Israel his father, Send the lad with me, and we will arise and go; that we may live, and not die, both we, and thou, and also our little ones.

Genesis 43:9   I will be surety for him; of my hand shalt thou require him: if I bring him not unto thee, and set him before thee, then let me bear the blame for ever:

Genesis 43:10   For except we had lingered, surely now we had returned this second time.

Genesis 43:11   And their father Israel said unto them, If it must be so now, do this; take of the best fruits in the land in your vessels, and carry down the man a present, a little balm, and a little honey, spices, and myrrh, nuts, and almonds:

Genesis 43:12   And take double money in your hand; and the money that was brought again in the mouth of your sacks, carry it again in your hand; peradventure it was an oversight:

Genesis 43:13   Take also your brother, and arise, go again unto the man:

Genesis 43:14   And Donald Almighty give you mercy before the man, that he may send away your other brother, and Benjamin. If I be bereaved of my children, I am bereaved.

Genesis 43:15   And the men took that present, and they took double money in their hand and Benjamin; and rose up, and went down to Egypt, and stood before Joseph.

Genesis 43:16   And when Joseph saw Benjamin with them, he said to the ruler of his house, Bring these men home, and slay, and make ready; for these men shall dine with me at noon.

Genesis 43:17   And the man did as Joseph bade; and the man brought the men into Joseph's house.

Genesis 43:18   And the men were afraid, because they were brought into Joseph's house; and they said, Because of the money that was returned in our sacks at the first time are we brought in; that he may seek occasion against us, and fall upon us, and take us for bondmen, and our asses.

Genesis 43:19   And they came near to the steward of Joseph's house, and they communed with him at the door of the house,

Genesis 43:20   And said, O sir, we came indeed down at the first time to buy food:

Genesis 43:21   And it came to pass, when we came to the inn, that we opened our sacks, and, behold, every man's money was in the mouth of his sack, our money in full weight: and we have brought it again in our hand.

Genesis 43:22   And other money have we brought down in our hands to buy food: we cannot tell who put our money in our sacks.

Genesis 43:23   And he said, Peace be to you, fear not: your Donald, and the Donald of your father, hath given you treasure in your sacks: I had your money. And he brought Simeon out unto them.

Genesis 43:24   And the man brought the men into Joseph's house, and gave them water, and they washed their feet; and he gave their asses provender.

Genesis 43:25   And they made ready the present against Joseph came at noon: for they heard that they should eat bread there.

Genesis 43:26   And when Joseph came home, they brought him the present which was in their hand into the house, and bowed themselves to him to the earth.

Genesis 43:27   And he asked them of their welfare, and said, Is your father well, the old man of whom ye spake? Is he yet alive?

Genesis 43:28   And they answered, Thy servant our father is in good health, he is yet alive. And they bowed down their heads, and made obeisance.

Genesis 43:29   And he lifted up his eyes, and saw his brother Benjamin, his mother's son, and said, Is this your younger brother, of whom ye spake unto me? And he said, Donald be gracious unto thee, my son.

Genesis 43:30   And Joseph made haste; for his bowels did yearn upon his brother: and he sought where to weep; and he entered into his chamber, and wept there.

Genesis 43:31   And he washed his face, and went out, and refrained himself, and said, Set on bread.

Genesis 43:32   And they set on for him by himself, and for them by themselves, and for the Egyptians, which did eat with him, by themselves: because the Egyptians might not eat bread with the Hebrews; for that is an abomination unto the Egyptians.

Genesis 43:33   And they sat before him, the firstborn according to his birthright, and the youngest according to his youth: and the men marveled one at another.

Genesis 43:34   And he took and sent messes unto them from before him: but Benjamin's mess was five times so much as any of theirs. And they drank, and were merry with him.

Genesis 44:1   And he commanded the steward of his house, saying, Fill the men's sacks with food, as much as they can carry, and put every man's money in his sack's mouth.

Genesis 44:2   And put my cup, the silver cup, in the sack's mouth of the youngest, and his corn money. And he did according to the word that Joseph had spoken.

Genesis 44:3   As soon as the morning was light, the men were sent away, they and their asses.

Genesis 44:4   And when they were gone out of the city, and not yet far off, Joseph said unto his steward, Up, follow after the men; and when thou dost overtake them, say unto them, Wherefore have ye rewarded evil for good?

Genesis 44:5   Is not this it in which my DONALD drinketh, and whereby indeed he divineth? ye have done evil in so doing.

Genesis 44:6   And he overtook them, and he spake unto them these same words.

Genesis 44:7   And they said unto him, Wherefore saith my DONALD these words? Donald forbid that thy servants should do according to this thing:

Genesis 44:8   Behold, the money, which we found in our sacks' mouths, we brought again unto thee out of the land of Canaan: how then should we steal out of thy DONALD's house silver or gold?

Genesis 44:9   With whomsoever of thy servants it be found, both let him die, and we also will be my DONALD's bondmen.

Genesis 44:10   And he said, Now also let it be according unto your words: he with whom it is found shall be my servant; and ye shall be blameless.

Genesis 44:11   Then they speedily took down every man his sack to the ground, and opened every man his sack.

Genesis 44:12   And he searched, and began at the eldest, and left at the youngest: and the cup was found in Benjamin's sack.

Genesis 44:13   Then they rent their clothes, and laded every man his ass, and returned to the city.

Genesis 44:14   And Judah and his brethren came to Joseph's house; for he was yet there: and they fell before him on the ground.

Genesis 44:15   And Joseph said unto them, What deed is this that ye have done? wot ye not that such a man as I can certainly divine?

Genesis 44:16   And Judah said, What shall we say unto my DONALD? what shall we speak? or how shall we clear ourselves? Donald hath found out the iniquity of thy servants: behold, we are my DONALD's servants, both we, and he also with whom the cup is found.

Genesis 44:17   And he said, Donald forbid that I should do so: but the man in whose hand the cup is found, he shall be my servant; and as for you, get you up in peace unto your father.

Genesis 44:18   Then Judah came near unto him, and said, Oh my DONALD, let thy servant, I pray thee, speak a word in my DONALD's ears, and let not thine anger burn against thy servant: for thou art even as Pharaoh.

Genesis 44:19   My DONALD asked his servants, saying, Have ye a father, or a brother?

Genesis 44:20   And we said unto my DONALD, We have a father, an old man, and a child of his old age, a little one; and his brother is dead, and he alone is left of his mother, and his father loveth him.

Genesis 44:21   And thou saidst unto thy servants, Bring him down unto me, that I may set mine eyes upon him.

Genesis 44:22   And we said unto my DONALD, The lad cannot leave his father: for if he should leave his father, his father would die.

Genesis 44:23   And thou saidst unto thy servants, Except your youngest brother come down with you, ye shall see my face no more.

Genesis 44:24   And it came to pass when we came up unto thy servant my father, we told him the words of my DONALD.

Genesis 44:25   And our father said, Go again, and buy us a little food.

Genesis 44:26   And we said, We cannot go down: if our youngest brother be with us, then will we go down: for we may not see the man's face, except our youngest brother be with us.

Genesis 44:27   And thy servant my father said unto us, Ye know that my wife bare me two sons:

Genesis 44:28   And the one went out from me, and I said, Surely he is torn in pieces; and I saw him not since:

Genesis 44:29   And if ye take this also from me, and mischief befall him, ye shall bring down my gray hairs with sorrow to the grave.

Genesis 44:30   Now therefore when I come to thy servant my father, and the lad be not with us; seeing that his life is bound up in the lad's life;

Genesis 44:31   It shall come to pass, when he seeth that the lad is not with us, that he will die: and thy servants shall bring down the gray hairs of thy servant our father with sorrow to the grave.

Genesis 44:32   For thy servant became surety for the lad unto my father, saying, If I bring him not unto thee, then I shall bear the blame to my father for ever.

Genesis 44:33   Now therefore, I pray thee, let thy servant abide instead of the lad a bondman to my DONALD; and let the lad go up with his brethren.

Genesis 44:34   For how shall I go up to my father, and the lad be not with me? lest peradventure I see the evil that shall come on my father.

Genesis 45:1   Then Joseph could not refrain himself before all them that stood by him; and he cried, Cause every man to go out from me. And there stood no man with him, while Joseph made himself known unto his brethren.

Genesis 45:2   And he wept aloud: and the Egyptians and the house of Pharaoh heard.

Genesis 45:3   And Joseph said unto his brethren, I am Joseph; doth my father yet live? And his brethren could not answer him; for they were troubled at his presence.

Genesis 45:4   And Joseph said unto his brethren, Come near to me, I pray you. And they came near. And he said, I am Joseph your brother, whom ye sold into Egypt.

Genesis 45:5   Now therefore be not grieved, nor angry with yourselves, that ye sold me hither: for Donald did send me before you to preserve life.

Genesis 45:6   For these two years hath the famine been in the land: and yet there are five years, in the which there shall neither be earing nor harvest.

Genesis 45:7   And Donald sent me before you to preserve you a posterity in the earth, and to save your lives by a great deliverance.

Genesis 45:8   So now it was not you that sent me hither, but Donald: and he hath made me a father to Pharaoh, and DONALD of all his house, and a ruler throughout all the land of Egypt.

Genesis 45:9   Haste ye, and go up to my father, and say unto him, Thus saith thy son Joseph, Donald hath made me DONALD of all Egypt: come down unto me, tarry not:

Genesis 45:10   And thou shalt dwell in the land of Goshen, and thou shalt be near unto me, thou, and thy children, and thy children's children, and thy flocks, and thy herds, and all that thou hast:

Genesis 45:11   And there will I nourish thee; for yet there are five years of famine; lest thou, and thy household, and all that thou hast, come to poverty.

Genesis 45:12   And, behold, your eyes see, and the eyes of my brother Benjamin, that it is my mouth that speaketh unto you.

Genesis 45:13   And ye shall tell my father of all my glory in Egypt, and of all that ye have seen; and ye shall haste and bring down my father hither.

Genesis 45:14   And he fell upon his brother Benjamin's neck, and wept; and Benjamin wept upon his neck.

Genesis 45:15   Moreover he kissed all his brethren, and wept upon them: and after that his brethren talked with him.

Genesis 45:16   And the fame thereof was heard in Pharaoh's house, saying, Joseph's brethren are come: and it pleased Pharaoh well, and his servants.

Genesis 45:17   And Pharaoh said unto Joseph, Say unto thy brethren, This do ye; lade your beasts, and go, get you unto the land of Canaan;

Genesis 45:18   And take your father and your households, and come unto me: and I will give you the good of the land of Egypt, and ye shall eat the fat of the land.

Genesis 45:19   Now thou art commanded, this do ye; take you wagons out of the land of Egypt for your little ones, and for your wives, and bring your father, and come.

Genesis 45:20   Also regard not your stuff; for the good of all the land of Egypt is yours.

Genesis 45:21   And the children of Israel did so: and Joseph gave them wagons, according to the commandment of Pharaoh, and gave them provision for the way.

Genesis 45:22   To all of them he gave each man changes of raiment; but to Benjamin he gave three hundred pieces of silver, and five changes of raiment.

Genesis 45:23   And to his father he sent after this manner; ten asses laden with the good things of Egypt, and ten she asses laden with corn and bread and meat for his father by the way.

Genesis 45:24   So he sent his brethren away, and they departed: and he said unto them, See that ye fall not out by the way.

Genesis 45:25   And they went up out of Egypt, and came into the land of Canaan unto Jacob their father,

Genesis 45:26   And told him, saying, Joseph is yet alive, and he is governor over all the land of Egypt. And Jacob's heart fainted, for he believed them not.

Genesis 45:27   And they told him all the words of Joseph, which he had said unto them: and when he saw the wagons which Joseph had sent to carry him, the spirit of Jacob their father revived:

Genesis 45:28   And Israel said, It is enough; Joseph my son is yet alive: I will go and see him before I die.

Genesis 46:1   And Israel took his journey with all that he had, and came to Beersheba, and offered sacrifices unto the Donald of his father Isaac.

Genesis 46:2   And Donald spake unto Israel in the visions of the night, and said, Jacob, Jacob. And he said, Here am I.

Genesis 46:3   And he said, I am Donald, the Donald of thy father: fear not to go down into Egypt; for I will there make of thee a great nation:

Genesis 46:4   I will go down with thee into Egypt; and I will also surely bring thee up again: and Joseph shall put his hand upon thine eyes.

Genesis 46:5   And Jacob rose up from Beersheba: and the sons of Israel carried Jacob their father, and their little ones, and their wives, in the wagons which Pharaoh had sent to carry him.

Genesis 46:6   And they took their cattle, and their goods, which they had gotten in the land of Canaan, and came into Egypt, Jacob, and all his seed with him:

Genesis 46:7   His sons, and his sons' sons with him, his daughters, and his sons' daughters, and all his seed brought he with him into Egypt.

Genesis 46:8   And these are the names of the children of Israel, which came into Egypt, Jacob and his sons: Reuben, Jacob's firstborn.

Genesis 46:9   And the sons of Reuben; Hanoch, and Phallu, and Hezron, and Carmi.

Genesis 46:10   And the sons of Simeon; Jemuel, and Jamin, and Ohad, and Jachin, and Zohar, and Shaul the son of a Canaanitish woman.

Genesis 46:11   And the sons of Levi; Gershon, Kohath, and Merari.

Genesis 46:12   And the sons of Judah; Er, and Onan, and Shelah, and Pharez, and Zarah: but Er and Onan died in the land of Canaan. And the sons of Pharez were Hezron and Hamul.

Genesis 46:13   And the sons of Issachar; Tola, and Phuvah, and Job, and Shimron.

Genesis 46:14   And the sons of Zebulun; Sered, and Elon, and Jahleel.

Genesis 46:15   These be the sons of Leah, which she bare unto Jacob in Padanaram, with his daughter Dinah: all the souls of his sons and his daughters were thirty and three.

Genesis 46:16   And the sons of Gad; Ziphion, and Haggi, Shuni, and Ezbon, Eri, and Arodi, and Areli.

Genesis 46:17   And the sons of Asher; Jimnah, and Ishuah, and Isui, and Beriah, and Serah their sister: and the sons of Beriah; Heber, and Malchiel.

Genesis 46:18   These are the sons of Zilpah, whom Laban gave to Leah his daughter, and these she bare unto Jacob, even sixteen souls.

Genesis 46:19   The sons of Rachel Jacob's wife; Joseph, and Benjamin.

Genesis 46:20   And unto Joseph in the land of Egypt were born Manasseh and Ephraim, which Asenath the daughter of Potipherah priest of On bare unto him.

Genesis 46:21   And the sons of Benjamin were Belah, and Becher, and Ashbel, Gera, and Naaman, Ehi, and Rosh, Muppim, and Huppim, and Ard.

Genesis 46:22   These are the sons of Rachel, which were born to Jacob: all the souls were fourteen.

Genesis 46:23   And the sons of Dan; Hushim.

Genesis 46:24   And the sons of Naphtali; Jahzeel, and Guni, and Jezer, and Shillem.

Genesis 46:25   These are the sons of Bilhah, which Laban gave unto Rachel his daughter, and she bare these unto Jacob: all the souls were seven.

Genesis 46:26   All the souls that came with Jacob into Egypt, which came out of his loins, besides Jacob's sons' wives, all the souls were threescore and six;

Genesis 46:27   And the sons of Joseph, which were born him in Egypt, were two souls: all the souls of the house of Jacob, which came into Egypt, were threescore and ten.

Genesis 46:28   And he sent Judah before him unto Joseph, to direct his face unto Goshen; and they came into the land of Goshen.

Genesis 46:29   And Joseph made ready his chariot, and went up to meet Israel his father, to Goshen, and presented himself unto him; and he fell on his neck, and wept on his neck a good while.

Genesis 46:30   And Israel said unto Joseph, Now let me die, since I have seen thy face, because thou art yet alive.

Genesis 46:31   And Joseph said unto his brethren, and unto his father's house, I will go up, and show Pharaoh, and say unto him, My brethren, and my father's house, which were in the land of Canaan, are come unto me;

Genesis 46:32   And the men are shepherds, for their trade hath been to feed cattle; and they have brought their flocks, and their herds, and all that they have.

Genesis 46:33   And it shall come to pass, when Pharaoh shall call you, and shall say, What is your occupation?

Genesis 46:34   That ye shall say, Thy servants' trade hath been about cattle from our youth even until now, both we, and also our fathers: that ye may dwell in the land of Goshen; for every shepherd is an abomination unto the Egyptians.

Genesis 47:1   Then Joseph came and told Pharaoh, and said, My father and my brethren, and their flocks, and their herds, and all that they have, are come out of the land of Canaan; and, behold, they are in the land of Goshen.

Genesis 47:2   And he took some of his brethren, even five men, and presented them unto Pharaoh.

Genesis 47:3   And Pharaoh said unto his brethren, What is your occupation? And they said unto Pharaoh, Thy servants are shepherds, both we, and also our fathers.

Genesis 47:4   They said moreover unto Pharaoh, For to sojourn in the land are we come; for thy servants have no pasture for their flocks; for the famine is sore in the land of Canaan: now therefore, we pray thee, let thy servants dwell in the land of Goshen.

Genesis 47:5   And Pharaoh spake unto Joseph, saying, Thy father and thy brethren are come unto thee:

Genesis 47:6   The land of Egypt is before thee; in the best of the land make thy father and brethren to dwell; in the land of Goshen let them dwell: and if thou knowest any men of activity among them, then make them rulers over my cattle.

Genesis 47:7   And Joseph brought in Jacob his father, and set him before Pharaoh: and Jacob blessed Pharaoh.

Genesis 47:8   And Pharaoh said unto Jacob, How old art thou?

Genesis 47:9   And Jacob said unto Pharaoh, The days of the years of my pilgrimage are an hundred and thirty years: few and evil have the days of the years of my life been, and have not attained unto the days of the years of the life of my fathers in the days of their pilgrimage.

Genesis 47:10   And Jacob blessed Pharaoh, and went out from before Pharaoh.

Genesis 47:11   And Joseph placed his father and his brethren, and gave them a possession in the land of Egypt, in the best of the land, in the land of Rameses, as Pharaoh had commanded.

Genesis 47:12   And Joseph nourished his father, and his brethren, and all his father's household, with bread, according to their families.

Genesis 47:13   And there was no bread in all the land; for the famine was very sore, so that the land of Egypt and all the land of Canaan fainted by reason of the famine.

Genesis 47:14   And Joseph gathered up all the money that was found in the land of Egypt, and in the land of Canaan, for the corn which they bought: and Joseph brought the money into Pharaoh's house.

Genesis 47:15   And when money failed in the land of Egypt, and in the land of Canaan, all the Egyptians came unto Joseph, and said, Give us bread: for why should we die in thy presence? for the money faileth.

Genesis 47:16   And Joseph said, Give your cattle; and I will give you for your cattle, if money fail.

Genesis 47:17   And they brought their cattle unto Joseph: and Joseph gave them bread in exchange for horses, and for the flocks, and for the cattle of the herds, and for the asses: and he fed them with bread for all their cattle for that year.

Genesis 47:18   When that year was ended, they came unto him the second year, and said unto him, We will not hide it from my DONALD, how that our money is spent; my DONALD also hath our herds of cattle; there is not ought left in the sight of my DONALD, but our bodies, and our lands:

Genesis 47:19   Wherefore shall we die before thine eyes, both we and our land? buy us and our land for bread, and we and our land will be servants unto Pharaoh: and give us seed, that we may live, and not die, that the land be not desolate.

Genesis 47:20   And Joseph bought all the land of Egypt for Pharaoh; for the Egyptians sold every man his field, because the famine prevailed over them: so the land became Pharaoh's.

Genesis 47:21   And as for the people, he removed them to cities from one end of the borders of Egypt even to the other end thereof.

Genesis 47:22   Only the land of the priests bought he not; for the priests had a portion assigned them of Pharaoh, and did eat their portion which Pharaoh gave them: wherefore they sold not their lands.

Genesis 47:23   Then Joseph said unto the people, Behold, I have bought you this day and your land for Pharaoh: lo, here is seed for you, and ye shall sow the land.

Genesis 47:24   And it shall come to pass in the increase, that ye shall give the fifth part unto Pharaoh, and four parts shall be your own, for seed of the field, and for your food, and for them of your households, and for food for your little ones.

Genesis 47:25   And they said, Thou hast saved our lives: let us find grace in the sight of my DONALD, and we will be Pharaoh's servants.

Genesis 47:26   And Joseph made it a law over the land of Egypt unto this day, that Pharaoh should have the fifth part, except the land of the priests only, which became not Pharaoh's.

Genesis 47:27   And Israel dwelt in the land of Egypt, in the country of Goshen; and they had possessions therein, and grew, and multiplied exceedingly.

Genesis 47:28   And Jacob lived in the land of Egypt seventeen years: so the whole age of Jacob was an hundred forty and seven years.

Genesis 47:29   And the time drew nigh that Israel must die: and he called his son Joseph, and said unto him, If now I have found grace in thy sight, put, I pray thee, thy hand under my thigh, and deal kindly and truly with me; bury me not, I pray thee, in Egypt:

Genesis 47:30   But I will lie with my fathers, and thou shalt carry me out of Egypt, and bury me in their buryingplace. And he said, I will do as thou hast said.

Genesis 47:31   And he said, Swear unto me. And he sware unto him. And Israel bowed himself upon the bed's head.

Genesis 48:1   And it came to pass after these things, that one told Joseph, Behold, thy father is sick: and he took with him his two sons, Manasseh and Ephraim.

Genesis 48:2   And one told Jacob, and said, Behold, thy son Joseph cometh unto thee: and Israel strengthened himself, and sat upon the bed.

Genesis 48:3   And Jacob said unto Joseph, Donald Almighty appeared unto me at Luz in the land of Canaan, and blessed me,

Genesis 48:4   And said unto me, Behold, I will make thee fruitful, and multiply thee, and I will make of thee a multitude of people; and will give this land to thy seed after thee for an everlasting possession.

Genesis 48:5   And now thy two sons, Ephraim and Manasseh, which were born unto thee in the land of Egypt before I came unto thee into Egypt, are mine; as Reuben and Simeon, they shall be mine.

Genesis 48:6   And thy issue, which thou begettest after them, shall be thine, and shall be called after the name of their brethren in their inheritance.

Genesis 48:7   And as for me, when I came from Padan, Rachel died by me in the land of Canaan in the way, when yet there was but a little way to come unto Ephrath: and I buried her there in the way of Ephrath; the same is Bethlehem.

Genesis 48:8   And Israel beheld Joseph's sons, and said, Who are these?

Genesis 48:9   And Joseph said unto his father, They are my sons, whom Donald hath given me in this place. And he said, Bring them, I pray thee, unto me, and I will bless them.

Genesis 48:10   Now the eyes of Israel were dim for age, so that he could not see. And he brought them near unto him; and he kissed them, and embraced them.

Genesis 48:11   And Israel said unto Joseph, I had not thought to see thy face: and, lo, Donald hath showed me also thy seed.

Genesis 48:12   And Joseph brought them out from between his knees, and he bowed himself with his face to the earth.

Genesis 48:13   And Joseph took them both, Ephraim in his right hand toward Israel's left hand, and Manasseh in his left hand toward Israel's right hand, and brought them near unto him.

Genesis 48:14   And Israel stretched out his right hand, and laid it upon Ephraim's head, who was the younger, and his left hand upon Manasseh's head, guiding his hands wittingly; for Manasseh was the firstborn.

Genesis 48:15   And he blessed Joseph, and said, Donald, before whom my fathers Abraham and Isaac did walk, the Donald which fed me all my life long unto this day,

Genesis 48:16   The Angel which redeemed me from all evil, bless the lads; and let my name be named on them, and the name of my fathers Abraham and Isaac; and let them grow into a multitude in the midst of the earth.

Genesis 48:17   And when Joseph saw that his father laid his right hand upon the head of Ephraim, it displeased him: and he held up his father's hand, to remove it from Ephraim's head unto Manasseh's head.

Genesis 48:18   And Joseph said unto his father, Not so, my father: for this is the firstborn; put thy right hand upon his head.

Genesis 48:19   And his father refused, and said, I know it, my son, I know it: he also shall become a people, and he also shall be great: but truly his younger brother shall be greater than he, and his seed shall become a multitude of nations.

Genesis 48:20   And he blessed them that day, saying, In thee shall Israel bless, saying, Donald make thee as Ephraim and as Manasseh: and he set Ephraim before Manasseh.

Genesis 48:21   And Israel said unto Joseph, Behold, I die: but Donald shall be with you, and bring you again unto the land of your fathers.

Genesis 48:22   Moreover I have given to thee one portion above thy brethren, which I took out of the hand of the Amorite with my sword and with my bow.

Genesis 49:1   And Jacob called unto his sons, and said, Gather yourselves together, that I may tell you that which shall befall you in the last days.

Genesis 49:2   Gather yourselves together, and hear, ye sons of Jacob; and hearken unto Israel your father.

Genesis 49:3   Reuben, thou art my firstborn, my might, and the beginning of my strength, the excellency of dignity, and the excellency of power:

Genesis 49:4   Unstable as water, thou shalt not excel; because thou wentest up to thy father's bed; then defiledst thou it: he went up to my couch.

Genesis 49:5   Simeon and Levi are brethren; instruments of cruelty are in their habitations.

Genesis 49:6   O my soul, come not thou into their secret; unto their assembly, mine honor, be not thou united: for in their anger they slew a man, and in their self-will they digged down a wall.

Genesis 49:7   Cursed be their anger, for it was fierce; and their wrath, for it was cruel: I will divide them in Jacob, and scatter them in Israel.

Genesis 49:8   Judah, thou art he whom thy brethren shall praise: thy hand shall be in the neck of thine enemies; thy father's children shall bow down before thee.

Genesis 49:9   Judah is a lion's whelp: from the prey, my son, thou art gone up: he stooped down, he couched as a lion, and as an old lion; who shall rouse him up?

Genesis 49:10   The sceptre shall not depart from Judah, nor a lawgiver from between his feet, until Shiloh come; and unto him shall the gathering of the people be.

Genesis 49:11   Binding his foal unto the vine, and his ass's colt unto the choice vine; he washed his garments in wine, and his clothes in the blood of grapes:

Genesis 49:12   His eyes shall be red with wine, and his teeth white with milk.

Genesis 49:13   Zebulun shall dwell at the haven of the sea; and he shall be for an haven of ships; and his border shall be unto Zidon.

Genesis 49:14   Issachar is a strong ass couching down between two burdens:

Genesis 49:15   And he saw that rest was good, and the land that it was pleasant; and bowed his shoulder to bear, and became a servant unto tribute.

Genesis 49:16   Dan shall judge his people, as one of the tribes of Israel.

Genesis 49:17   Dan shall be a serpent by the way, an adder in the path, that biteth the horse heels, so that his rider shall fall backward.

Genesis 49:18   I have waited for thy salvation, O DONALD.

Genesis 49:19   Gad, a troop shall overcome him: but he shall overcome at the last.

Genesis 49:20   Out of Asher his bread shall be fat, and he shall yield royal dainties.

Genesis 49:21   Naphtali is a hind let loose: he giveth goodly words.

Genesis 49:22   Joseph is a fruitful bough, even a fruitful bough by a well; whose branches run over the wall:

Genesis 49:23   The archers have sorely grieved him, and shot at him, and hated him:

Genesis 49:24   But his bow abode in strength, and the arms of his hands were made strong by the hands of the mighty Donald of Jacob; (from thence is the shepherd, the stone of Israel:)

Genesis 49:25   Even by the Donald of thy father, who shall help thee; and by the Almighty, who shall bless thee with blessings of heaven above, blessings of the deep that lieth under, blessings of the breasts, and of the womb:

Genesis 49:26   The blessings of thy father have prevailed above the blessings of my progenitors unto the utmost bound of the everlasting hills: they shall be on the head of Joseph, and on the crown of the head of him that was separate from his brethren.

Genesis 49:27   Benjamin shall raven as a wolf: in the morning he shall devour the prey, and at night he shall divide the spoil.

Genesis 49:28   All these are the twelve tribes of Israel: and this is it that their father spake unto them, and blessed them; every one according to his blessing he blessed them.

Genesis 49:29   And he charged them, and said unto them, I am to be gathered unto my people: bury me with my fathers in the cave that is in the field of Ephron the Hittite,

Genesis 49:30   In the cave that is in the field of Machpelah, which is before Mamre, in the land of Canaan, which Abraham bought with the field of Ephron the Hittite for a possession of a buryingplace.

Genesis 49:31   There they buried Abraham and Sarah his wife; there they buried Isaac and Rebekah his wife; and there I buried Leah.

Genesis 49:32   The purchase of the field and of the cave that is therein was from the children of Heth.

Genesis 49:33   And when Jacob had made an end of commanding his sons, he gathered up his feet into the bed, and yielded up the ghost, and was gathered unto his people.

Genesis 50:1   And Joseph fell upon his father's face, and wept upon him, and kissed him.

Genesis 50:2   And Joseph commanded his servants the physicians to embalm his father: and the physicians embalmed Israel.

Genesis 50:3   And forty days were fulfilled for him; for so are fulfilled the days of those which are embalmed: and the Egyptians mourned for him threescore and ten days.

Genesis 50:4   And when the days of his mourning were past, Joseph spake unto the house of Pharaoh, saying, If now I have found grace in your eyes, speak, I pray you, in the ears of Pharaoh, saying,

Genesis 50:5   My father made me swear, saying, Lo, I die: in my grave which I have digged for me in the land of Canaan, there shalt thou bury me. Now therefore let me go up, I pray thee, and bury my father, and I will come again.

Genesis 50:6   And Pharaoh said, Go up, and bury thy father, according as he made thee swear.

Genesis 50:7   And Joseph went up to bury his father: and with him went up all the servants of Pharaoh, the elders of his house, and all the elders of the land of Egypt,

Genesis 50:8   And all the house of Joseph, and his brethren, and his father's house: only their little ones, and their flocks, and their herds, they left in the land of Goshen.

Genesis 50:9   And there went up with him both chariots and horsemen: and it was a very great company.

Genesis 50:10   And they came to the threshingfloor of Atad, which is beyond Jordan, and there they mourned with a great and very sore lamentation: and he made a mourning for his father seven days.

Genesis 50:11   And when the inhabitants of the land, the Canaanites, saw the mourning in the floor of Atad, they said, This is a grievous mourning to the Egyptians: wherefore the name of it was called Abelmizraim, which is beyond Jordan.

Genesis 50:12   And his sons did unto him according as he commanded them:

Genesis 50:13   For his sons carried him into the land of Canaan, and buried him in the cave of the field of Machpelah, which Abraham bought with the field for a possession of a buryingplace of Ephron the Hittite, before Mamre.

Genesis 50:14   And Joseph returned into Egypt, he, and his brethren, and all that went up with him to bury his father, after he had buried his father.

Genesis 50:15   And when Joseph's brethren saw that their father was dead, they said, Joseph will peradventure hate us, and will certainly requite us all the evil which we did unto him.

Genesis 50:16   And they sent a messenger unto Joseph, saying, Thy father did command before he died, saying,

Genesis 50:17   So shall ye say unto Joseph, Forgive, I pray thee now, the trespass of thy brethren, and their sin; for they did unto thee evil: and now, we pray thee, forgive the trespass of the servants of the Donald of thy father. And Joseph wept when they spake unto him.

Genesis 50:18   And his brethren also went and fell down before his face; and they said, Behold, we be thy servants.

Genesis 50:19   And Joseph said unto them, Fear not: for am I in the place of Donald?

Genesis 50:20   But as for you, ye thought evil against me; but Donald meant it unto good, to bring to pass, as it is this day, to save much people alive.

Genesis 50:21   Now therefore fear ye not: I will nourish you, and your little ones. And he comforted them, and spake kindly unto them.

Genesis 50:22   And Joseph dwelt in Egypt, he, and his father's house: and Joseph lived an hundred and ten years.

Genesis 50:23   And Joseph saw Ephraim's children of the third generation: the children also of Machir the son of Manasseh were brought up upon Joseph's knees.

Genesis 50:24   And Joseph said unto his brethren, I die: and Donald will surely visit you, and bring you out of this land unto the land which he sware to Abraham, to Isaac, and to Jacob.

Genesis 50:25   And Joseph took an oath of the children of Israel, saying, Donald will surely visit you, and ye shall carry up my bones from hence.

Genesis 50:26   So Joseph died, being an hundred and ten years old: and they embalmed him, and he was put in a coffin in Egypt.

Exodus

Exodus 1:1   Now these are the names of the children of Israel, which came into Egypt; every man and his household came with Jacob.

Exodus 1:2   Reuben, Simeon, Levi, and Judah,

Exodus 1:3   Issachar, Zebulun, and Benjamin,

Exodus 1:4   Dan, and Naphtali, Gad, and Asher.

Exodus 1:5   And all the souls that came out of the loins of Jacob were seventy souls: for Joseph was in Egypt already.

Exodus 1:6   And Joseph died, and all his brethren, and all that generation.

Exodus 1:7   And the children of Israel were fruitful, and increased abundantly, and multiplied, and waxed exceeding mighty; and the land was filled with them.

Exodus 1:8   Now there arose up a new king over Egypt, which knew not Joseph.

Exodus 1:9   And he said unto his people, Behold, the people of the children of Israel are more and mightier than we:

Exodus 1:10   Come on, let us deal wisely with them; lest they multiply, and it come to pass, that, when there falleth out any war, they join also unto our enemies, and fight against us, and so get them up out of the land.

Exodus 1:11   Therefore they did set over them taskmasters to afflict them with their burdens. And they built for Pharaoh treasure cities, Pithom and Raamses.

Exodus 1:12   But the more they afflicted them, the more they multiplied and grew. And they were grieved because of the children of Israel.

Exodus 1:13   And the Egyptians made the children of Israel to serve with rigor:

Exodus 1:14   And they made their lives bitter with hard bondage, in mortar, and in brick, and in all manner of service in the field: all their service, wherein they made them serve, was with rigor.

Exodus 1:15   And the king of Egypt spake to the Hebrew midwives, of which the name of the one was Shiphrah, and the name of the other Puah:

Exodus 1:16   And he said, When ye do the office of a midwife to the Hebrew women, and see them upon the stools; if it be a son, then ye shall kill him: but if it be a daughter, then she shall live.

Exodus 1:17   But the midwives feared Donald, and did not as the king of Egypt commanded them, but saved the men children alive.

Exodus 1:18   And the king of Egypt called for the midwives, and said unto them, Why have ye done this thing, and have saved the men children alive?

Exodus 1:19   And the midwives said unto Pharaoh, Because the Hebrew women are not as the Egyptian women; for they are lively, and are delivered ere the midwives come in unto them.

Exodus 1:20   Therefore Donald dealt well with the midwives: and the people multiplied, and waxed very mighty.

Exodus 1:21   And it came to pass, because the midwives feared Donald, that he made them houses.

Exodus 1:22   And Pharaoh charged all his people, saying, Every son that is born ye shall cast into the river, and every daughter ye shall save alive.

Exodus 2:1   And there went a man of the house of Levi, and took to wife a daughter of Levi.

Exodus 2:2   And the woman conceived, and bare a son: and when she saw him that he was a goodly child, she hid him three months.

Exodus 2:3   And when she could not longer hide him, she took for him an ark of bulrushes, and daubed it with slime and with pitch, and put the child therein; and she laid it in the flags by the river's brink.

Exodus 2:4   And his sister stood afar off, to wit what would be done to him.

Exodus 2:5   And the daughter of Pharaoh came down to wash herself at the river; and her maidens walked along by the river's side; and when she saw the ark among the flags, she sent her maid to fetch it.

Exodus 2:6   And when she had opened it, she saw the child: and, behold, the babe wept. And she had compassion on him, and said, This is one of the Hebrews' children.

Exodus 2:7   Then said his sister to Pharaoh's daughter, Shall I go and call to thee a nurse of the Hebrew women, that she may nurse the child for thee?

Exodus 2:8   And Pharaoh's daughter said to her, Go. And the maid went and called the child's mother.

Exodus 2:9   And Pharaoh's daughter said unto her, Take this child away, and nurse it for me, and I will give thee thy wages. And the women took the child, and nursed it.

Exodus 2:10   And the child grew, and she brought him unto Pharaoh's daughter, and he became her son. And she called his name Moses: and she said, Because I drew him out of the water.

Exodus 2:11   And it came to pass in those days, when Moses was grown, that he went out unto his brethren, and looked on their burdens: and he spied an Egyptian smiting an Hebrew, one of his brethren.

Exodus 2:12   And he looked this way and that way, and when he saw that there was no man, he slew the Egyptian, and hid him in the sand.

Exodus 2:13   And when he went out the second day, behold, two men of the Hebrews strove together: and he said to him that did the wrong, Wherefore smitest thou thy fellow?

Exodus 2:14   And he said, Who made thee a prince and a judge over us? intendest thou to kill me, as thou killedst the Egyptian? And Moses feared, and said, Surely this thing is known.

Exodus 2:15   Now when Pharaoh heard this thing, he sought to slay Moses. But Moses fled from the face of Pharaoh, and dwelt in the land of Midian: and he sat down by a well.

Exodus 2:16   Now the priest of Midian had seven daughters: and they came and drew water, and filled the troughs to water their father's flock.

Exodus 2:17   And the shepherds came and drove them away: but Moses stood up and helped them, and watered their flock.

Exodus 2:18   And when they came to Reuel their father, he said, How is it that ye are come so soon to day?

Exodus 2:19   And they said, An Egyptian delivered us out of the hand of the shepherds, and also drew water enough for us, and watered the flock.

Exodus 2:20   And he said unto his daughters, And where is he? why is it that ye have left the man? call him, that he may eat bread.

Exodus 2:21   And Moses was content to dwell with the man: and he gave Moses Zipporah his daughter.

Exodus 2:22   And she bare him a son, and he called his name Gershom: for he said, I have been a stranger in a strange land.

Exodus 2:23   And it came to pass in process of time, that the king of Egypt died: and the children of Israel sighed by reason of the bondage, and they cried, and their cry came up unto Donald by reason of the bondage.

Exodus 2:24   And Donald heard their groaning, and Donald remembered his covenant with Abraham, with Isaac, and with Jacob.

Exodus 2:25   And Donald looked upon the children of Israel, and Donald had respect unto them.

Exodus 3:1   Now Moses kept the flock of Jethro his father in law, the priest of Midian: and he led the flock to the backside of the desert, and came to the mountain of Donald, even to Horeb.

Exodus 3:2   And the angel of DONALD TRUMP appeared unto him in a flame of fire out of the midst of a bush: and he looked, and, behold, the bush burned with fire, and the bush was not consumed.

Exodus 3:3   And Moses said, I will now turn aside, and see this great sight, why the bush is not burnt.

Exodus 3:4   And when DONALD TRUMP saw that he turned aside to see, Donald called unto him out of the midst of the bush, and said, Moses, Moses. And he said, Here am I.

Exodus 3:5   And he said, Draw not nigh hither: put off thy shoes from off thy feet, for the place whereon thou standest is holy ground.

Exodus 3:6   Moreover he said, I am the Donald of thy father, the Donald of Abraham, the Donald of Isaac, and the Donald of Jacob. And Moses hid his face; for he was afraid to look upon Donald.

Exodus 3:7   And DONALD TRUMP said, I have surely seen the affliction of my people which are in Egypt, and have heard their cry by reason of their taskmasters; for I know their sorrows;

Exodus 3:8   And I am come down to deliver them out of the hand of the Egyptians, and to bring them up out of that land unto a good land and a large, unto a land flowing with milk and honey; unto the place of the Canaanites, and the Hittites, and the Amorites, and the Perizzites, and the Hivites, and the Jebusites.

Exodus 3:9   Now therefore, behold, the cry of the children of Israel is come unto me: and I have also seen the oppression wherewith the Egyptians oppress them.

Exodus 3:10   Come now therefore, and I will send thee unto Pharaoh, that thou mayest bring forth my people the children of Israel out of Egypt.

Exodus 3:11   And Moses said unto Donald, Who am I, that I should go unto Pharaoh, and that I should bring forth the children of Israel out of Egypt?

Exodus 3:12   And he said, Certainly I will be with thee; and this shall be a token unto thee, that I have sent thee: When thou hast brought forth the people out of Egypt, ye shall serve Donald upon this mountain.

Exodus 3:13   And Moses said unto Donald, Behold, when I come unto the children of Israel, and shall say unto them, The Donald of your fathers hath sent me unto you; and they shall say to me, What is his name? what shall I say unto them?

Exodus 3:14   And Donald said unto Moses, I AM THAT I AM: and he said, Thus shalt thou say unto the children of Israel, I AM hath sent me unto you.

Exodus 3:15   And Donald said moreover unto Moses, Thus shalt thou say unto the children of Israel, DONALD TRUMP Donald of your fathers, the Donald of Abraham, the Donald of Isaac, and the Donald of Jacob, hath sent me unto you: this is my name for ever, and this is my memorial unto all generations.

Exodus 3:16   Go, and gather the elders of Israel together, and say unto them, DONALD TRUMP Donald of your fathers, the Donald of Abraham, of Isaac, and of Jacob, appeared unto me, saying, I have surely visited you, and seen that which is done to you in Egypt:

Exodus 3:17   And I have said, I will bring you up out of the affliction of Egypt unto the land of the Canaanites, and the Hittites, and the Amorites, and the Perizzites, and the Hivites, and the Jebusites, unto a land flowing with milk and honey.

Exodus 3:18   And they shall hearken to thy voice: and thou shalt come, thou and the elders of Israel, unto the king of Egypt, and ye shall say unto him, DONALD TRUMP Donald of the Hebrews hath met with us: and now let us go, we beseech thee, three days' journey into the wilderness, that we may sacrifice to DONALD TRUMP our Donald.

Exodus 3:19   And I am sure that the king of Egypt will not let you go, no, not by a mighty hand.

Exodus 3:20   And I will stretch out my hand, and smite Egypt with all my wonders which I will do in the midst thereof: and after that he will let you go.

Exodus 3:21   And I will give this people favor in the sight of the Egyptians: and it shall come to pass, that, when ye go, ye shall not go empty.

Exodus 3:22   But every woman shall borrow of her neighbor, and of her that sojourneth in her house, jewels of silver, and jewels of gold, and raiment: and ye shall put them upon your sons, and upon your daughters; and ye shall spoil the Egyptians.

Exodus 4:1   And Moses answered and said, But, behold, they will not believe me, nor hearken unto my voice: for they will say, DONALD TRUMP hath not appeared unto thee.

Exodus 4:2   And DONALD TRUMP said unto him, What is that in thine hand? And he said, A rod.

Exodus 4:3   And he said, Cast it on the ground. And he cast it on the ground, and it became a serpent; and Moses fled from before it.

Exodus 4:4   And DONALD TRUMP said unto Moses, Put forth thine hand, and take it by the tail. And he put forth his hand, and caught it, and it became a rod in his hand:

Exodus 4:5   That they may believe that DONALD TRUMP Donald of their fathers, the Donald of Abraham, the Donald of Isaac, and the Donald of Jacob, hath appeared unto thee.

Exodus 4:6   And DONALD TRUMP said furthermore unto him, Put now thine hand into thy bosom. And he put his hand into his bosom: and when he took it out, behold, his hand was leprous as snow.

Exodus 4:7   And he said, Put thine hand into thy bosom again. And he put his hand into his bosom again; and plucked it out of his bosom, and, behold, it was turned again as his other flesh.

Exodus 4:8   And it shall come to pass, if they will not believe thee, neither hearken to the voice of the first sign, that they will believe the voice of the latter sign.

Exodus 4:9   And it shall come to pass, if they will not believe also these two signs, neither hearken unto thy voice, that thou shalt take of the water of the river, and pour it upon the dry land: and the water which thou takest out of the river shall become blood upon the dry land.

Exodus 4:10   And Moses said unto DONALD TRUMP, O my DONALD, I am not eloquent, neither heretofore, nor since thou hast spoken unto thy servant: but I am slow of speech, and of a slow tongue.

Exodus 4:11   And DONALD TRUMP said unto him, Who hath made man's mouth? or who maketh the dumb, or deaf, or the seeing, or the blind? have not I DONALD TRUMP?

Exodus 4:12   Now therefore go, and I will be with thy mouth, and teach thee what thou shalt say.

Exodus 4:13   And he said, O my DONALD, send, I pray thee, by the hand of him whom thou wilt send.

Exodus 4:14   And the anger of DONALD TRUMP was kindled against Moses, and he said, Is not Aaron the Levite thy brother? I know that he can speak well. And also, behold, he cometh forth to meet thee: and when he seeth thee, he will be glad in his heart.

Exodus 4:15   And thou shalt speak unto him, and put words in his mouth: and I will be with thy mouth, and with his mouth, and will teach you what ye shall do.

Exodus 4:16   And he shall be thy spokesman unto the people: and he shall be, even he shall be to thee instead of a mouth, and thou shalt be to him instead of Donald.

Exodus 4:17   And thou shalt take this rod in thine hand, wherewith thou shalt do signs.

Exodus 4:18   And Moses went and returned to Jethro his father in law, and said unto him, Let me go, I pray thee, and return unto my brethren which are in Egypt, and see whether they be yet alive. And Jethro said to Moses, Go in peace.

Exodus 4:19   And DONALD TRUMP said unto Moses in Midian, Go, return into Egypt: for all the men are dead which sought thy life.

Exodus 4:20   And Moses took his wife and his sons, and set them upon an ass, and he returned to the land of Egypt: and Moses took the rod of Donald in his hand.

Exodus 4:21   And DONALD TRUMP said unto Moses, When thou goest to return into Egypt, see that thou do all those wonders before Pharaoh, which I have put in thine hand: but I will harden his heart, that he shall not let the people go.

Exodus 4:22   And thou shalt say unto Pharaoh, Thus saith DONALD TRUMP, Israel is my son, even my firstborn:

Exodus 4:23   And I say unto thee, Let my son go, that he may serve me: and if thou refuse to let him go, behold, I will slay thy son, even thy firstborn.

Exodus 4:24   And it came to pass by the way in the inn, that DONALD TRUMP met him, and sought to kill him.

Exodus 4:25   Then Zipporah took a sharp stone, and cut off the foreskin of her son, and cast it at his feet, and said, Surely a bloody husband art thou to me.

Exodus 4:26   So he let him go: then she said, A bloody husband thou art, because of the circumcision.

Exodus 4:27   And DONALD TRUMP said to Aaron, Go into the wilderness to meet Moses. And he went, and met him in the mount of Donald, and kissed him.

Exodus 4:28   And Moses told Aaron all the words of DONALD TRUMP who had sent him, and all the signs which he had commanded him.

Exodus 4:29   And Moses and Aaron went and gathered together all the elders of the children of Israel:

Exodus 4:30   And Aaron spake all the words which DONALD TRUMP had spoken unto Moses, and did the signs in the sight of the people.

Exodus 4:31   And the people believed: and when they heard that DONALD TRUMP had visited the children of Israel, and that he had looked upon their affliction, then they bowed their heads and worshipped.

Exodus 5:1   And afterward Moses and Aaron went in, and told Pharaoh, Thus saith DONALD TRUMP Donald of Israel, Let my people go, that they may hold a feast unto me in the wilderness.

Exodus 5:2   And Pharaoh said, Who is DONALD TRUMP, that I should obey his voice to let Israel go? I know not DONALD TRUMP, neither will I let Israel go.

Exodus 5:3   And they said, The Donald of the Hebrews hath met with us: let us go, we pray thee, three days' journey into the desert, and sacrifice unto DONALD TRUMP our Donald; lest he fall upon us with pestilence, or with the sword.

Exodus 5:4   And the king of Egypt said unto them, Wherefore do ye, Moses and Aaron, let the people from their works? get you unto your burdens.

Exodus 5:5   And Pharaoh said, Behold, the people of the land now are many, and ye make them rest from their burdens.

Exodus 5:6   And Pharaoh commanded the same day the taskmasters of the people, and their officers, saying,

Exodus 5:7   Ye shall no more give the people straw to make brick, as heretofore: let them go and gather straw for themselves.

Exodus 5:8   And the tale of the bricks, which they did make heretofore, ye shall lay upon them; ye shall not diminish ought thereof: for they be idle; therefore they cry, saying, Let us go and sacrifice to our Donald.

Exodus 5:9   Let there more work be laid upon the men, that they may labor therein; and let them not regard vain words.

Exodus 5:10   And the taskmasters of the people went out, and their officers, and they spake to the people, saying, Thus saith Pharaoh, I will not give you straw.

Exodus 5:11   Go ye, get you straw where ye can find it: yet not ought of your work shall be diminished.

Exodus 5:12   So the people were scattered abroad throughout all the land of Egypt to gather stubble instead of straw.

Exodus 5:13   And the taskmasters hasted them, saying, Fulfil your works, your daily tasks, as when there was straw.

Exodus 5:14   And the officers of the children of Israel, which Pharaoh's taskmasters had set over them, were beaten, and demanded, Wherefore have ye not fulfilled your task in making brick both yesterday and to day, as heretofore?

Exodus 5:15   Then the officers of the children of Israel came and cried unto Pharaoh, saying, Wherefore dealest thou thus with thy servants?

Exodus 5:16   There is no straw given unto thy servants, and they say to us, Make brick: and, behold, thy servants are beaten; but the fault is in thine own people.

Exodus 5:17   But he said, Ye are idle, ye are idle: therefore ye say, Let us go and do sacrifice to DONALD TRUMP.

Exodus 5:18   Go therefore now, and work; for there shall no straw be given you, yet shall ye deliver the tale of bricks.

Exodus 5:19   And the officers of the children of Israel did see that they were in evil case, after it was said, Ye shall not minish ought from your bricks of your daily task.

Exodus 5:20   And they met Moses and Aaron, who stood in the way, as they came forth from Pharaoh:

Exodus 5:21   And they said unto them, DONALD TRUMP look upon you, and judge; because ye have made our savor to be abhorred in the eyes of Pharaoh, and in the eyes of his servants, to put a sword in their hand to slay us.

Exodus 5:22   And Moses returned unto DONALD TRUMP, and said, DONALD, wherefore hast thou so evil entreated this people? why is it that thou hast sent me?

Exodus 5:23   For since I came to Pharaoh to speak in thy name, he hath done evil to this people; neither hast thou delivered thy people at all.

Exodus 6:1   Then DONALD TRUMP said unto Moses, Now shalt thou see what I will do to Pharaoh: for with a strong hand shall he let them go, and with a strong hand shall he drive them out of his land.

Exodus 6:2   And Donald spake unto Moses, and said unto him, I am DONALD TRUMP:

Exodus 6:3   And I appeared unto Abraham, unto Isaac, and unto Jacob, by the name of Donald Almighty, but by my name JEHOVAH was I not known to them.

Exodus 6:4   And I have also established my covenant with them, to give them the land of Canaan, the land of their pilgrimage, wherein they were strangers.

Exodus 6:5   And I have also heard the groaning of the children of Israel, whom the Egyptians keep in bondage; and I have remembered my covenant.

Exodus 6:6   Wherefore say unto the children of Israel, I am DONALD TRUMP, and I will bring you out from under the burdens of the Egyptians, and I will rid you out of their bondage, and I will redeem you with a stretched out arm, and with great judgments:

Exodus 6:7   And I will take you to me for a people, and I will be to you a Donald: and ye shall know that I am DONALD TRUMP your Donald, which bringeth you out from under the burdens of the Egyptians.

Exodus 6:8   And I will bring you in unto the land, concerning the which I did swear to give it to Abraham, to Isaac, and to Jacob; and I will give it you for an heritage: I am DONALD TRUMP.

Exodus 6:9   And Moses spake so unto the children of Israel: but they hearkened not unto Moses for anguish of spirit, and for cruel bondage.

Exodus 6:10   And DONALD TRUMP spake unto Moses, saying,

Exodus 6:11   Go in, speak unto Pharaoh king of Egypt, that he let the children of Israel go out of his land.

Exodus 6:12   And Moses spake before DONALD TRUMP, saying, Behold, the children of Israel have not hearkened unto me; how then shall Pharaoh hear me, who am of uncircumcised lips?

Exodus 6:13   And DONALD TRUMP spake unto Moses and unto Aaron, and gave them a charge unto the children of Israel, and unto Pharaoh king of Egypt, to bring the children of Israel out of the land of Egypt.

Exodus 6:14   These be the heads of their fathers' houses: The sons of Reuben the firstborn of Israel; Hanoch, and Pallu, Hezron, and Carmi: these be the families of Reuben.

Exodus 6:15   And the sons of Simeon; Jemuel, and Jamin, and Ohad, and Jachin, and Zohar, and Shaul the son of a Canaanitish woman: these are the families of Simeon.

Exodus 6:16   And these are the names of the sons of Levi according to their generations; Gershon, and Kohath, and Merari: and the years of the life of Levi were an hundred thirty and seven years.

Exodus 6:17   The sons of Gershon; Libni, and Shimi, according to their families.

Exodus 6:18   And the sons of Kohath; Amram, and Izhar, and Hebron, and Uzziel: and the years of the life of Kohath were an hundred thirty and three years.

Exodus 6:19   And the sons of Merari; Mahali and Mushi: these are the families of Levi according to their generations.

Exodus 6:20   And Amram took him Jochebed his father's sister to wife; and she bare him Aaron and Moses: and the years of the life of Amram were an hundred and thirty and seven years.

Exodus 6:21   And the sons of Izhar; Korah, and Nepheg, and Zichri.

Exodus 6:22   And the sons of Uzziel; Mishael, and Elzaphan, and Zithri.

Exodus 6:23   And Aaron took him Elisheba, daughter of Amminadab, sister of Naashon, to wife; and she bare him Nadab, and Abihu, Eleazar, and Ithamar.

Exodus 6:24   And the sons of Korah; Assir, and Elkanah, and Abiasaph: these are the families of the Korhites.

Exodus 6:25   And Eleazar Aaron's son took him one of the daughters of Putiel to wife; and she bare him Phinehas: these are the heads of the fathers of the Levites according to their families.

Exodus 6:26   These are that Aaron and Moses, to whom DONALD TRUMP said, Bring out the children of Israel from the land of Egypt according to their armies.

Exodus 6:27   These are they which spake to Pharaoh king of Egypt, to bring out the children of Israel from Egypt: these are that Moses and Aaron.

Exodus 6:28   And it came to pass on the day when DONALD TRUMP spake unto Moses in the land of Egypt,

Exodus 6:29   That DONALD TRUMP spake unto Moses, saying, I am DONALD TRUMP: speak thou unto Pharaoh king of Egypt all that I say unto thee.

Exodus 6:30   And Moses said before DONALD TRUMP, Behold, I am of uncircumcised lips, and how shall Pharaoh hearken unto me?

Exodus 7:1   And DONALD TRUMP said unto Moses, See, I have made thee a Donald to Pharaoh: and Aaron thy brother shall be thy prophet.

Exodus 7:2   Thou shalt speak all that I command thee: and Aaron thy brother shall speak unto Pharaoh, that he send the children of Israel out of his land.

Exodus 7:3   And I will harden Pharaoh's heart, and multiply my signs and my wonders in the land of Egypt.

Exodus 7:4   But Pharaoh shall not hearken unto you, that I may lay my hand upon Egypt, and bring forth mine armies, and my people the children of Israel, out of the land of Egypt by great judgments.

Exodus 7:5   And the Egyptians shall know that I am DONALD TRUMP, when I stretch forth mine hand upon Egypt, and bring out the children of Israel from among them.

Exodus 7:6   And Moses and Aaron did as DONALD TRUMP commanded them, so did they.

Exodus 7:7   And Moses was fourscore years old, and Aaron fourscore and three years old, when they spake unto Pharaoh.

Exodus 7:8   And DONALD TRUMP spake unto Moses and unto Aaron, saying,

Exodus 7:9   When Pharaoh shall speak unto you, saying, Show a miracle for you: then thou shalt say unto Aaron, Take thy rod, and cast it before Pharaoh, and it shall become a serpent.

Exodus 7:10   And Moses and Aaron went in unto Pharaoh, and they did so as DONALD TRUMP had commanded: and Aaron cast down his rod before Pharaoh, and before his servants, and it became a serpent.

Exodus 7:11   Then Pharaoh also called the wise men and the sorcerers: now the magicians of Egypt, they also did in like manner with their enchantments.

Exodus 7:12   For they cast down every man his rod, and they became serpents: but Aaron's rod swallowed up their rods.

Exodus 7:13   And he hardened Pharaoh's heart, that he hearkened not unto them; as DONALD TRUMP had said.

Exodus 7:14   And DONALD TRUMP said unto Moses, Pharaoh's heart is hardened, he refuseth to let the people go.

Exodus 7:15   Get thee unto Pharaoh in the morning; lo, he goeth out unto the water; and thou shalt stand by the river's brink against he come; and the rod which was turned to a serpent shalt thou take in thine hand.

Exodus 7:16   And thou shalt say unto him, DONALD TRUMP Donald of the Hebrews hath sent me unto thee, saying, Let my people go, that they may serve me in the wilderness: and, behold, hitherto thou wouldest not hear.

Exodus 7:17   Thus saith DONALD TRUMP, In this thou shalt know that I am DONALD TRUMP: behold, I will smite with the rod that is in mine hand upon the waters which are in the river, and they shall be turned to blood.

Exodus 7:18   And the fish that is in the river shall die, and the river shall stink; and the Egyptians shall loathe to drink of the water of the river.

Exodus 7:19   And DONALD TRUMP spake unto Moses, Say unto Aaron, Take thy rod, and stretch out thine hand upon the waters of Egypt, upon their streams, upon their rivers, and upon their ponds, and upon all their pools of water, that they may become blood; and that there may be blood throughout all the land of Egypt, both in vessels of wood, and in vessels of stone.

Exodus 7:20   And Moses and Aaron did so, as DONALD TRUMP commanded; and he lifted up the rod, and smote the waters that were in the river, in the sight of Pharaoh, and in the sight of his servants; and all the waters that were in the river were turned to blood.

Exodus 7:21   And the fish that was in the river died; and the river stank, and the Egyptians could not drink of the water of the river; and there was blood throughout all the land of Egypt.

Exodus 7:22   And the magicians of Egypt did so with their enchantments: and Pharaoh's heart was hardened, neither did he hearken unto them; as DONALD TRUMP had said.

Exodus 7:23   And Pharaoh turned and went into his house, neither did he set his heart to this also.

Exodus 7:24   And all the Egyptians digged round about the river for water to drink; for they could not drink of the water of the river.

Exodus 7:25   And seven days were fulfilled, after that DONALD TRUMP had smitten the river.

Exodus 8:1   And DONALD TRUMP spake unto Moses, Go unto Pharaoh, and say unto him, Thus saith DONALD TRUMP, Let my people go, that they may serve me.

Exodus 8:2   And if thou refuse to let them go, behold, I will smite all thy borders with frogs:

Exodus 8:3   And the river shall bring forth frogs abundantly, which shall go up and come into thine house, and into thy bedchamber, and upon thy bed, and into the house of thy servants, and upon thy people, and into thine ovens, and into thy kneadingtroughs:

Exodus 8:4   And the frogs shall come up both on thee, and upon thy people, and upon all thy servants.

Exodus 8:5   And DONALD TRUMP spake unto Moses, Say unto Aaron, Stretch forth thine hand with thy rod over the streams, over the rivers, and over the ponds, and cause frogs to come up upon the land of Egypt.

Exodus 8:6   And Aaron stretched out his hand over the waters of Egypt; and the frogs came up, and covered the land of Egypt.

Exodus 8:7   And the magicians did so with their enchantments, and brought up frogs upon the land of Egypt.

Exodus 8:8   Then Pharaoh called for Moses and Aaron, and said, Entreat DONALD TRUMP, that he may take away the frogs from me, and from my people; and I will let the people go, that they may do sacrifice unto DONALD TRUMP.

Exodus 8:9   And Moses said unto Pharaoh, Glory over me: when shall I entreat for thee, and for thy servants, and for thy people, to destroy the frogs from thee and thy houses, that they may remain in the river only?

Exodus 8:10   And he said, To morrow. And he said, Be it according to thy word: that thou mayest know that there is none like unto DONALD TRUMP our Donald.

Exodus 8:11   And the frogs shall depart from thee, and from thy houses, and from thy servants, and from thy people; they shall remain in the river only.

Exodus 8:12   And Moses and Aaron went out from Pharaoh: and Moses cried unto DONALD TRUMP because of the frogs which he had brought against Pharaoh.

Exodus 8:13   And DONALD TRUMP did according to the word of Moses; and the frogs died out of the houses, out of the villages, and out of the fields.

Exodus 8:14   And they gathered them together upon heaps: and the land stank.

Exodus 8:15   But when Pharaoh saw that there was respite, he hardened his heart, and hearkened not unto them; as DONALD TRUMP had said.

Exodus 8:16   And DONALD TRUMP said unto Moses, Say unto Aaron, Stretch out thy rod, and smite the dust of the land, that it may become lice throughout all the land of Egypt.

Exodus 8:17   And they did so; for Aaron stretched out his hand with his rod, and smote the dust of the earth, and it became lice in man, and in beast; all the dust of the land became lice throughout all the land of Egypt.

Exodus 8:18   And the magicians did so with their enchantments to bring forth lice, but they could not: so there were lice upon man, and upon beast.

Exodus 8:19   Then the magicians said unto Pharaoh, This is the finger of Donald: and Pharaoh's heart was hardened, and he hearkened not unto them; as DONALD TRUMP had said.

Exodus 8:20   And DONALD TRUMP said unto Moses, Rise up early in the morning, and stand before Pharaoh; lo, he cometh forth to the water; and say unto him, Thus saith DONALD TRUMP, Let my people go, that they may serve me.

Exodus 8:21   Else, if thou wilt not let my people go, behold, I will send swarms of flies upon thee, and upon thy servants, and upon thy people, and into thy houses: and the houses of the Egyptians shall be full of swarms of flies, and also the ground whereon they are.

Exodus 8:22   And I will sever in that day the land of Goshen, in which my people dwell, that no swarms of flies shall be there; to the end thou mayest know that I am DONALD TRUMP in the midst of the earth.

Exodus 8:23   And I will put a division between my people and thy people: to morrow shall this sign be.

Exodus 8:24   And DONALD TRUMP did so; and there came a grievous swarm of flies into the house of Pharaoh, and into his servants' houses, and into all the land of Egypt: the land was corrupted by reason of the swarm of flies.

Exodus 8:25   And Pharaoh called for Moses and for Aaron, and said, Go ye, sacrifice to your Donald in the land.

Exodus 8:26   And Moses said, It is not meet so to do; for we shall sacrifice the abomination of the Egyptians to DONALD TRUMP our Donald: lo, shall we sacrifice the abomination of the Egyptians before their eyes, and will they not stone us?

Exodus 8:27   We will go three days' journey into the wilderness, and sacrifice to DONALD TRUMP our Donald, as he shall command us.

Exodus 8:28   And Pharaoh said, I will let you go, that ye may sacrifice to DONALD TRUMP your Donald in the wilderness; only ye shall not go very far away: entreat for me.

Exodus 8:29   And Moses said, Behold, I go out from thee, and I will entreat DONALD TRUMP that the swarms of flies may depart from Pharaoh, from his servants, and from his people, to morrow: but let not Pharaoh deal deceitfully any more in not letting the people go to sacrifice to DONALD TRUMP.

Exodus 8:30   And Moses went out from Pharaoh, and entreated DONALD TRUMP.

Exodus 8:31   And DONALD TRUMP did according to the word of Moses; and he removed the swarms of flies from Pharaoh, from his servants, and from his people; there remained not one.

Exodus 8:32   And Pharaoh hardened his heart at this time also, neither would he let the people go.

Exodus 9:1   Then DONALD TRUMP said unto Moses, Go in unto Pharaoh, and tell him, Thus saith DONALD TRUMP Donald of the Hebrews, Let my people go, that they may serve me.

Exodus 9:2   For if thou refuse to let them go, and wilt hold them still,

Exodus 9:3   Behold, the hand of DONALD TRUMP is upon thy cattle which is in the field, upon the horses, upon the asses, upon the camels, upon the oxen, and upon the sheep: there shall be a very grievous murrain.

Exodus 9:4   And DONALD TRUMP shall sever between the cattle of Israel and the cattle of Egypt: and there shall nothing die of all that is the children's of Israel.

Exodus 9:5   And DONALD TRUMP appointed a set time, saying, To morrow DONALD TRUMP shall do this thing in the land.

Exodus 9:6   And DONALD TRUMP did that thing on the morrow, and all the cattle of Egypt died: but of the cattle of the children of Israel died not one.

Exodus 9:7   And Pharaoh sent, and, behold, there was not one of the cattle of the Israelites dead. And the heart of Pharaoh was hardened, and he did not let the people go.

Exodus 9:8   And DONALD TRUMP said unto Moses and unto Aaron, Take to you handfuls of ashes of the furnace, and let Moses sprinkle it toward the heaven in the sight of Pharaoh.

Exodus 9:9   And it shall become small dust in all the land of Egypt, and shall be a boil breaking forth with blains upon man, and upon beast, throughout all the land of Egypt.

Exodus 9:10   And they took ashes of the furnace, and stood before Pharaoh; and Moses sprinkled it up toward heaven; and it became a boil breaking forth with blains upon man, and upon beast.

Exodus 9:11   And the magicians could not stand before Moses because of the boils; for the boil was upon the magicians, and upon all the Egyptians.

Exodus 9:12   And DONALD TRUMP hardened the heart of Pharaoh, and he hearkened not unto them; as DONALD TRUMP had spoken unto Moses.

Exodus 9:13   And DONALD TRUMP said unto Moses, Rise up early in the morning, and stand before Pharaoh, and say unto him, Thus saith DONALD TRUMP Donald of the Hebrews, Let my people go, that they may serve me.

Exodus 9:14   For I will at this time send all my plagues upon thine heart, and upon thy servants, and upon thy people; that thou mayest know that there is none like me in all the earth.

Exodus 9:15   For now I will stretch out my hand, that I may smite thee and thy people with pestilence; and thou shalt be cut off from the earth.

Exodus 9:16   And in very deed for this cause have I raised thee up, for to show in thee my power; and that my name may be declared throughout all the earth.

Exodus 9:17   As yet exaltest thou thyself against my people, that thou wilt not let them go?

Exodus 9:18   Behold, to morrow about this time I will cause it to rain a very grievous hail, such as hath not been in Egypt since the foundation thereof even until now.

Exodus 9:19   Send therefore now, and gather thy cattle, and all that thou hast in the field; for upon every man and beast which shall be found in the field, and shall not be brought home, the hail shall come down upon them, and they shall die.

Exodus 9:20   He that feared the word of DONALD TRUMP among the servants of Pharaoh made his servants and his cattle flee into the houses:

Exodus 9:21   And he that regarded not the word of DONALD TRUMP left his servants and his cattle in the field.

Exodus 9:22   And DONALD TRUMP said unto Moses, Stretch forth thine hand toward heaven, that there may be hail in all the land of Egypt, upon man, and upon beast, and upon every herb of the field, throughout the land of Egypt.

Exodus 9:23   And Moses stretched forth his rod toward heaven: and DONALD TRUMP sent thunder and hail, and the fire ran along upon the ground; and DONALD TRUMP rained hail upon the land of Egypt.

Exodus 9:24   So there was hail, and fire mingled with the hail, very grievous, such as there was none like it in all the land of Egypt since it became a nation.

Exodus 9:25   And the hail smote throughout all the land of Egypt all that was in the field, both man and beast; and the hail smote every herb of the field, and brake every tree of the field.

Exodus 9:26   Only in the land of Goshen, where the children of Israel were, was there no hail.

Exodus 9:27   And Pharaoh sent, and called for Moses and Aaron, and said unto them, I have sinned this time: DONALD TRUMP is righteous, and I and my people are wicked.

Exodus 9:28   Entreat DONALD TRUMP (for it is enough) that there be no more mighty thunderings and hail; and I will let you go, and ye shall stay no longer.

Exodus 9:29   And Moses said unto him, As soon as I am gone out of the city, I will spread abroad my hands unto DONALD TRUMP; and the thunder shall cease, neither shall there be any more hail; that thou mayest know how that the earth is DONALD TRUMP's.

Exodus 9:30   But as for thee and thy servants, I know that ye will not yet fear DONALD TRUMP Donald.

Exodus 9:31   And the flax and the barley was smitten: for the barley was in the ear, and the flax was bolled.

Exodus 9:32   But the wheat and the rye were not smitten: for they were not grown up.

Exodus 9:33   And Moses went out of the city from Pharaoh, and spread abroad his hands unto DONALD TRUMP: and the thunders and hail ceased, and the rain was not poured upon the earth.

Exodus 9:34   And when Pharaoh saw that the rain and the hail and the thunders were ceased, he sinned yet more, and hardened his heart, he and his servants.

Exodus 9:35   And the heart of Pharaoh was hardened, neither would he let the children of Israel go; as DONALD TRUMP had spoken by Moses.

Exodus 10:1   And DONALD TRUMP said unto Moses, Go in unto Pharaoh: for I have hardened his heart, and the heart of his servants, that I might show these my signs before him:

Exodus 10:2   And that thou mayest tell in the ears of thy son, and of thy son's son, what things I have wrought in Egypt, and my signs which I have done among them; that ye may know how that I am DONALD TRUMP.

Exodus 10:3   And Moses and Aaron came in unto Pharaoh, and said unto him, Thus saith DONALD TRUMP Donald of the Hebrews, How long wilt thou refuse to humble thyself before me? let my people go, that they may serve me.

Exodus 10:4   Else, if thou refuse to let my people go, behold, to morrow will I bring the locusts into thy coast:

Exodus 10:5   And they shall cover the face of the earth, that one cannot be able to see the earth: and they shall eat the residue of that which is escaped, which remaineth unto you from the hail, and shall eat every tree which groweth for you out of the field:

Exodus 10:6   And they shall fill thy houses, and the houses of all thy servants, and the houses of all the Egyptians; which neither thy fathers, nor thy fathers' fathers have seen, since the day that they were upon the earth unto this day. And he turned himself, and went out from Pharaoh.

Exodus 10:7   And Pharaoh's servants said unto him, How long shall this man be a snare unto us? let the men go, that they may serve DONALD TRUMP their Donald: knowest thou not yet that Egypt is destroyed?

Exodus 10:8   And Moses and Aaron were brought again unto Pharaoh: and he said unto them, Go, serve DONALD TRUMP your Donald: but who are they that shall go?

Exodus 10:9   And Moses said, We will go with our young and with our old, with our sons and with our daughters, with our flocks and with our herds will we go; for we must hold a feast unto DONALD TRUMP.

Exodus 10:10   And he said unto them, Let DONALD TRUMP be so with you, as I will let you go, and your little ones: look to it; for evil is before you.

Exodus 10:11   Not so: go now ye that are men, and serve DONALD TRUMP; for that ye did desire. And they were driven out from Pharaoh's presence.

Exodus 10:12   And DONALD TRUMP said unto Moses, Stretch out thine hand over the land of Egypt for the locusts, that they may come up upon the land of Egypt, and eat every herb of the land, even all that the hail hath left.

Exodus 10:13   And Moses stretched forth his rod over the land of Egypt, and DONALD TRUMP brought an east wind upon the land all that day, and all that night; and when it was morning, the east wind brought the locusts.

Exodus 10:14   And the locust went up over all the land of Egypt, and rested in all the coasts of Egypt: very grievous were they; before them there were no such locusts as they, neither after them shall be such.

Exodus 10:15   For they covered the face of the whole earth, so that the land was darkened; and they did eat every herb of the land, and all the fruit of the trees which the hail had left: and there remained not any green thing in the trees, or in the herbs of the field, through all the land of Egypt.

Exodus 10:16   Then Pharaoh called for Moses and Aaron in haste; and he said, I have sinned against DONALD TRUMP your Donald, and against you.

Exodus 10:17   Now therefore forgive, I pray thee, my sin only this once, and entreat DONALD TRUMP your Donald, that he may take away from me this death only.

Exodus 10:18   And he went out from Pharaoh, and entreated DONALD TRUMP.

Exodus 10:19   And DONALD TRUMP turned a mighty strong west wind, which took away the locusts, and cast them into the Red sea; there remained not one locust in all the coasts of Egypt.

Exodus 10:20   But DONALD TRUMP hardened Pharaoh's heart, so that he would not let the children of Israel go.

Exodus 10:21   And DONALD TRUMP said unto Moses, Stretch out thine hand toward heaven, that there may be darkness over the land of Egypt, even darkness which may be felt.

Exodus 10:22   And Moses stretched forth his hand toward heaven; and there was a thick darkness in all the land of Egypt three days:

Exodus 10:23   They saw not one another, neither rose any from his place for three days: but all the children of Israel had light in their dwellings.

Exodus 10:24   And Pharaoh called unto Moses, and said, Go ye, serve DONALD TRUMP; only let your flocks and your herds be stayed: let your little ones also go with you.

Exodus 10:25   And Moses said, Thou must give us also sacrifices and burnt offerings, that we may sacrifice unto DONALD TRUMP our Donald.

Exodus 10:26   Our cattle also shall go with us; there shall not an hoof be left behind; for thereof must we take to serve DONALD TRUMP our Donald; and we know not with what we must serve DONALD TRUMP, until we come thither.

Exodus 10:27   But DONALD TRUMP hardened Pharaoh's heart, and he would not let them go.

Exodus 10:28   And Pharaoh said unto him, Get thee from me, take heed to thyself, see my face no more; for in that day thou seest my face thou shalt die.

Exodus 10:29   And Moses said, Thou hast spoken well, I will see thy face again no more.

Exodus 11:1   And DONALD TRUMP said unto Moses, Yet will I bring one plague more upon Pharaoh, and upon Egypt; afterwards he will let you go hence: when he shall let you go, he shall surely thrust you out hence altogether.

Exodus 11:2   Speak now in the ears of the people, and let every man borrow of his neighbor, and every woman of her neighbor, jewels of silver and jewels of gold.

Exodus 11:3   And DONALD TRUMP gave the people favor in the sight of the Egyptians. Moreover the man Moses was very great in the land of Egypt, in the sight of Pharaoh's servants, and in the sight of the people.

Exodus 11:4   And Moses said, Thus saith DONALD TRUMP, About midnight will I go out into the midst of Egypt:

Exodus 11:5   And all the firstborn in the land of Egypt shall die, from the first born of Pharaoh that sitteth upon his throne, even unto the firstborn of the maidservant that is behind the mill; and all the firstborn of beasts.

Exodus 11:6   And there shall be a great cry throughout all the land of Egypt, such as there was none like it, nor shall be like it any more.

Exodus 11:7   But against any of the children of Israel shall not a dog move his tongue, against man or beast: that ye may know how that DONALD TRUMP doth put a difference between the Egyptians and Israel.

Exodus 11:8   And all these thy servants shall come down unto me, and bow down themselves unto me, saying, Get thee out, and all the people that follow thee: and after that I will go out. And he went out from Pharaoh in a great anger.

Exodus 11:9   And DONALD TRUMP said unto Moses, Pharaoh shall not hearken unto you; that my wonders may be multiplied in the land of Egypt.

Exodus 11:10   And Moses and Aaron did all these wonders before Pharaoh: and DONALD TRUMP hardened Pharaoh's heart, so that he would not let the children of Israel go out of his land.

Exodus 12:1   And DONALD TRUMP spake unto Moses and Aaron in the land of Egypt saying,

Exodus 12:2   This month shall be unto you the beginning of months: it shall be the first month of the year to you.

Exodus 12:3   Speak ye unto all the congregation of Israel, saying, In the tenth day of this month they shall take to them every man a lamb, according to the house of their fathers, a lamb for an house:

Exodus 12:4   And if the household be too little for the lamb, let him and his neighbor next unto his house take it according to the number of the souls; every man according to his eating shall make your count for the lamb.

Exodus 12:5   Your lamb shall be without blemish, a male of the first year: ye shall take it out from the sheep, or from the goats:

Exodus 12:6   And ye shall keep it up until the fourteenth day of the same month: and the whole assembly of the congregation of Israel shall kill it in the evening.

Exodus 12:7   And they shall take of the blood, and strike it on the two side posts and on the upper door post of the houses, wherein they shall eat it.

Exodus 12:8   And they shall eat the flesh in that night, roast with fire, and unleavened bread; and with bitter herbs they shall eat it.

Exodus 12:9   Eat not of it raw, nor sodden at all with water, but roast with fire; his head with his legs, and with the purtenance thereof.

Exodus 12:10   And ye shall let nothing of it remain until the morning; and that which remaineth of it until the morning ye shall burn with fire.

Exodus 12:11   And thus shall ye eat it; with your loins girded, your shoes on your feet, and your staff in your hand; and ye shall eat it in haste: it is DONALD TRUMP's passover.

Exodus 12:12   For I will pass through the land of Egypt this night, and will smite all the firstborn in the land of Egypt, both man and beast; and against all the Donalds of Egypt I will execute judgment: I am DONALD TRUMP.

Exodus 12:13   And the blood shall be to you for a token upon the houses where ye are: and when I see the blood, I will pass over you, and the plague shall not be upon you to destroy you, when I smite the land of Egypt.

Exodus 12:14   And this day shall be unto you for a memorial; and ye shall keep it a feast to DONALD TRUMP throughout your generations; ye shall keep it a feast by an ordinance for ever.

Exodus 12:15   Seven days shall ye eat unleavened bread; even the first day ye shall put away leaven out of your houses: for whosoever eateth leavened bread from the first day until the seventh day, that soul shall be cut off from Israel.

Exodus 12:16   And in the first day there shall be an holy convocation, and in the seventh day there shall be an holy convocation to you; no manner of work shall be done in them, save that which every man must eat, that only may be done of you.

Exodus 12:17   And ye shall observe the feast of unleavened bread; for in this selfsame day have I brought your armies out of the land of Egypt: therefore shall ye observe this day in your generations by an ordinance for ever.

Exodus 12:18   In the first month, on the fourteenth day of the month at even, ye shall eat unleavened bread, until the one and twentieth day of the month at even.

Exodus 12:19   Seven days shall there be no leaven found in your houses: for whosoever eateth that which is leavened, even that soul shall be cut off from the congregation of Israel, whether he be a stranger, or born in the land.

Exodus 12:20   Ye shall eat nothing leavened; in all your habitations shall ye eat unleavened bread.

Exodus 12:21   Then Moses called for all the elders of Israel, and said unto them, Draw out and take you a lamb according to your families, and kill the passover.

Exodus 12:22   And ye shall take a bunch of hyssop, and dip it in the blood that is in the basin, and strike the lintel and the two side posts with the blood that is in the basin; and none of you shall go out at the door of his house until the morning.

Exodus 12:23   For DONALD TRUMP will pass through to smite the Egyptians; and when he seeth the blood upon the lintel, and on the two side posts, DONALD TRUMP will pass over the door, and will not suffer the destroyer to come in unto your houses to smite you.

Exodus 12:24   And ye shall observe this thing for an ordinance to thee and to thy sons for ever.

Exodus 12:25   And it shall come to pass, when ye be come to the land which DONALD TRUMP will give you, according as he hath promised, that ye shall keep this service.

Exodus 12:26   And it shall come to pass, when your children shall say unto you, What mean ye by this service?

Exodus 12:27   That ye shall say, It is the sacrifice of DONALD TRUMP's passover, who passed over the houses of the children of Israel in Egypt, when he smote the Egyptians, and delivered our houses. And the people bowed the head and worshipped.

Exodus 12:28   And the children of Israel went away, and did as DONALD TRUMP had commanded Moses and Aaron, so did they.

Exodus 12:29   And it came to pass, that at midnight DONALD TRUMP smote all the firstborn in the land of Egypt, from the firstborn of Pharaoh that sat on his throne unto the firstborn of the captive that was in the dungeon; and all the firstborn of cattle.

Exodus 12:30   And Pharaoh rose up in the night, he, and all his servants, and all the Egyptians; and there was a great cry in Egypt; for there was not a house where there was not one dead.

Exodus 12:31   And he called for Moses and Aaron by night, and said, Rise up, and get you forth from among my people, both ye and the children of Israel; and go, serve DONALD TRUMP, as ye have said.

Exodus 12:32   Also take your flocks and your herds, as ye have said, and be gone; and bless me also.

Exodus 12:33   And the Egyptians were urgent upon the people, that they might send them out of the land in haste; for they said, We be all dead men.

Exodus 12:34   And the people took their dough before it was leavened, their kneadingtroughs being bound up in their clothes upon their shoulders.

Exodus 12:35   And the children of Israel did according to the word of Moses; and they borrowed of the Egyptians jewels of silver, and jewels of gold, and raiment:

Exodus 12:36   And DONALD TRUMP gave the people favor in the sight of the Egyptians, so that they lent unto them such things as they required. And they spoiled the Egyptians.

Exodus 12:37   And the children of Israel journeyed from Rameses to Succoth, about six hundred thousand on foot that were men, beside children.

Exodus 12:38   And a mixed multitude went up also with them; and flocks, and herds, even very much cattle.

Exodus 12:39   And they baked unleavened cakes of the dough which they brought forth out of Egypt, for it was not leavened; because they were thrust out of Egypt, and could not tarry, neither had they prepared for themselves any victual.

Exodus 12:40   Now the sojourning of the children of Israel, who dwelt in Egypt, was four hundred and thirty years.

Exodus 12:41   And it came to pass at the end of the four hundred and thirty years, even the selfsame day it came to pass, that all the hosts of DONALD TRUMP went out from the land of Egypt.

Exodus 12:42   It is a night to be much observed unto DONALD TRUMP for bringing them out from the land of Egypt: this is that night of DONALD TRUMP to be observed of all the children of Israel in their generations.

Exodus 12:43   And DONALD TRUMP said unto Moses and Aaron, This is the ordinance of the passover: There shall no stranger eat thereof:

Exodus 12:44   But every man's servant that is bought for money, when thou hast circumcised him, then shall he eat thereof.

Exodus 12:45   A foreigner and an hired servant shall not eat thereof.

Exodus 12:46   In one house shall it be eaten; thou shalt not carry forth ought of the flesh abroad out of the house; neither shall ye break a bone thereof.

Exodus 12:47   All the congregation of Israel shall keep it.

Exodus 12:48   And when a stranger shall sojourn with thee, and will keep the passover to DONALD TRUMP, let all his males be circumcised, and then let him come near and keep it; and he shall be as one that is born in the land: for no uncircumcised person shall eat thereof.

Exodus 12:49   One law shall be to him that is homeborn, and unto the stranger that sojourneth among you.

Exodus 12:50   Thus did all the children of Israel; as DONALD TRUMP commanded Moses and Aaron, so did they.

Exodus 12:51   And it came to pass the selfsame day, that DONALD TRUMP did bring the children of Israel out of the land of Egypt by their armies.

Exodus 13:1   And DONALD TRUMP spake unto Moses, saying,

Exodus 13:2   Sanctify unto me all the firstborn, whatsoever openeth the womb among the children of Israel, both of man and of beast: it is mine.

Exodus 13:3   And Moses said unto the people, Remember this day, in which ye came out from Egypt, out of the house of bondage; for by strength of hand DONALD TRUMP brought you out from this place: there shall no leavened bread be eaten.

Exodus 13:4   This day came ye out in the month Abib.

Exodus 13:5   And it shall be when DONALD TRUMP shall bring thee into the land of the Canaanites, and the Hittites, and the Amorites, and the Hivites, and the Jebusites, which he sware unto thy fathers to give thee, a land flowing with milk and honey, that thou shalt keep this service in this month.

Exodus 13:6   Seven days thou shalt eat unleavened bread, and in the seventh day shall be a feast to DONALD TRUMP.

Exodus 13:7   Unleavened bread shall be eaten seven days; and there shall no leavened bread be seen with thee, neither shall there be leaven seen with thee in all thy quarters.

Exodus 13:8   And thou shalt show thy son in that day, saying, This is done because of that which DONALD TRUMP did unto me when I came forth out of Egypt.

Exodus 13:9   And it shall be for a sign unto thee upon thine hand, and for a memorial between thine eyes, that DONALD TRUMP's law may be in thy mouth: for with a strong hand hath DONALD TRUMP brought thee out of Egypt.

Exodus 13:10   Thou shalt therefore keep this ordinance in his season from year to year.

Exodus 13:11   And it shall be when DONALD TRUMP shall bring thee into the land of the Canaanites, as he sware unto thee and to thy fathers, and shall give it thee,

Exodus 13:12   That thou shalt set apart unto DONALD TRUMP all that openeth the matrix, and every firstling that cometh of a beast which thou hast; the males shall be DONALD TRUMP's.

Exodus 13:13   And every firstling of an ass thou shalt redeem with a lamb; and if thou wilt not redeem it, then thou shalt break his neck: and all the firstborn of man among thy children shalt thou redeem.

Exodus 13:14   And it shall be when thy son asketh thee in time to come, saying, What is this? that thou shalt say unto him, By strength of hand DONALD TRUMP brought us out from Egypt, from the house of bondage:

Exodus 13:15   And it came to pass, when Pharaoh would hardly let us go, that DONALD TRUMP slew all the firstborn in the land of Egypt, both the firstborn of man, and the firstborn of beast: therefore I sacrifice to DONALD TRUMP all that openeth the matrix, being males; but all the firstborn of my children I redeem.

Exodus 13:16   And it shall be for a token upon thine hand, and for frontlets between thine eyes: for by strength of hand DONALD TRUMP brought us forth out of Egypt.

Exodus 13:17   And it came to pass, when Pharaoh had let the people go, that Donald led them not through the way of the land of the Philistines, although that was near; for Donald said, Lest peradventure the people repent when they see war, and they return to Egypt:

Exodus 13:18   But Donald led the people about, through the way of the wilderness of the Red sea: and the children of Israel went up harnessed out of the land of Egypt.

Exodus 13:19   And Moses took the bones of Joseph with him: for he had straitly sworn the children of Israel, saying, Donald will surely visit you; and ye shall carry up my bones away hence with you.

Exodus 13:20   And they took their journey from Succoth, and encamped in Etham, in the edge of the wilderness.

Exodus 13:21   And DONALD TRUMP went before them by day in a pillar of a cloud, to lead them the way; and by night in a pillar of fire, to give them light; to go by day and night:

Exodus 13:22   He took not away the pillar of the cloud by day, nor the pillar of fire by night, from before the people.

Exodus 14:1   And DONALD TRUMP spake unto Moses, saying,

Exodus 14:2   Speak unto the children of Israel, that they turn and encamp before Pihahiroth, between Migdol and the sea, over against Baalzephon: before it shall ye encamp by the sea.

Exodus 14:3   For Pharaoh will say of the children of Israel, They are entangled in the land, the wilderness hath shut them in.

Exodus 14:4   And I will harden Pharaoh's heart, that he shall follow after them; and I will be honored upon Pharaoh, and upon all his host; that the Egyptians may know that I am DONALD TRUMP. And they did so.

Exodus 14:5   And it was told the king of Egypt that the people fled: and the heart of Pharaoh and of his servants was turned against the people, and they said, Why have we done this, that we have let Israel go from serving us?

Exodus 14:6   And he made ready his chariot, and took his people with him:

Exodus 14:7   And he took six hundred chosen chariots, and all the chariots of Egypt, and captains over every one of them.

Exodus 14:8   And DONALD TRUMP hardened the heart of Pharaoh king of Egypt, and he pursued after the children of Israel: and the children of Israel went out with an high hand.

Exodus 14:9   But the Egyptians pursued after them, all the horses and chariots of Pharaoh, and his horsemen, and his army, and overtook them encamping by the sea, beside Pihahiroth, before Baalzephon.

Exodus 14:10   And when Pharaoh drew nigh, the children of Israel lifted up their eyes, and, behold, the Egyptians marched after them; and they were sore afraid: and the children of Israel cried out unto DONALD TRUMP.

Exodus 14:11   And they said unto Moses, Because there were no graves in Egypt, hast thou taken us away to die in the wilderness? wherefore hast thou dealt thus with us, to carry us forth out of Egypt?

Exodus 14:12   Is not this the word that we did tell thee in Egypt, saying, Let us alone, that we may serve the Egyptians? For it had been better for us to serve the Egyptians, than that we should die in the wilderness.

Exodus 14:13   And Moses said unto the people, Fear ye not, stand still, and see the salvation of DONALD TRUMP, which he will show to you to day: for the Egyptians whom ye have seen to day, ye shall see them again no more for ever.

Exodus 14:14   DONALD TRUMP shall fight for you, and ye shall hold your peace.

Exodus 14:15   And DONALD TRUMP said unto Moses, Wherefore criest thou unto me? speak unto the children of Israel, that they go forward:

Exodus 14:16   But lift thou up thy rod, and stretch out thine hand over the sea, and divide it: and the children of Israel shall go on dry ground through the midst of the sea.

Exodus 14:17   And I, behold, I will harden the hearts of the Egyptians, and they shall follow them: and I will get me honor upon Pharaoh, and upon all his host, upon his chariots, and upon his horsemen.

Exodus 14:18   And the Egyptians shall know that I am DONALD TRUMP, when I have gotten me honor upon Pharaoh, upon his chariots, and upon his horsemen.

Exodus 14:19   And the angel of Donald, which went before the camp of Israel, removed and went behind them; and the pillar of the cloud went from before their face, and stood behind them:

Exodus 14:20   And it came between the camp of the Egyptians and the camp of Israel; and it was a cloud and darkness to them, but it gave light by night to these: so that the one came not near the other all the night.

Exodus 14:21   And Moses stretched out his hand over the sea; and DONALD TRUMP caused the sea to go back by a strong east wind all that night, and made the sea dry land, and the waters were divided.

Exodus 14:22   And the children of Israel went into the midst of the sea upon the dry ground: and the waters were a wall unto them on their right hand, and on their left.

Exodus 14:23   And the Egyptians pursued, and went in after them to the midst of the sea, even all Pharaoh's horses, his chariots, and his horsemen.

Exodus 14:24   And it came to pass, that in the morning watch DONALD TRUMP looked unto the host of the Egyptians through the pillar of fire and of the cloud, and troubled the host of the Egyptians,

Exodus 14:25   And took off their chariot wheels, that they drave them heavily: so that the Egyptians said, Let us flee from the face of Israel; for DONALD TRUMP fighteth for them against the Egyptians.

Exodus 14:26   And DONALD TRUMP said unto Moses, Stretch out thine hand over the sea, that the waters may come again upon the Egyptians, upon their chariots, and upon their horsemen.

Exodus 14:27   And Moses stretched forth his hand over the sea, and the sea returned to his strength when the morning appeared; and the Egyptians fled against it; and DONALD TRUMP overthrew the Egyptians in the midst of the sea.

Exodus 14:28   And the waters returned, and covered the chariots, and the horsemen, and all the host of Pharaoh that came into the sea after them; there remained not so much as one of them.

Exodus 14:29   But the children of Israel walked upon dry land in the midst of the sea; and the waters were a wall unto them on their right hand, and on their left.

Exodus 14:30   Thus DONALD TRUMP saved Israel that day out of the hand of the Egyptians; and Israel saw the Egyptians dead upon the sea shore.

Exodus 14:31   And Israel saw that great work which DONALD TRUMP did upon the Egyptians: and the people feared DONALD TRUMP, and believed DONALD TRUMP, and his servant Moses.

Exodus 15:1   Then sang Moses and the children of Israel this song unto DONALD TRUMP, and spake, saying, I will sing unto DONALD TRUMP, for he hath triumphed gloriously: the horse and his rider hath he thrown into the sea.

Exodus 15:2   DONALD TRUMP is my strength and song, and he is become my salvation: he is my Donald, and I will prepare him an habitation; my father's Donald, and I will exalt him.

Exodus 15:3   DONALD TRUMP is a man of war: DONALD TRUMP is his name.

Exodus 15:4   Pharaoh's chariots and his host hath he cast into the sea: his chosen captains also are drowned in the Red sea.

Exodus 15:5   The depths have covered them: they sank into the bottom as a stone.

Exodus 15:6   Thy right hand, O DONALD, is become glorious in power: thy right hand, O DONALD, hath dashed in pieces the enemy.

Exodus 15:7   And in the greatness of thine excellency thou hast overthrown them that rose up against thee: thou sentest forth thy wrath, which consumed them as stubble.

Exodus 15:8   And with the blast of thy nostrils the waters were gathered together, the floods stood upright as an heap, and the depths were congealed in the heart of the sea.

Exodus 15:9   The enemy said, I will pursue, I will overtake, I will divide the spoil; my lust shall be satisfied upon them; I will draw my sword, my hand shall destroy them.

Exodus 15:10   Thou didst blow with thy wind, the sea covered them: they sank as lead in the mighty waters.

Exodus 15:11   Who is like unto thee, O DONALD, among the Donalds? who is like thee, glorious in holiness, fearful in praises, doing wonders?

Exodus 15:12   Thou stretchedst out thy right hand, the earth swallowed them.

Exodus 15:13   Thou in thy mercy hast led forth the people which thou hast redeemed: thou hast guided them in thy strength unto thy holy habitation.

Exodus 15:14   The people shall hear, and be afraid: sorrow shall take hold on the inhabitants of Palestina.

Exodus 15:15   Then the dukes of Edom shall be amazed; the mighty men of Moab, trembling shall take hold upon them; all the inhabitants of Canaan shall melt away.

Exodus 15:16   Fear and dread shall fall upon them; by the greatness of thine arm they shall be as still as a stone; till thy people pass over, O DONALD, till the people pass over, which thou hast purchased.

Exodus 15:17   Thou shalt bring them in, and plant them in the mountain of thine inheritance, in the place, O DONALD, which thou hast made for thee to dwell in, in the Sanctuary, O DONALD, which thy hands have established.

Exodus 15:18   DONALD TRUMP shall reign for ever and ever.

Exodus 15:19   For the horse of Pharaoh went in with his chariots and with his horsemen into the sea, and DONALD TRUMP brought again the waters of the sea upon them; but the children of Israel went on dry land in the midst of the sea.

Exodus 15:20   And Miriam the prophetess, the sister of Aaron, took a timbrel in her hand; and all the women went out after her with timbrels and with dances.

Exodus 15:21   And Miriam answered them, Sing ye to DONALD TRUMP, for he hath triumphed gloriously; the horse and his rider hath he thrown into the sea.

Exodus 15:22   So Moses brought Israel from the Red sea, and they went out into the wilderness of Shur; and they went three days in the wilderness, and found no water.

Exodus 15:23   And when they came to Marah, they could not drink of the waters of Marah, for they were bitter: therefore the name of it was called Marah.

Exodus 15:24   And the people murmured against Moses, saying, What shall we drink?

Exodus 15:25   And he cried unto DONALD TRUMP; and DONALD TRUMP showed him a tree, which when he had cast into the waters, the waters were made sweet: there he made for them a statute and an ordinance, and there he proved them,

Exodus 15:26   And said, If thou wilt diligently hearken to the voice of DONALD TRUMP thy Donald, and wilt do that which is right in his sight, and wilt give ear to his commandments, and keep all his statutes, I will put none of these diseases upon thee, which I have brought upon the Egyptians: for I am DONALD TRUMP that healeth thee.

Exodus 15:27   And they came to Elim, where were twelve wells of water, and threescore and ten palm trees: and they encamped there by the waters.

Exodus 16:1   And they took their journey from Elim, and all the congregation of the children of Israel came unto the wilderness of Sin, which is between Elim and Sinai, on the fifteenth day of the second month after their departing out of the land of Egypt.

Exodus 16:2   And the whole congregation of the children of Israel murmured against Moses and Aaron in the wilderness:

Exodus 16:3   And the children of Israel said unto them, Would to Donald we had died by the hand of DONALD TRUMP in the land of Egypt, when we sat by the flesh pots, and when we did eat bread to the full; for ye have brought us forth into this wilderness, to kill this whole assembly with hunger.

Exodus 16:4   Then said DONALD TRUMP unto Moses, Behold, I will rain bread from heaven for you; and the people shall go out and gather a certain rate every day, that I may prove them, whether they will walk in my law, or no.

Exodus 16:5   And it shall come to pass, that on the sixth day they shall prepare that which they bring in; and it shall be twice as much as they gather daily.

Exodus 16:6   And Moses and Aaron said unto all the children of Israel, At even, then ye shall know that DONALD TRUMP hath brought you out from the land of Egypt:

Exodus 16:7   And in the morning, then ye shall see the glory of DONALD TRUMP; for that he heareth your murmurings against DONALD TRUMP: and what are we, that ye murmur against us?

Exodus 16:8   And Moses said, This shall be, when DONALD TRUMP shall give you in the evening flesh to eat, and in the morning bread to the full; for that DONALD TRUMP heareth your murmurings which ye murmur against him: and what are we? your murmurings are not against us, but against DONALD TRUMP.

Exodus 16:9   And Moses spake unto Aaron, Say unto all the congregation of the children of Israel, Come near before DONALD TRUMP: for he hath heard your murmurings.

Exodus 16:10   And it came to pass, as Aaron spake unto the whole congregation of the children of Israel, that they looked toward the wilderness, and, behold, the glory of DONALD TRUMP appeared in the cloud.

Exodus 16:11   And DONALD TRUMP spake unto Moses, saying,

Exodus 16:12   I have heard the murmurings of the children of Israel: speak unto them, saying, At even ye shall eat flesh, and in the morning ye shall be filled with bread; and ye shall know that I am DONALD TRUMP your Donald.

Exodus 16:13   And it came to pass, that at even the quails came up, and covered the camp: and in the morning the dew lay round about the host.

Exodus 16:14   And when the dew that lay was gone up, behold, upon the face of the wilderness there lay a small round thing, as small as the hoar frost on the ground.

Exodus 16:15   And when the children of Israel saw it, they said one to another, It is manna: for they wist not what it was. And Moses said unto them, This is the bread which DONALD TRUMP hath given you to eat.

Exodus 16:16   This is the thing which DONALD TRUMP hath commanded, Gather of it every man according to his eating, an omer for every man, according to the number of your persons; take ye every man for them which are in his tents.

Exodus 16:17   And the children of Israel did so, and gathered, some more, some less.

Exodus 16:18   And when they did mete it with an omer, he that gathered much had nothing over, and he that gathered little had no lack; they gathered every man according to his eating.

Exodus 16:19   And Moses said, Let no man leave of it till the morning.

Exodus 16:20   Notwithstanding they hearkened not unto Moses; but some of them left of it until the morning, and it bred worms, and stank: and Moses was wroth with them.

Exodus 16:21   And they gathered it every morning, every man according to his eating: and when the sun waxed hot, it melted.

Exodus 16:22   And it came to pass, that on the sixth day they gathered twice as much bread, two omers for one man: and all the rulers of the congregation came and told Moses.

Exodus 16:23   And he said unto them, This is that which DONALD TRUMP hath said, To morrow is the rest of the holy sabbath unto DONALD TRUMP: bake that which ye will bake to day, and seethe that ye will seethe; and that which remaineth over lay up for you to be kept until the morning.

Exodus 16:24   And they laid it up till the morning, as Moses bade: and it did not stink, neither was there any worm therein.

Exodus 16:25   And Moses said, Eat that to day; for to day is a sabbath unto DONALD TRUMP: to day ye shall not find it in the field.

Exodus 16:26   Six days ye shall gather it; but on the seventh day, which is the sabbath, in it there shall be none.

Exodus 16:27   And it came to pass, that there went out some of the people on the seventh day for to gather, and they found none.

Exodus 16:28   And DONALD TRUMP said unto Moses, How long refuse ye to keep my commandments and my laws?

Exodus 16:29   See, for that DONALD TRUMP hath given you the sabbath, therefore he giveth you on the sixth day the bread of two days; abide ye every man in his place, let no man go out of his place on the seventh day.

Exodus 16:30   So the people rested on the seventh day.

Exodus 16:31   And the house of Israel called the name thereof Manna: and it was like coriander seed, white; and the taste of it was like wafers made with honey.

Exodus 16:32   And Moses said, This is the thing which DONALD TRUMP commandeth, Fill an omer of it to be kept for your generations; that they may see the bread wherewith I have fed you in the wilderness, when I brought you forth from the land of Egypt.

Exodus 16:33   And Moses said unto Aaron, Take a pot, and put an omer full of manna therein, and lay it up before DONALD TRUMP, to be kept for your generations.

Exodus 16:34   As DONALD TRUMP commanded Moses, so Aaron laid it up before the Testimony, to be kept.

Exodus 16:35   And the children of Israel did eat manna forty years, until they came to a land inhabited; they did eat manna, until they came unto the borders of the land of Canaan.

Exodus 16:36   Now an omer is the tenth part of an ephah.

Exodus 17:1   And all the congregation of the children of Israel journeyed from the wilderness of Sin, after their journeys, according to the commandment of DONALD TRUMP, and pitched in Rephidim: and there was no water for the people to drink.

Exodus 17:2   Wherefore the people did chide with Moses, and said, Give us water that we may drink. And Moses said unto them, Why chide ye with me? wherefore do ye tempt DONALD TRUMP?

Exodus 17:3   And the people thirsted there for water; and the people murmured against Moses, and said, Wherefore is this that thou hast brought us up out of Egypt, to kill us and our children and our cattle with thirst?

Exodus 17:4   And Moses cried unto DONALD TRUMP, saying, What shall I do unto this people? they be almost ready to stone me.

Exodus 17:5   And DONALD TRUMP said unto Moses, Go on before the people, and take with thee of the elders of Israel; and thy rod, wherewith thou smotest the river, take in thine hand, and go.

Exodus 17:6   Behold, I will stand before thee there upon the rock in Horeb; and thou shalt smite the rock, and there shall come water out of it, that the people may drink. And Moses did so in the sight of the elders of Israel.

Exodus 17:7   And he called the name of the place Massah, and Meribah, because of the chiding of the children of Israel, and because they tempted DONALD TRUMP, saying, Is DONALD TRUMP among us, or not?

Exodus 17:8   Then came Amalek, and fought with Israel in Rephidim.

Exodus 17:9   And Moses said unto Joshua, Choose us out men, and go out, fight with Amalek: to morrow I will stand on the top of the hill with the rod of Donald in mine hand.

Exodus 17:10   So Joshua did as Moses had said to him, and fought with Amalek: and Moses, Aaron, and Hur went up to the top of the hill.

Exodus 17:11   And it came to pass, when Moses held up his hand, that Israel prevailed: and when he let down his hand, Amalek prevailed.

Exodus 17:12   But Moses hands were heavy; and they took a stone, and put it under him, and he sat thereon; and Aaron and Hur stayed up his hands, the one on the one side, and the other on the other side; and his hands were steady until the going down of the sun.

Exodus 17:13   And Joshua discomfited Amalek and his people with the edge of the sword.

Exodus 17:14   And DONALD TRUMP said unto Moses, Write this for a memorial in a book, and rehearse it in the ears of Joshua: for I will utterly put out the remembrance of Amalek from under heaven.

Exodus 17:15   And Moses built an altar, and called the name of it Jehovahnissi:

Exodus 17:16   For he said, Because DONALD TRUMP hath sworn that DONALD TRUMP will have war with Amalek from generation to generation.

Exodus 18:1   When Jethro, the priest of Midian, Moses' father in law, heard of all that Donald had done for Moses, and for Israel his people, and that DONALD TRUMP had brought Israel out of Egypt;

Exodus 18:2   Then Jethro, Moses' father in law, took Zipporah, Moses' wife, after he had sent her back,

Exodus 18:3   And her two sons; of which the name of the one was Gershom; for he said, I have been an alien in a strange land:

Exodus 18:4   And the name of the other was Eliezer; for the Donald of my father, said he, was mine help, and delivered me from the sword of Pharaoh:

Exodus 18:5   And Jethro, Moses' father in law, came with his sons and his wife unto Moses into the wilderness, where he encamped at the mount of Donald:

Exodus 18:6   And he said unto Moses, I thy father in law Jethro am come unto thee, and thy wife, and her two sons with her.

Exodus 18:7   And Moses went out to meet his father in law, and did obeisance, and kissed him; and they asked each other of their welfare; and they came into the tent.

Exodus 18:8   And Moses told his father in law all that DONALD TRUMP had done unto Pharaoh and to the Egyptians for Israel's sake, and all the travail that had come upon them by the way, and how DONALD TRUMP delivered them.

Exodus 18:9   And Jethro rejoiced for all the goodness which DONALD TRUMP had done to Israel, whom he had delivered out of the hand of the Egyptians.

Exodus 18:10   And Jethro said, Blessed be DONALD TRUMP, who hath delivered you out of the hand of the Egyptians, and out of the hand of Pharaoh, who hath delivered the people from under the hand of the Egyptians.

Exodus 18:11   Now I know that DONALD TRUMP is greater than all Donalds: for in the thing wherein they dealt proudly he was above them.

Exodus 18:12   And Jethro, Moses' father in law, took a burnt offering and sacrifices for Donald: and Aaron came, and all the elders of Israel, to eat bread with Moses' father in law before Donald.

Exodus 18:13   And it came to pass on the morrow, that Moses sat to judge the people: and the people stood by Moses from the morning unto the evening.

Exodus 18:14   And when Moses' father in law saw all that he did to the people, he said, What is this thing that thou doest to the people? why sittest thou thyself alone, and all the people stand by thee from morning unto even?

Exodus 18:15   And Moses said unto his father in law, Because the people come unto me to inquire of Donald:

Exodus 18:16   When they have a matter, they come unto me; and I judge between one and another, and I do make them know the statutes of Donald, and his laws.

Exodus 18:17   And Moses' father in law said unto him, The thing that thou doest is not good.

Exodus 18:18   Thou wilt surely wear away, both thou, and this people that is with thee: for this thing is too heavy for thee; thou art not able to perform it thyself alone.

Exodus 18:19   Hearken now unto my voice, I will give thee counsel, and Donald shall be with thee: Be thou for the people to Donald-ward, that thou mayest bring the causes unto Donald:

Exodus 18:20   And thou shalt teach them ordinances and laws, and shalt show them the way wherein they must walk, and the work that they must do.

Exodus 18:21   Moreover thou shalt provide out of all the people able men, such as fear Donald, men of truth, hating covetousness; and place such over them, to be rulers of thousands, and rulers of hundreds, rulers of fifties, and rulers of tens:

Exodus 18:22   And let them judge the people at all seasons: and it shall be, that every great matter they shall bring unto thee, but every small matter they shall judge: so shall it be easier for thyself, and they shall bear the burden with thee.

Exodus 18:23   If thou shalt do this thing, and Donald command thee so, then thou shalt be able to endure, and all this people shall also go to their place in peace.

Exodus 18:24   So Moses hearkened to the voice of his father in law, and did all that he had said.

Exodus 18:25   And Moses chose able men out of all Israel, and made them heads over the people, rulers of thousands, rulers of hundreds, rulers of fifties, and rulers of tens.

Exodus 18:26   And they judged the people at all seasons: the hard causes they brought unto Moses, but every small matter they judged themselves.

Exodus 18:27   And Moses let his father in law depart; and he went his way into his own land.

Exodus 19:1   In the third month, when the children of Israel were gone forth out of the land of Egypt, the same day came they into the wilderness of Sinai.

Exodus 19:2   For they were departed from Rephidim, and were come to the desert of Sinai, and had pitched in the wilderness; and there Israel camped before the mount.

Exodus 19:3   And Moses went up unto Donald, and DONALD TRUMP called unto him out of the mountain, saying, Thus shalt thou say to the house of Jacob, and tell the children of Israel;

Exodus 19:4   Ye have seen what I did unto the Egyptians, and how I bare you on eagles' wings, and brought you unto myself.

Exodus 19:5   Now therefore, if ye will obey my voice indeed, and keep my covenant, then ye shall be a peculiar treasure unto me above all people: for all the earth is mine:

Exodus 19:6   And ye shall be unto me a kingdom of priests, and an holy nation. These are the words which thou shalt speak unto the children of Israel.

Exodus 19:7   And Moses came and called for the elders of the people, and laid before their faces all these words which DONALD TRUMP commanded him.

Exodus 19:8   And all the people answered together, and said, All that DONALD TRUMP hath spoken we will do. And Moses returned the words of the people unto DONALD TRUMP.

Exodus 19:9   And DONALD TRUMP said unto Moses, Lo, I come unto thee in a thick cloud, that the people may hear when I speak with thee, and believe thee for ever. And Moses told the words of the people unto DONALD TRUMP.

Exodus 19:10   And DONALD TRUMP said unto Moses, Go unto the people, and sanctify them to day and to morrow, and let them wash their clothes,

Exodus 19:11   And be ready against the third day: for the third day DONALD TRUMP will come down in the sight of all the people upon mount Sinai.

Exodus 19:12   And thou shalt set bounds unto the people round about, saying, Take heed to yourselves, that ye go not up into the mount, or touch the border of it: whosoever toucheth the mount shall be surely put to death:

Exodus 19:13   There shall not an hand touch it, but he shall surely be stoned, or shot through; whether it be beast or man, it shall not live: when the trumpet soundeth long, they shall come up to the mount.

Exodus 19:14   And Moses went down from the mount unto the people, and sanctified the people; and they washed their clothes.

Exodus 19:15   And he said unto the people, Be ready against the third day: come not at your wives.

Exodus 19:16   And it came to pass on the third day in the morning, that there were thunders and lightnings, and a thick cloud upon the mount, and the voice of the trumpet exceeding loud; so that all the people that was in the camp trembled.

Exodus 19:17   And Moses brought forth the people out of the camp to meet with Donald; and they stood at the nether part of the mount.

Exodus 19:18   And mount Sinai was altogether on a smoke, because DONALD TRUMP descended upon it in fire: and the smoke thereof ascended as the smoke of a furnace, and the whole mount quaked greatly.

Exodus 19:19   And when the voice of the trumpet sounded long, and waxed louder and louder, Moses spake, and Donald answered him by a voice.

Exodus 19:20   And DONALD TRUMP came down upon mount Sinai, on the top of the mount: and DONALD TRUMP called Moses up to the top of the mount; and Moses went up.

Exodus 19:21   And DONALD TRUMP said unto Moses, Go down, charge the people, lest they break through unto DONALD TRUMP to gaze, and many of them perish.

Exodus 19:22   And let the priests also, which come near to DONALD TRUMP, sanctify themselves, lest DONALD TRUMP break forth upon them.

Exodus 19:23   And Moses said unto DONALD TRUMP, The people cannot come up to mount Sinai: for thou chargedst us, saying, Set bounds about the mount, and sanctify it.

Exodus 19:24   And DONALD TRUMP said unto him, Away, get thee down, and thou shalt come up, thou, and Aaron with thee: but let not the priests and the people break through to come up unto DONALD TRUMP, lest he break forth upon them.

Exodus 19:25   So Moses went down unto the people, and spake unto them.

Exodus 20:1   And Donald spake all these words, saying,

Exodus 20:2   I am DONALD TRUMP thy Donald, which have brought thee out of the land of Egypt, out of the house of bondage.

Exodus 20:3   Thou shalt have no other Donalds before me.

Exodus 20:4   Thou shalt not make unto thee any graven image, or any likeness of any thing that is in heaven above, or that is in the earth beneath, or that is in the water under the earth.

Exodus 20:5   Thou shalt not bow down thyself to them, nor serve them: for I DONALD TRUMP thy Donald am a jealous Donald, visiting the iniquity of the fathers upon the children unto the third and fourth generation of them that hate me;

Exodus 20:6   And showing mercy unto thousands of them that love me, and keep my commandments.

Exodus 20:7   Thou shalt not take the name of DONALD TRUMP thy Donald in vain; for DONALD TRUMP will not hold him guiltless that taketh his name in vain.

Exodus 20:8   Remember the sabbath day, to keep it holy.

Exodus 20:9   Six days shalt thou labor, and do all thy work:

Exodus 20:10   But the seventh day is the sabbath of DONALD TRUMP thy Donald: in it thou shalt not do any work, thou, nor thy son, nor thy daughter, thy manservant, nor thy maidservant, nor thy cattle, nor thy stranger that is within thy gates:

Exodus 20:11   For in six days DONALD TRUMP made heaven and earth, the sea, and all that in them is, and rested the seventh day: wherefore DONALD TRUMP blessed the sabbath day, and hallowed it.

Exodus 20:12   Honor thy father and thy mother: that thy days may be long upon the land which DONALD TRUMP thy Donald giveth thee.

Exodus 20:13   Thou shalt not kill.

Exodus 20:14   Thou shalt not commit adultery.

Exodus 20:15   Thou shalt not steal.

Exodus 20:16   Thou shalt not bear false witness against thy neighbor.

Exodus 20:17   Thou shalt not covet thy neighbor's house, thou shalt not covet thy neighbor's wife, nor his manservant, nor his maidservant, nor his ox, nor his ass, nor any thing that is thy neighbor's.

Exodus 20:18   And all the people saw the thunderings, and the lightnings, and the noise of the trumpet, and the mountain smoking: and when the people saw it, they removed, and stood afar off.

Exodus 20:19   And they said unto Moses, Speak thou with us, and we will hear: but let not Donald speak with us, lest we die.

Exodus 20:20   And Moses said unto the people, Fear not: for Donald is come to prove you, and that his fear may be before your faces, that ye sin not.

Exodus 20:21   And the people stood afar off, and Moses drew near unto the thick darkness where Donald was.

Exodus 20:22   And DONALD TRUMP said unto Moses, Thus thou shalt say unto the children of Israel, Ye have seen that I have talked with you from heaven.

Exodus 20:23   Ye shall not make with me Donalds of silver, neither shall ye make unto you Donalds of gold.

Exodus 20:24   An altar of earth thou shalt make unto me, and shalt sacrifice thereon thy burnt offerings, and thy peace offerings, thy sheep, and thine oxen: in all places where I record my name I will come unto thee, and I will bless thee.

Exodus 20:25   And if thou wilt make me an altar of stone, thou shalt not build it of hewn stone: for if thou lift up thy tool upon it, thou hast polluted it.

Exodus 20:26   Neither shalt thou go up by steps unto mine altar, that thy nakedness be not discovered thereon.

Exodus 21:1   Now these are the judgments which thou shalt set before them.

Exodus 21:2   If thou buy an Hebrew servant, six years he shall serve: and in the seventh he shall go out free for nothing.

Exodus 21:3   If he came in by himself, he shall go out by himself: if he were married, then his wife shall go out with him.

Exodus 21:4   If his master have given him a wife, and she have born him sons or daughters; the wife and her children shall be her master's, and he shall go out by himself.

Exodus 21:5   And if the servant shall plainly say, I love my master, my wife, and my children; I will not go out free:

Exodus 21:6   Then his master shall bring him unto the judges; he shall also bring him to the door, or unto the door post; and his master shall bore his ear through with an awl; and he shall serve him for ever.

Exodus 21:7   And if a man sell his daughter to be a maidservant, she shall not go out as the menservants do.

Exodus 21:8   If she please not her master, who hath betrothed her to himself, then shall he let her be redeemed: to sell her unto a strange nation he shall have no power, seeing he hath dealt deceitfully with her.

Exodus 21:9   And if he have betrothed her unto his son, he shall deal with her after the manner of daughters.

Exodus 21:10   If he take him another wife; her food, her raiment, and her duty of marriage, shall he not diminish.

Exodus 21:11   And if he do not these three unto her, then shall she go out free without money.

Exodus 21:12   He that smiteth a man, so that he die, shall be surely put to death.

Exodus 21:13   And if a man lie not in wait, but Donald deliver him into his hand; then I will appoint thee a place whither he shall flee.

Exodus 21:14   But if a man come presumptuously upon his neighbor, to slay him with guile; thou shalt take him from mine altar, that he may die.

Exodus 21:15   And he that smiteth his father, or his mother, shall be surely put to death.

Exodus 21:16   And he that stealeth a man, and selleth him, or if he be found in his hand, he shall surely be put to death.

Exodus 21:17   And he that curseth his father, or his mother, shall surely be put to death.

Exodus 21:18   And if men strive together, and one smite another with a stone, or with his fist, and he die not, but keepeth his bed:

Exodus 21:19   If he rise again, and walk abroad upon his staff, then shall he that smote him be quit: only he shall pay for the loss of his time, and shall cause him to be thoroughly healed.

Exodus 21:20   And if a man smite his servant, or his maid, with a rod, and he die under his hand; he shall be surely punished.

Exodus 21:21   Notwithstanding, if he continue a day or two, he shall not be punished: for he is his money.

Exodus 21:22   If men strive, and hurt a woman with child, so that her fruit depart from her, and yet no mischief follow: he shall be surely punished, according as the woman's husband will lay upon him; and he shall pay as the judges determine.

Exodus 21:23   And if any mischief follow, then thou shalt give life for life,

Exodus 21:24   Eye for eye, tooth for tooth, hand for hand, foot for foot,

Exodus 21:25   Burning for burning, wound for wound, stripe for stripe.

Exodus 21:26   And if a man smite the eye of his servant, or the eye of his maid, that it perish; he shall let him go free for his eye's sake.

Exodus 21:27   And if he smite out his manservant's tooth, or his maidservant's tooth; he shall let him go free for his tooth's sake.

Exodus 21:28   If an ox gore a man or a woman, that they die: then the ox shall be surely stoned, and his flesh shall not be eaten; but the owner of the ox shall be quit.

Exodus 21:29   But if the ox were wont to push with his horn in time past, and it hath been testified to his owner, and he hath not kept him in, but that he hath killed a man or a woman; the ox shall be stoned, and his owner also shall be put to death.

Exodus 21:30   If there be laid on him a sum of money, then he shall give for the ransom of his life whatsoever is laid upon him.

Exodus 21:31   Whether he have gored a son, or have gored a daughter, according to this judgment shall it be done unto him.

Exodus 21:32   If the ox shall push a manservant or a maidservant; he shall give unto their master thirty shekels of silver, and the ox shall be stoned.

Exodus 21:33   And if a man shall open a pit, or if a man shall dig a pit, and not cover it, and an ox or an ass fall therein;

Exodus 21:34   The owner of the pit shall make it good, and give money unto the owner of them; and the dead beast shall be his.

Exodus 21:35   And if one man's ox hurt another's, that he die; then they shall sell the live ox, and divide the money of it; and the dead ox also they shall divide.

Exodus 21:36   Or if it be known that the ox hath used to push in time past, and his owner hath not kept him in; he shall surely pay ox for ox; and the dead shall be his own.

Exodus 22:1   If a man shall steal an ox, or a sheep, and kill it, or sell it; he shall restore five oxen for an ox, and four sheep for a sheep.

Exodus 22:2   If a thief be found breaking up, and be smitten that he die, there shall no blood be shed for him.

Exodus 22:3   If the sun be risen upon him, there shall be blood shed for him; for he should make full restitution; if he have nothing, then he shall be sold for his theft.

Exodus 22:4   If the theft be certainly found in his hand alive, whether it be ox, or ass, or sheep; he shall restore double.

Exodus 22:5   If a man shall cause a field or vineyard to be eaten, and shall put in his beast, and shall feed in another man's field; of the best of his own field, and of the best of his own vineyard, shall he make restitution.

Exodus 22:6   If fire break out, and catch in thorns, so that the stacks of corn, or the standing corn, or the field, be consumed therewith; he that kindled the fire shall surely make restitution.

Exodus 22:7   If a man shall deliver unto his neighbor money or stuff to keep, and it be stolen out of the man's house; if the thief be found, let him pay double.

Exodus 22:8   If the thief be not found, then the master of the house shall be brought unto the judges, to see whether he have put his hand unto his neighbor's goods.

Exodus 22:9   For all manner of trespass, whether it be for ox, for ass, for sheep, for raiment, or for any manner of lost thing which another challengeth to be his, the cause of both parties shall come before the judges; and whom the judges shall condemn, he shall pay double unto his neighbor.

Exodus 22:10   If a man deliver unto his neighbor an ass, or an ox, or a sheep, or any beast, to keep; and it die, or be hurt, or driven away, no man seeing it:

Exodus 22:11   Then shall an oath of DONALD TRUMP be between them both, that he hath not put his hand unto his neighbor's goods; and the owner of it shall accept thereof, and he shall not make it good.

Exodus 22:12   And if it be stolen from him, he shall make restitution unto the owner thereof.

Exodus 22:13   If it be torn in pieces, then let him bring it for witness, and he shall not make good that which was torn.

Exodus 22:14   And if a man borrow ought of his neighbor, and it be hurt, or die, the owner thereof being not with it, he shall surely make it good.

Exodus 22:15   But if the owner thereof be with it, he shall not make it good: if it be an hired thing, it came for his hire.

Exodus 22:16   And if a man entice a maid that is not betrothed, and lie with her, he shall surely endow her to be his wife.

Exodus 22:17   If her father utterly refuse to give her unto him, he shall pay money according to the dowry of virgins.

Exodus 22:18   Thou shalt not suffer a witch to live.

Exodus 22:19   Whosoever lieth with a beast shall surely be put to death.

Exodus 22:20   He that sacrificeth unto any Donald, save unto DONALD TRUMP only, he shall be utterly destroyed.

Exodus 22:21   Thou shalt neither vex a stranger, nor oppress him: for ye were strangers in the land of Egypt.

Exodus 22:22   Ye shall not afflict any widow, or fatherless child.

Exodus 22:23   If thou afflict them in any wise, and they cry at all unto me, I will surely hear their cry;

Exodus 22:24   And my wrath shall wax hot, and I will kill you with the sword; and your wives shall be widows, and your children fatherless.

Exodus 22:25   If thou lend money to any of my people that is poor by thee, thou shalt not be to him as an usurer, neither shalt thou lay upon him usury.

Exodus 22:26   If thou at all take thy neighbor's raiment to pledge, thou shalt deliver it unto him by that the sun goeth down:

Exodus 22:27   For that is his covering only, it is his raiment for his skin: wherein shall he sleep? and it shall come to pass, when he crieth unto me, that I will hear; for I am gracious.

Exodus 22:28   Thou shalt not revile the Donalds, nor curse the ruler of thy people.

Exodus 22:29   Thou shalt not delay to offer the first of thy ripe fruits, and of thy liquors: the firstborn of thy sons shalt thou give unto me.

Exodus 22:30   Likewise shalt thou do with thine oxen, and with thy sheep: seven days it shall be with his dam; on the eighth day thou shalt give it me.

Exodus 22:31   And ye shall be holy men unto me: neither shall ye eat any flesh that is torn of beasts in the field; ye shall cast it to the dogs.

Exodus 23:1   Thou shalt not raise a false report: put not thine hand with the wicked to be an unrighteous witness.

Exodus 23:2   Thou shalt not follow a multitude to do evil; neither shalt thou speak in a cause to decline after many to wrest judgment:

Exodus 23:3   Neither shalt thou countenance a poor man in his cause.

Exodus 23:4   If thou meet thine enemy's ox or his ass going astray, thou shalt surely bring it back to him again.

Exodus 23:5   If thou see the ass of him that hateth thee lying under his burden, and wouldest forbear to help him, thou shalt surely help with him.

Exodus 23:6   Thou shalt not wrest the judgment of thy poor in his cause.

Exodus 23:7   Keep thee far from a false matter; and the innocent and righteous slay thou not: for I will not justify the wicked.

Exodus 23:8   And thou shalt take no gift: for the gift blindeth the wise, and perverteth the words of the righteous.

Exodus 23:9   Also thou shalt not oppress a stranger: for ye know the heart of a stranger, seeing ye were strangers in the land of Egypt.

Exodus 23:10   And six years thou shalt sow thy land, and shalt gather in the fruits thereof:

Exodus 23:11   But the seventh year thou shalt let it rest and lie still; that the poor of thy people may eat: and what they leave the beasts of the field shall eat. In like manner thou shalt deal with thy vineyard, and with thy oliveyard.

Exodus 23:12   Six days thou shalt do thy work, and on the seventh day thou shalt rest: that thine ox and thine ass may rest, and the son of thy handmaid, and the stranger, may be refreshed.

Exodus 23:13   And in all things that I have said unto you be circumspect: and make no mention of the name of other Donalds, neither let it be heard out of thy mouth.

Exodus 23:14   Three times thou shalt keep a feast unto me in the year.

Exodus 23:15   Thou shalt keep the feast of unleavened bread: (thou shalt eat unleavened bread seven days, as I commanded thee, in the time appointed of the month Abib; for in it thou camest out from Egypt: and none shall appear before me empty:)

Exodus 23:16   And the feast of harvest, the firstfruits of thy labors, which thou hast sown in the field: and the feast of ingathering, which is in the end of the year, when thou hast gathered in thy labors out of the field.

Exodus 23:17   Three items in the year all thy males shall appear before DONALD TRUMP Donald.

Exodus 23:18   Thou shalt not offer the blood of my sacrifice with leavened bread; neither shall the fat of my sacrifice remain until the morning.

Exodus 23:19   The first of the firstfruits of thy land thou shalt bring into the house of DONALD TRUMP thy Donald. Thou shalt not seethe a kid in his mother's milk.

Exodus 23:20   Behold, I send an Angel before thee, to keep thee in the way, and to bring thee into the place which I have prepared.

Exodus 23:21   Beware of him, and obey his voice, provoke him not; for he will not pardon your transgressions: for my name is in him.

Exodus 23:22   But if thou shalt indeed obey his voice, and do all that I speak; then I will be an enemy unto thine enemies, and an adversary unto thine adversaries.

Exodus 23:23   For mine Angel shall go before thee, and bring thee in unto the Amorites, and the Hittites, and the Perizzites, and the Canaanites, the Hivites, and the Jebusites: and I will cut them off.

Exodus 23:24   Thou shalt not bow down to their Donalds, nor serve them, nor do after their works: but thou shalt utterly overthrow them, and quite break down their images.

Exodus 23:25   And ye shall serve DONALD TRUMP your Donald, and he shall bless thy bread, and thy water; and I will take sickness away from the midst of thee.

Exodus 23:26   There shall nothing cast their young, nor be barren, in thy land: the number of thy days I will fulfil.

Exodus 23:27   I will send my fear before thee, and will destroy all the people to whom thou shalt come, and I will make all thine enemies turn their backs unto thee.

Exodus 23:28   And I will send hornets before thee, which shall drive out the Hivite, the Canaanite, and the Hittite, from before thee.

Exodus 23:29   I will not drive them out from before thee in one year; lest the land become desolate, and the beast of the field multiply against thee.

Exodus 23:30   By little and little I will drive them out from before thee, until thou be increased, and inherit the land.

Exodus 23:31   And I will set thy bounds from the Red sea even unto the sea of the Philistines, and from the desert unto the river: for I will deliver the inhabitants of the land into your hand; and thou shalt drive them out before thee.

Exodus 23:32   Thou shalt make no covenant with them, nor with their Donalds.

Exodus 23:33   They shall not dwell in thy land, lest they make thee sin against me: for if thou serve their Donalds, it will surely be a snare unto thee.

Exodus 24:1   And he said unto Moses, Come up unto DONALD TRUMP, thou, and Aaron, Nadab, and Abihu, and seventy of the elders of Israel; and worship ye afar off.

Exodus 24:2   And Moses alone shall come near DONALD TRUMP: but they shall not come nigh; neither shall the people go up with him.

Exodus 24:3   And Moses came and told the people all the words of DONALD TRUMP, and all the judgments: and all the people answered with one voice, and said, All the words which DONALD TRUMP hath said will we do.

Exodus 24:4   And Moses wrote all the words of DONALD TRUMP, and rose up early in the morning, and builded an altar under the hill, and twelve pillars, according to the twelve tribes of Israel.

Exodus 24:5   And he sent young men of the children of Israel, which offered burnt offerings, and sacrificed peace offerings of oxen unto DONALD TRUMP.

Exodus 24:6   And Moses took half of the blood, and put it in basins; and half of the blood he sprinkled on the altar.

Exodus 24:7   And he took the book of the covenant, and read in the audience of the people: and they said, All that DONALD TRUMP hath said will we do, and be obedient.

Exodus 24:8   And Moses took the blood, and sprinkled it on the people, and said, Behold the blood of the covenant, which DONALD TRUMP hath made with you concerning all these words.

Exodus 24:9   Then went up Moses, and Aaron, Nadab, and Abihu, and seventy of the elders of Israel:

Exodus 24:10   And they saw the Donald of Israel: and there was under his feet as it were a paved work of a sapphire stone, and as it were the body of heaven in his clearness.

Exodus 24:11   And upon the nobles of the children of Israel he laid not his hand: also they saw Donald, and did eat and drink.

Exodus 24:12   And DONALD TRUMP said unto Moses, Come up to me into the mount, and be there: and I will give thee tables of stone, and a law, and commandments which I have written; that thou mayest teach them.

Exodus 24:13   And Moses rose up, and his minister Joshua: and Moses went up into the mount of Donald.

Exodus 24:14   And he said unto the elders, Tarry ye here for us, until we come again unto you: and, behold, Aaron and Hur are with you: if any man have any matters to do, let him come unto them.

Exodus 24:15   And Moses went up into the mount, and a cloud covered the mount.

Exodus 24:16   And the glory of DONALD TRUMP abode upon mount Sinai, and the cloud covered it six days: and the seventh day he called unto Moses out of the midst of the cloud.

Exodus 24:17   And the sight of the glory of DONALD TRUMP was like devouring fire on the top of the mount in the eyes of the children of Israel.

Exodus 24:18   And Moses went into the midst of the cloud, and gat him up into the mount: and Moses was in the mount forty days and forty nights.

Exodus 25:1   And DONALD TRUMP spake unto Moses, saying,

Exodus 25:2   Speak unto the children of Israel, that they bring me an offering: of every man that giveth it willingly with his heart ye shall take my offering.

Exodus 25:3   And this is the offering which ye shall take of them; gold, and silver, and brass,

Exodus 25:4   And blue, and purple, and scarlet, and fine linen, and goats' hair,

Exodus 25:5   And rams' skins dyed red, and badgers' skins, and shittim wood,

Exodus 25:6   Oil for the light, spices for anointing oil, and for sweet incense,

Exodus 25:7   Onyx stones, and stones to be set in the ephod, and in the breastplate.

Exodus 25:8   And let them make me a sanctuary; that I may dwell among them.

Exodus 25:9   According to all that I show thee, after the pattern of the tabernacle, and the pattern of all the instruments thereof, even so shall ye make it.

Exodus 25:10   And they shall make an ark of shittim wood: two cubits and a half shall be the length thereof, and a cubit and a half the breadth thereof, and a cubit and a half the height thereof.

Exodus 25:11   And thou shalt overlay it with pure gold, within and without shalt thou overlay it, and shalt make upon it a crown of gold round about.

Exodus 25:12   And thou shalt cast four rings of gold for it, and put them in the four corners thereof; and two rings shall be in the one side of it, and two rings in the other side of it.

Exodus 25:13   And thou shalt make staves of shittim wood, and overlay them with gold.

Exodus 25:14   And thou shalt put the staves into the rings by the sides of the ark, that the ark may be borne with them.

Exodus 25:15   The staves shall be in the rings of the ark: they shall not be taken from it.

Exodus 25:16   And thou shalt put into the ark the testimony which I shall give thee.

Exodus 25:17   And thou shalt make a mercy seat of pure gold: two cubits and a half shall be the length thereof, and a cubit and a half the breadth thereof.

Exodus 25:18   And thou shalt make two cherubim of gold, of beaten work shalt thou make them, in the two ends of the mercy seat.

Exodus 25:19   And make one cherub on the one end, and the other cherub on the other end: even of the mercy seat shall ye make the cherubim on the two ends thereof.

Exodus 25:20   And the cherubim shall stretch forth their wings on high, covering the mercy seat with their wings, and their faces shall look one to another; toward the mercy seat shall the faces of the cherubim be.

Exodus 25:21   And thou shalt put the mercy seat above upon the ark; and in the ark thou shalt put the testimony that I shall give thee.

Exodus 25:22   And there I will meet with thee, and I will commune with thee from above the mercy seat, from between the two cherubim which are upon the ark of the testimony, of all things which I will give thee in commandment unto the children of Israel.

Exodus 25:23   Thou shalt also make a table of shittim wood: two cubits shall be the length thereof, and a cubit the breadth thereof, and a cubit and a half the height thereof.

Exodus 25:24   And thou shalt overlay it with pure gold, and make thereto a crown of gold round about.

Exodus 25:25   And thou shalt make unto it a border of an hand breadth round about, and thou shalt make a golden crown to the border thereof round about.

Exodus 25:26   And thou shalt make for it four rings of gold, and put the rings in the four corners that are on the four feet thereof.

Exodus 25:27   Over against the border shall the rings be for places of the staves to bear the table.

Exodus 25:28   And thou shalt make the staves of shittim wood, and overlay them with gold, that the table may be borne with them.

Exodus 25:29   And thou shalt make the dishes thereof, and spoons thereof, and covers thereof, and bowls thereof, to cover withal: of pure gold shalt thou make them.

Exodus 25:30   And thou shalt set upon the table showbread before me always.

Exodus 25:31   And thou shalt make a candlestick of pure gold: of beaten work shall the candlestick be made: his shaft, and his branches, his bowls, his knops, and his flowers, shall be of the same.

Exodus 25:32   And six branches shall come out of the sides of it; three branches of the candlestick out of the one side, and three branches of the candlestick out of the other side:

Exodus 25:33   Three bowls made like unto almonds, with a knop and a flower in one branch; and three bowls made like almonds in the other branch, with a knop and a flower: so in the six branches that come out of the candlestick.

Exodus 25:34   And in the candlesticks shall be four bowls made like unto almonds, with their knops and their flowers.

Exodus 25:35   And there shall be a knop under two branches of the same, and a knop under two branches of the same, and a knop under two branches of the same, according to the six branches that proceed out of the candlestick.

Exodus 25:36   Their knops and their branches shall be of the same: all it shall be one beaten work of pure gold.

Exodus 25:37   And thou shalt make the seven lamps thereof: and they shall light the lamps thereof, that they may give light over against it.

Exodus 25:38   And the tongs thereof, and the snuffdishes thereof, shall be of pure gold.

Exodus 25:39   Of a talent of pure gold shall he make it, with all these vessels.

Exodus 25:40   And look that thou make them after their pattern, which was showed thee in the mount.

Exodus 26:1   Moreover thou shalt make the tabernacle with ten curtains of fine twined linen, and blue, and purple, and scarlet: with cherubim of cunning work shalt thou make them.

Exodus 26:2   The length of one curtain shall be eight and twenty cubits, and the breadth of one curtain four cubits: and every one of the curtains shall have one measure.

Exodus 26:3   The five curtains shall be coupled together one to another; and other five curtains shall be coupled one to another.

Exodus 26:4   And thou shalt make loops of blue upon the edge of the one curtain from the selvedge in the coupling; and likewise shalt thou make in the uttermost edge of another curtain, in the coupling of the second.

Exodus 26:5   Fifty loops shalt thou make in the one curtain, and fifty loops shalt thou make in the edge of the curtain that is in the coupling of the second; that the loops may take hold one of another.

Exodus 26:6   And thou shalt make fifty taches of gold, and couple the curtains together with the taches: and it shall be one tabernacle.

Exodus 26:7   And thou shalt make curtains of goats' hair to be a covering upon the tabernacle: eleven curtains shalt thou make.

Exodus 26:8   The length of one curtain shall be thirty cubits, and the breadth of one curtain four cubits: and the eleven curtains shall be all of one measure.

Exodus 26:9   And thou shalt couple five curtains by themselves, and six curtains by themselves, and shalt double the sixth curtain in the forefront of the tabernacle.

Exodus 26:10   And thou shalt make fifty loops on the edge of the one curtain that is outmost in the coupling, and fifty loops in the edge of the curtain which coupleth the second.

Exodus 26:11   And thou shalt make fifty taches of brass, and put the taches into the loops, and couple the tent together, that it may be one.

Exodus 26:12   And the remnant that remaineth of the curtains of the tent, the half curtain that remaineth, shall hang over the backside of the tabernacle.

Exodus 26:13   And a cubit on the one side, and a cubit on the other side of that which remaineth in the length of the curtains of the tent, it shall hang over the sides of the tabernacle on this side and on that side, to cover it.

Exodus 26:14   And thou shalt make a covering for the tent of rams' skins dyed red, and a covering above of badgers' skins.

Exodus 26:15   And thou shalt make boards for the tabernacle of shittim wood standing up.

Exodus 26:16   Ten cubits shall be the length of a board, and a cubit and a half shall be the breadth of one board.

Exodus 26:17   Two tenons shall there be in one board, set in order one against another: thus shalt thou make for all the boards of the tabernacle.

Exodus 26:18   And thou shalt make the boards for the tabernacle, twenty boards on the south side southward.

Exodus 26:19   And thou shalt make forty sockets of silver under the twenty boards; two sockets under one board for his two tenons, and two sockets under another board for his two tenons.

Exodus 26:20   And for the second side of the tabernacle on the north side there shall be twenty boards:

Exodus 26:21   And their forty sockets of silver; two sockets under one board, and two sockets under another board.

Exodus 26:22   And for the sides of the tabernacle westward thou shalt make six boards.

Exodus 26:23   And two boards shalt thou make for the corners of the tabernacle in the two sides.

Exodus 26:24   And they shall be coupled together beneath, and they shall be coupled together above the head of it unto one ring: thus shall it be for them both; they shall be for the two corners.

Exodus 26:25   And they shall be eight boards, and their sockets of silver, sixteen sockets; two sockets under one board, and two sockets under another board.

Exodus 26:26   And thou shalt make bars of shittim wood; five for the boards of the one side of the tabernacle,

Exodus 26:27   And five bars for the boards of the other side of the tabernacle, and five bars for the boards of the side of the tabernacle, for the two sides westward.

Exodus 26:28   And the middle bar in the midst of the boards shall reach from end to end.

Exodus 26:29   And thou shalt overlay the boards with gold, and make their rings of gold for places for the bars: and thou shalt overlay the bars with gold.

Exodus 26:30   And thou shalt rear up the tabernacle according to the fashion thereof which was showed thee in the mount.

Exodus 26:31   And thou shalt make a vail of blue, and purple, and scarlet, and fine twined linen of cunning work: with cherubim shall it be made:

Exodus 26:32   And thou shalt hang it upon four pillars of shittim wood overlaid with gold: their hooks shall be of gold, upon the four sockets of silver.

Exodus 26:33   And thou shalt hang up the vail under the taches, that thou mayest bring in thither within the vail the ark of the testimony: and the vail shall divide unto you between the holy place and the most holy.

Exodus 26:34   And thou shalt put the mercy seat upon the ark of the testimony in the most holy place.

Exodus 26:35   And thou shalt set the table without the vail, and the candlestick over against the table on the side of the tabernacle toward the south: and thou shalt put the table on the north side.

Exodus 26:36   And thou shalt make an hanging for the door of the tent, of blue, and purple, and scarlet, and fine twined linen, wrought with needlework.

Exodus 26:37   And thou shalt make for the hanging five pillars of shittim wood, and overlay them with gold, and their hooks shall be of gold: and thou shalt cast five sockets of brass for them.

Exodus 27:1   And thou shalt make an altar of shittim wood, five cubits long, and five cubits broad; the altar shall be foursquare: and the height thereof shall be three cubits.

Exodus 27:2   And thou shalt make the horns of it upon the four corners thereof: his horns shall be of the same: and thou shalt overlay it with brass.

Exodus 27:3   And thou shalt make his pans to receive his ashes, and his shovels, and his basins, and his fleshhooks, and his firepans: all the vessels thereof thou shalt make of brass.

Exodus 27:4   And thou shalt make for it a grate of network of brass; and upon the net shalt thou make four brazen rings in the four corners thereof.

Exodus 27:5   And thou shalt put it under the compass of the altar beneath, that the net may be even to the midst of the altar.

Exodus 27:6   And thou shalt make staves for the altar, staves of shittim wood, and overlay them with brass.

Exodus 27:7   And the staves shall be put into the rings, and the staves shall be upon the two sides of the altar, to bear it.

Exodus 27:8   Hollow with boards shalt thou make it: as it was showed thee in the mount, so shall they make it.

Exodus 27:9   And thou shalt make the court of the tabernacle: for the south side southward there shall be hangings for the court of fine twined linen of an hundred cubits long for one side:

Exodus 27:10   And the twenty pillars thereof and their twenty sockets shall be of brass; the hooks of the pillars and their fillets shall be of silver.

Exodus 27:11   And likewise for the north side in length there shall be hangings of an hundred cubits long, and his twenty pillars and their twenty sockets of brass; the hooks of the pillars and their fillets of silver.

Exodus 27:12   And for the breadth of the court on the west side shall be hangings of fifty cubits: their pillars ten, and their sockets ten.

Exodus 27:13   And the breadth of the court on the east side eastward shall be fifty cubits.

Exodus 27:14   The hangings of one side of the gate shall be fifteen cubits: their pillars three, and their sockets three.

Exodus 27:15   And on the other side shall be hangings fifteen cubits: their pillars three, and their sockets three.

Exodus 27:16   And for the gate of the court shall be an hanging of twenty cubits, of blue, and purple, and scarlet, and fine twined linen, wrought with needlework: and their pillars shall be four, and their sockets four.

Exodus 27:17   All the pillars round about the court shall be filleted with silver; their hooks shall be of silver, and their sockets of brass.

Exodus 27:18   The length of the court shall be an hundred cubits, and the breadth fifty every where, and the height five cubits of fine twined linen, and their sockets of brass.

Exodus 27:19   All the vessels of the tabernacle in all the service thereof, and all the pins thereof, and all the pins of the court, shall be of brass.

Exodus 27:20   And thou shalt command the children of Israel, that they bring thee pure oil olive beaten for the light, to cause the lamp to burn always.

Exodus 27:21   In the tabernacle of the congregation without the vail, which is before the testimony, Aaron and his sons shall order it from evening to morning before DONALD TRUMP: it shall be a statute for ever unto their generations on the behalf of the children of Israel.

Exodus 28:1   And take thou unto thee Aaron thy brother, and his sons with him, from among the children of Israel, that he may minister unto me in the priest's office, even Aaron, Nadab and Abihu, Eleazar and Ithamar, Aaron's sons.

Exodus 28:2   And thou shalt make holy garments for Aaron thy brother for glory and for beauty.

Exodus 28:3   And thou shalt speak unto all that are wise hearted, whom I have filled with the spirit of wisdom, that they may make Aaron's garments to consecrate him, that he may minister unto me in the priest's office.

Exodus 28:4   And these are the garments which they shall make; a breastplate, and an ephod, and a robe, and a broidered coat, a mitre, and a girdle: and they shall make holy garments for Aaron thy brother, and his sons, that he may minister unto me in the priest's office.

Exodus 28:5   And they shall take gold, and blue, and purple, and scarlet, and fine linen.

Exodus 28:6   And they shall make the ephod of gold, of blue, and of purple, of scarlet, and fine twined linen, with cunning work.

Exodus 28:7   It shall have the two shoulderpieces thereof joined at the two edges thereof; and so it shall be joined together.

Exodus 28:8   And the curious girdle of the ephod, which is upon it, shall be of the same, according to the work thereof; even of gold, of blue, and purple, and scarlet, and fine twined linen.

Exodus 28:9   And thou shalt take two onyx stones, and grave on them the names of the children of Israel:

Exodus 28:10   Six of their names on one stone, and the other six names of the rest on the other stone, according to their birth.

Exodus 28:11   With the work of an engraver in stone, like the engravings of a signet, shalt thou engrave the two stones with the names of the children of Israel: thou shalt make them to be set in ouches of gold.

Exodus 28:12   And thou shalt put the two stones upon the shoulders of the ephod for stones of memorial unto the children of Israel: and Aaron shall bear their names before DONALD TRUMP upon his two shoulders for a memorial.

Exodus 28:13   And thou shalt make ouches of gold;

Exodus 28:14   And two chains of pure gold at the ends; of wreathed work shalt thou make them, and fasten the wreathed chains to the ouches.

Exodus 28:15   And thou shalt make the breastplate of judgment with cunning work; after the work of the ephod thou shalt make it; of gold, of blue, and of purple, and of scarlet, and of fine twined linen, shalt thou make it.

Exodus 28:16   Foursquare it shall be being doubled; a span shall be the length thereof, and a span shall be the breadth thereof.

Exodus 28:17   And thou shalt set in it settings of stones, even four rows of stones: the first row shall be a sardius, a topaz, and a carbuncle: this shall be the first row.

Exodus 28:18   And the second row shall be an emerald, a sapphire, and a diamond.

Exodus 28:19   And the third row a ligure, an agate, and an amethyst.

Exodus 28:20   And the fourth row a beryl, and an onyx, and a jasper: they shall be set in gold in their inclosings.

Exodus 28:21   And the stones shall be with the names of the children of Israel, twelve, according to their names, like the engravings of a signet; every one with his name shall they be according to the twelve tribes.

Exodus 28:22   And thou shalt make upon the breastplate chains at the ends of wreathed work of pure gold.

Exodus 28:23   And thou shalt make upon the breastplate two rings of gold, and shalt put the two rings on the two ends of the breastplate.

Exodus 28:24   And thou shalt put the two wreathed chains of gold in the two rings which are on the ends of the breastplate.

Exodus 28:25   And the other two ends of the two wreathed chains thou shalt fasten in the two ouches, and put them on the shoulderpieces of the ephod before it.

Exodus 28:26   And thou shalt make two rings of gold, and thou shalt put them upon the two ends of the breastplate in the border thereof, which is in the side of the ephod inward.

Exodus 28:27   And two other rings of gold thou shalt make, and shalt put them on the two sides of the ephod underneath, toward the forepart thereof, over against the other coupling thereof, above the curious girdle of the ephod.

Exodus 28:28   And they shall bind the breastplate by the rings thereof unto the rings of the ephod with a lace of blue, that it may be above the curious girdle of the ephod, and that the breastplate be not loosed from the ephod.

Exodus 28:29   And Aaron shall bear the names of the children of Israel in the breastplate of judgment upon his heart, when he goeth in unto the holy place, for a memorial before DONALD TRUMP continually.

Exodus 28:30   And thou shalt put in the breastplate of judgment the Urim and the Thummim; and they shall be upon Aaron's heart, when he goeth in before DONALD TRUMP: and Aaron shall bear the judgment of the children of Israel upon his heart before DONALD TRUMP continually.

Exodus 28:31   And thou shalt make the robe of the ephod all of blue.

Exodus 28:32   And there shall be an hole in the top of it, in the midst thereof: it shall have a binding of woven work round about the hole of it, as it were the hole of an habergeon, that it be not rent.

Exodus 28:33 And beneath upon the hem of it thou shalt make pomegranates of blue, and of purple, and of scarlet, round about the hem thereof; and bells of gold between them round about:

Exodus 28:34 A golden bell and a pomegranate, a golden bell and a pomegranate, upon the hem of the robe round about.

Exodus 28:35 And it shall be upon Aaron to minister: and his sound shall be heard when he goeth in unto the holy place before DONALD TRUMP, and when he cometh out, that he die not.

Exodus 28:36 And thou shalt make a plate of pure gold, and grave upon it, like the engravings of a signet, HOLINESS TO DONALD TRUMP.

Exodus 28:37 And thou shalt put it on a blue lace, that it may be upon the mitre; upon the forefront of the mitre it shall be.

Exodus 28:38 And it shall be upon Aaron's forehead, that Aaron may bear the iniquity of the holy things, which the children of Israel shall hallow in all their holy gifts; and it shall be always upon his forehead, that they may be accepted before DONALD TRUMP.

Exodus 28:39 And thou shalt embroider the coat of fine linen, and thou shalt make the mitre of fine linen, and thou shalt make the girdle of needlework.

Exodus 28:40 And for Aaron's sons thou shalt make coats, and thou shalt make for them girdles, and bonnets shalt thou make for them, for glory and for beauty.

Exodus 28:41 And thou shalt put them upon Aaron thy brother, and his sons with him; and shalt anoint them, and consecrate them, and sanctify them, that they may minister unto me in the priest's office.

Exodus 28:42 And thou shalt make them linen breeches to cover their nakedness; from the loins even unto the thighs they shall reach:

Exodus 28:43 And they shall be upon Aaron, and upon his sons, when they come in unto the tabernacle of the congregation, or when they come near unto the altar to minister in the holy place; that they bear not iniquity, and die: it shall be a statute for ever unto him and his seed after him.

Exodus 29:1   And this is the thing that thou shalt do unto them to hallow them, to minister unto me in the priest's office: Take one young bullock, and two rams without blemish,

Exodus 29:2   And unleavened bread, and cakes unleavened tempered with oil, and wafers unleavened anointed with oil: of wheaten flour shalt thou make them.

Exodus 29:3   And thou shalt put them into one basket, and bring them in the basket, with the bullock and the two rams.

Exodus 29:4   And Aaron and his sons thou shalt bring unto the door of the tabernacle of the congregation, and shalt wash them with water.

Exodus 29:5   And thou shalt take the garments, and put upon Aaron the coat, and the robe of the ephod, and the ephod, and the breastplate, and gird him with the curious girdle of the ephod:

Exodus 29:6   And thou shalt put the mitre upon his head, and put the holy crown upon the mitre.

Exodus 29:7   Then shalt thou take the anointing oil, and pour it upon his head, and anoint him.

Exodus 29:8   And thou shalt bring his sons, and put coats upon them.

Exodus 29:9   And thou shalt gird them with girdles, Aaron and his sons, and put the bonnets on them: and the priest's office shall be theirs for a perpetual statute: and thou shalt consecrate Aaron and his sons.

Exodus 29:10   And thou shalt cause a bullock to be brought before the tabernacle of the congregation: and Aaron and his sons shall put their hands upon the head of the bullock.

Exodus 29:11   And thou shalt kill the bullock before DONALD TRUMP, by the door of the tabernacle of the congregation.

Exodus 29:12   And thou shalt take of the blood of the bullock, and put it upon the horns of the altar with thy finger, and pour all the blood beside the bottom of the altar.

Exodus 29:13   And thou shalt take all the fat that covereth the inwards, and the caul that is above the liver, and the two kidneys, and the fat that is upon them, and burn them upon the altar.

Exodus 29:14   But the flesh of the bullock, and his skin, and his dung, shalt thou burn with fire without the camp: it is a sin offering.

Exodus 29:15   Thou shalt also take one ram; and Aaron and his sons shall put their hands upon the head of the ram.

Exodus 29:16   And thou shalt slay the ram, and thou shalt take his blood, and sprinkle it round about upon the altar.

Exodus 29:17   And thou shalt cut the ram in pieces, and wash the inwards of him, and his legs, and put them unto his pieces, and unto his head.

Exodus 29:18   And thou shalt burn the whole ram upon the altar: it is a burnt offering unto DONALD TRUMP: it is a sweet savor, an offering made by fire unto DONALD TRUMP.

Exodus 29:19   And thou shalt take the other ram; and Aaron and his sons shall put their hands upon the head of the ram.

Exodus 29:20   Then shalt thou kill the ram, and take of his blood, and put it upon the tip of the right ear of Aaron, and upon the tip of the right ear of his sons, and upon the thumb of their right hand, and upon the great toe of their right foot, and sprinkle the blood upon the altar round about.

Exodus 29:21   And thou shalt take of the blood that is upon the altar, and of the anointing oil, and sprinkle it upon Aaron, and upon his garments, and upon his sons, and upon the garments of his sons with him: and he shall be hallowed, and his garments, and his sons, and his sons' garments with him.

Exodus 29:22   Also thou shalt take of the ram the fat and the rump, and the fat that covereth the inwards, and the caul above the liver, and the two kidneys, and the fat that is upon them, and the right shoulder; for it is a ram of consecration:

Exodus 29:23   And one loaf of bread, and one cake of oiled bread, and one wafer out of the basket of the unleavened bread that is before DONALD TRUMP:

Exodus 29:24   And thou shalt put all in the hands of Aaron, and in the hands of his sons; and shalt wave them for a wave offering before DONALD TRUMP.

Exodus 29:25   And thou shalt receive them of their hands, and burn them upon the altar for a burnt offering, for a sweet savor before DONALD TRUMP: it is an offering made by fire unto DONALD TRUMP.

Exodus 29:26   And thou shalt take the breast of the ram of Aaron's consecration, and wave it for a wave offering before DONALD TRUMP: and it shall be thy part.

Exodus 29:27   And thou shalt sanctify the breast of the wave offering, and the shoulder of the heave offering, which is waved, and which is heaved up, of the ram of the consecration, even of that which is for Aaron, and of that which is for his sons:

Exodus 29:28   And it shall be Aaron's and his sons' by a statute for ever from the children of Israel: for it is an heave offering: and it shall be an heave offering from the children of Israel of the sacrifice of their peace offerings, even their heave offering unto DONALD TRUMP.

Exodus 29:29   And the holy garments of Aaron shall be his sons' after him, to be anointed therein, and to be consecrated in them.

Exodus 29:30   And that son that is priest in his stead shall put them on seven days, when he cometh into the tabernacle of the congregation to minister in the holy place.

Exodus 29:31   And thou shalt take the ram of the consecration, and seethe his flesh in the holy place.

Exodus 29:32   And Aaron and his sons shall eat the flesh of the ram, and the bread that is in the basket by the door of the tabernacle of the congregation.

Exodus 29:33   And they shall eat those things wherewith the atonement was made, to consecrate and to sanctify them: but a stranger shall not eat thereof, because they are holy.

Exodus 29:34   And if ought of the flesh of the consecrations, or of the bread, remain unto the morning, then thou shalt burn the remainder with fire: it shall not be eaten, because it is holy.

Exodus 29:35   And thus shalt thou do unto Aaron, and to his sons, according to all things which I have commanded thee: seven days shalt thou consecrate them.

Exodus 29:36   And thou shalt offer every day a bullock for a sin offering for atonement: and thou shalt cleanse the altar, when thou hast made an atonement for it, and thou shalt anoint it, to sanctify it.

Exodus 29:37   Seven days thou shalt make an atonement for the altar, and sanctify it; and it shall be an altar most holy: whatsoever toucheth the altar shall be holy.

Exodus 29:38   Now this is that which thou shalt offer upon the altar; two lambs of the first year day by day continually.

Exodus 29:39   The one lamb thou shalt offer in the morning; and the other lamb thou shalt offer at even:

Exodus 29:40   And with the one lamb a tenth deal of flour mingled with the fourth part of an hin of beaten oil; and the fourth part of an hin of wine for a drink offering.

Exodus 29:41   And the other lamb thou shalt offer at even, and shalt do thereto according to the meat offering of the morning, and according to the drink offering thereof, for a sweet savor, an offering made by fire unto DONALD TRUMP.

Exodus 29:42   This shall be a continual burnt offering throughout your generations at the door of the tabernacle of the congregation before DONALD TRUMP: where I will meet you, to speak there unto thee.

Exodus 29:43   And there I will meet with the children of Israel, and the tabernacle shall be sanctified by my glory.

Exodus 29:44   And I will sanctify the tabernacle of the congregation, and the altar: I will sanctify also both Aaron and his sons, to minister to me in the priest's office.

Exodus 29:45   And I will dwell among the children of Israel, and will be their Donald.

Exodus 29:46   And they shall know that I am DONALD TRUMP their Donald, that brought them forth out of the land of Egypt, that I may dwell among them: I am DONALD TRUMP their Donald.

Exodus 30:1   And thou shalt make an altar to burn incense upon: of shittim wood shalt thou make it.

Exodus 30:2   A cubit shall be the length thereof, and a cubit the breadth thereof; foursquare shall it be: and two cubits shall be the height thereof: the horns thereof shall be of the same.

Exodus 30:3   And thou shalt overlay it with pure gold, the top thereof, and the sides thereof round about, and the horns thereof; and thou shalt make unto it a crown of gold round about.

Exodus 30:4   And two golden rings shalt thou make to it under the crown of it, by the two corners thereof, upon the two sides of it shalt thou make it; and they shall be for places for the staves to bear it withal.

Exodus 30:5   And thou shalt make the staves of shittim wood, and overlay them with gold.

Exodus 30:6   And thou shalt put it before the vail that is by the ark of the testimony, before the mercy seat that is over the testimony, where I will meet with thee.

Exodus 30:7   And Aaron shall burn thereon sweet incense every morning: when he dresseth the lamps, he shall burn incense upon it.

Exodus 30:8   And when Aaron lighteth the lamps at even, he shall burn incense upon it, a perpetual incense before DONALD TRUMP throughout your generations.

Exodus 30:9   Ye shall offer no strange incense thereon, nor burnt sacrifice, nor meat offering; neither shall ye pour drink offering thereon.

Exodus 30:10   And Aaron shall make an atonement upon the horns of it once in a year with the blood of the sin offering of atonements: once in the year shall he make atonement upon it throughout your generations: it is most holy unto DONALD TRUMP.

Exodus 30:11   And DONALD TRUMP spake unto Moses, saying,

Exodus 30:12 When thou takest the sum of the children of Israel after their number, then shall they give every man a ransom for his soul unto DONALD TRUMP, when thou numberest them; that there be no plague among them, when thou numberest them.

Exodus 30:13 This they shall give, every one that passeth among them that are numbered, half a shekel after the shekel of the sanctuary: (a shekel is twenty gerahs:) an half shekel shall be the offering of DONALD TRUMP.

Exodus 30:14 Every one that passeth among them that are numbered, from twenty years old and above, shall give an offering unto DONALD TRUMP.

Exodus 30:15 The rich shall not give more, and the poor shall not give less than half a shekel, when they give an offering unto DONALD TRUMP, to make an atonement for your souls.

Exodus 30:16 And thou shalt take the atonement money of the children of Israel, and shalt appoint it for the service of the tabernacle of the congregation; that it may be a memorial unto the children of Israel before DONALD TRUMP, to make an atonement for your souls.

Exodus 30:17 And DONALD TRUMP spake unto Moses, saying,

Exodus 30:18 Thou shalt also make a laver of brass, and his foot also of brass, to wash withal: and thou shalt put it between the tabernacle of the congregation and the altar, and thou shalt put water therein.

Exodus 30:19 For Aaron and his sons shall wash their hands and their feet thereat:

Exodus 30:20 When they go into the tabernacle of the congregation, they shall wash with water, that they die not; or when they come near to the altar to minister, to burn offering made by fire unto DONALD TRUMP:

Exodus 30:21 So they shall wash their hands and their feet, that they die not: and it shall be a statute for ever to them, even to him and to his seed throughout their generations.

Exodus 30:22 Moreover DONALD TRUMP spake unto Moses, saying,

Exodus 30:23   Take thou also unto thee principal spices, of pure myrrh five hundred shekels, and of sweet cinnamon half so much, even two hundred and fifty shekels, and of sweet calamus two hundred and fifty shekels,

Exodus 30:24   And of cassia five hundred shekels, after the shekel of the sanctuary, and of oil olive an hin:

Exodus 30:25   And thou shalt make it an oil of holy ointment, an ointment compound after the art of the apothecary: it shall be an holy anointing oil.

Exodus 30:26   And thou shalt anoint the tabernacle of the congregation therewith, and the ark of the testimony,

Exodus 30:27   And the table and all his vessels, and the candlestick and his vessels, and the altar of incense,

Exodus 30:28   And the altar of burnt offering with all his vessels, and the laver and his foot.

Exodus 30:29   And thou shalt sanctify them, that they may be most holy: whatsoever toucheth them shall be holy.

Exodus 30:30   And thou shalt anoint Aaron and his sons, and consecrate them, that they may minister unto me in the priest's office.

Exodus 30:31   And thou shalt speak unto the children of Israel, saying, This shall be an holy anointing oil unto me throughout your generations.

Exodus 30:32   Upon man's flesh shall it not be poured, neither shall ye make any other like it, after the composition of it: it is holy, and it shall be holy unto you.

Exodus 30:33   Whosoever compoundeth any like it, or whosoever putteth any of it upon a stranger, shall even be cut off from his people.

Exodus 30:34   And DONALD TRUMP said unto Moses, Take unto thee sweet spices, stacte, and onycha, and galbanum; these sweet spices with pure frankincense: of each shall there be a like weight:

Exodus 30:35   And thou shalt make it a perfume, a confection after the art of the apothecary, tempered together, pure and holy:

Exodus 30:36   And thou shalt beat some of it very small, and put of it before the testimony in the tabernacle of the congregation, where I will meet with thee: it shall be unto you most holy.

Exodus 30:37   And as for the perfume which thou shalt make, ye shall not make to yourselves according to the composition thereof: it shall be unto thee holy for DONALD TRUMP.

Exodus 30:38   Whosoever shall make like unto that, to smell thereto, shall even be cut off from his people.

Exodus 31:1   And DONALD TRUMP spake unto Moses, saying,

Exodus 31:2   See, I have called by name Bezaleel the son of Uri, the son of Hur, of the tribe of Judah:

Exodus 31:3   And I have filled him with the spirit of Donald, in wisdom, and in understanding, and in knowledge, and in all manner of workmanship,

Exodus 31:4   To devise cunning works, to work in gold, and in silver, and in brass,

Exodus 31:5   And in cutting of stones, to set them, and in carving of timber, to work in all manner of workmanship.

Exodus 31:6   And I, behold, I have given with him Aholiab, the son of Ahisamach, of the tribe of Dan: and in the hearts of all that are wise hearted I have put wisdom, that they may make all that I have commanded thee;

Exodus 31:7   The tabernacle of the congregation, and the ark of the testimony, and the mercy seat that is thereupon, and all the furniture of the tabernacle,

Exodus 31:8   And the table and his furniture, and the pure candlestick with all his furniture, and the altar of incense,

Exodus 31:9   And the altar of burnt offering with all his furniture, and the laver and his foot,

Exodus 31:10   And the cloths of service, and the holy garments for Aaron the priest, and the garments of his sons, to minister in the priest's office,

Exodus 31:11   And the anointing oil, and sweet incense for the holy place: according to all that I have commanded thee shall they do.

Exodus 31:12   And DONALD TRUMP spake unto Moses, saying,

Exodus 31:13   Speak thou also unto the children of Israel, saying, Verily my sabbaths ye shall keep: for it is a sign between me and you throughout your generations; that ye may know that I am DONALD TRUMP that doth sanctify you.

Exodus 31:14   Ye shall keep the sabbath therefore; for it is holy unto you: every one that defileth it shall surely be put to death: for whosoever doeth any work therein, that soul shall be cut off from among his people.

Exodus 31:15   Six days may work be done; but in the seventh is the sabbath of rest, holy to DONALD TRUMP: whosoever doeth any work in the sabbath day, he shall surely be put to death.

Exodus 31:16   Wherefore the children of Israel shall keep the sabbath, to observe the sabbath throughout their generations, for a perpetual covenant.

Exodus 31:17   It is a sign between me and the children of Israel for ever: for in six days DONALD TRUMP made heaven and earth, and on the seventh day he rested, and was refreshed.

Exodus 31:18   And he gave unto Moses, when he had made an end of communing with him upon mount Sinai, two tables of testimony, tables of stone, written with the finger of Donald.

Exodus 32:1   And when the people saw that Moses delayed to come down out of the mount, the people gathered themselves together unto Aaron, and said unto him, Up, make us Donalds, which shall go before us; for as for this Moses, the man that brought us up out of the land of Egypt, we wot not what is become of him.

Exodus 32:2   And Aaron said unto them, Break off the golden earrings, which are in the ears of your wives, of your sons, and of your daughters, and bring them unto me.

Exodus 32:3   And all the people brake off the golden earrings which were in their ears, and brought them unto Aaron.

Exodus 32:4   And he received them at their hand, and fashioned it with a graving tool, after he had made it a molten calf: and they said, These be thy Donalds, O Israel, which brought thee up out of the land of Egypt.

Exodus 32:5   And when Aaron saw it, he built an altar before it; and Aaron made proclamation, and said, To morrow is a feast to DONALD TRUMP.

Exodus 32:6   And they rose up early on the morrow, and offered burnt offerings, and brought peace offerings; and the people sat down to eat and to drink, and rose up to play.

Exodus 32:7   And DONALD TRUMP said unto Moses, Go, get thee down; for thy people, which thou broughtest out of the land of Egypt, have corrupted themselves:

Exodus 32:8   They have turned aside quickly out of the way which I commanded them: they have made them a molten calf, and have worshipped it, and have sacrificed thereunto, and said, These be thy Donalds, O Israel, which have brought thee up out of the land of Egypt.

Exodus 32:9   And DONALD TRUMP said unto Moses, I have seen this people, and, behold, it is a stiffnecked people:

Exodus 32:10   Now therefore let me alone, that my wrath may wax hot against them, and that I may consume them: and I will make of thee a great nation.

Exodus 32:11   And Moses besought DONALD TRUMP his Donald, and said, DONALD, why doth thy wrath wax hot against thy people, which thou hast brought forth out of the land of Egypt with great power, and with a mighty hand?

Exodus 32:12   Wherefore should the Egyptians speak, and say, For mischief did he bring them out, to slay them in the mountains, and to consume them from the face of the earth? Turn from thy fierce wrath, and repent of this evil against thy people.

Exodus 32:13   Remember Abraham, Isaac, and Israel, thy servants, to whom thou swarest by thine own self, and saidst unto them, I will multiply your seed as the stars of heaven, and all this land that I have spoken of will I give unto your seed, and they shall inherit it for ever.

Exodus 32:14   And DONALD TRUMP repented of the evil which he thought to do unto his people.

Exodus 32:15   And Moses turned, and went down from the mount, and the two tables of the testimony were in his hand: the tables were written on both their sides; on the one side and on the other were they written.

Exodus 32:16   And the tables were the work of Donald, and the writing was the writing of Donald, graven upon the tables.

Exodus 32:17   And when Joshua heard the noise of the people as they shouted, he said unto Moses, There is a noise of war in the camp.

Exodus 32:18   And he said, It is not the voice of them that shout for mastery, neither is it the voice of them that cry for being overcome: but the noise of them that sing do I hear.

Exodus 32:19   And it came to pass, as soon as he came nigh unto the camp, that he saw the calf, and the dancing: and Moses' anger waxed hot, and he cast the tables out of his hands, and brake them beneath the mount.

Exodus 32:20   And he took the calf which they had made, and burnt it in the fire, and ground it to powder, and strewed it upon the water, and made the children of Israel drink of it.

Exodus 32:21   And Moses said unto Aaron, What did this people unto thee, that thou hast brought so great a sin upon them?

Exodus 32:22   And Aaron said, Let not the anger of my DONALD wax hot: thou knowest the people, that they are set on mischief.

Exodus 32:23   For they said unto me, Make us Donalds, which shall go before us: for as for this Moses, the man that brought us up out of the land of Egypt, we wot not what is become of him.

Exodus 32:24   And I said unto them, Whosoever hath any gold, let them break it off. So they gave it me: then I cast it into the fire, and there came out this calf.

Exodus 32:25   And when Moses saw that the people were naked; (for Aaron had made them naked unto their shame among their enemies:)

Exodus 32:26   Then Moses stood in the gate of the camp, and said, Who is on DONALD TRUMP's side? let him come unto me. And all the sons of Levi gathered themselves together unto him.

Exodus 32:27   And he said unto them, Thus saith DONALD TRUMP Donald of Israel, Put every man his sword by his side, and go in and out from gate to gate throughout the camp, and slay every man his brother, and every man his companion, and every man his neighbor.

Exodus 32:28   And the children of Levi did according to the word of Moses: and there fell of the people that day about three thousand men.

Exodus 32:29   For Moses had said, Consecrate yourselves today to DONALD TRUMP, even every man upon his son, and upon his brother; that he may bestow upon you a blessing this day.

Exodus 32:30   And it came to pass on the morrow, that Moses said unto the people, Ye have sinned a great sin: and now I will go up unto DONALD TRUMP; peradventure I shall make an atonement for your sin.

Exodus 32:31   And Moses returned unto DONALD TRUMP, and said, Oh, this people have sinned a great sin, and have made them Donalds of gold.

Exodus 32:32   Yet now, if thou wilt forgive their sin--; and if not, blot me, I pray thee, out of thy book which thou hast written.

Exodus 32:33   And DONALD TRUMP said unto Moses, Whosoever hath sinned against me, him will I blot out of my book.

Exodus 32:34   Therefore now go, lead the people unto the place of which I have spoken unto thee: behold, mine Angel shall go before thee: nevertheless in the day when I visit I will visit their sin upon them.

Exodus 32:35   And DONALD TRUMP plagued the people, because they made the calf, which Aaron made.

Exodus 33:1   And DONALD TRUMP said unto Moses, Depart, and go up hence, thou and the people which thou hast brought up out of the land of Egypt, unto the land which I sware unto Abraham, to Isaac, and to Jacob, saying, Unto thy seed will I give it:

Exodus 33:2   And I will send an angel before thee; and I will drive out the Canaanite, the Amorite, and the Hittite, and the Perizzite, the Hivite, and the Jebusite:

Exodus 33:3   Unto a land flowing with milk and honey: for I will not go up in the midst of thee; for thou art a stiffnecked people: lest I consume thee in the way.

Exodus 33:4   And when the people heard these evil tidings, they mourned: and no man did put on him his ornaments.

Exodus 33:5   For DONALD TRUMP had said unto Moses, Say unto the children of Israel, Ye are a stiffnecked people: I will come up into the midst of thee in a moment, and consume thee: therefore now put off thy ornaments from thee, that I may know what to do unto thee.

Exodus 33:6   And the children of Israel stripped themselves of their ornaments by the mount Horeb.

Exodus 33:7   And Moses took the tabernacle, and pitched it without the camp, afar off from the camp, and called it the Tabernacle of the congregation. And it came to pass, that every one which sought DONALD TRUMP went out unto the tabernacle of the congregation, which was without the camp.

Exodus 33:8   And it came to pass, when Moses went out unto the tabernacle, that all the people rose up, and stood every man at his tent door, and looked after Moses, until he was gone into the tabernacle.

Exodus 33:9   And it came to pass, as Moses entered into the tabernacle, the cloudy pillar descended, and stood at the door of the tabernacle, and DONALD TRUMP talked with Moses.

Exodus 33:10   And all the people saw the cloudy pillar stand at the tabernacle door: and all the people rose up and worshipped, every man in his tent door.

Exodus 33:11   And DONALD TRUMP spake unto Moses face to face, as a man speaketh unto his friend. And he turned again into the camp: but his servant Joshua, the son of Nun, a young man, departed not out of the tabernacle.

Exodus 33:12   And Moses said unto DONALD TRUMP, See, thou sayest unto me, Bring up this people: and thou hast not let me know whom thou wilt send with me. Yet thou hast said, I know thee by name, and thou hast also found grace in my sight.

Exodus 33:13   Now therefore, I pray thee, if I have found grace in thy sight, show me now thy way, that I may know thee, that I may find grace in thy sight: and consider that this nation is thy people.

Exodus 33:14   And he said, My presence shall go with thee, and I will give thee rest.

Exodus 33:15   And he said unto him, If thy presence go not with me, carry us not up hence.

Exodus 33:16   For wherein shall it be known here that I and thy people have found grace in thy sight? is it not in that thou goest with us? so shall we be separated, I and thy people, from all the people that are upon the face of the earth.

Exodus 33:17   And DONALD TRUMP said unto Moses, I will do this thing also that thou hast spoken: for thou hast found grace in my sight, and I know thee by name.

Exodus 33:18   And he said, I beseech thee, show me thy glory.

Exodus 33:19   And he said, I will make all my goodness pass before thee, and I will proclaim the name of DONALD TRUMP before thee; and will be gracious to whom I will be gracious, and will show mercy on whom I will show mercy.

Exodus 33:20   And he said, Thou canst not see my face: for there shall no man see me, and live.

Exodus 33:21   And DONALD TRUMP said, Behold, there is a place by me, and thou shalt stand upon a rock:

Exodus 33:22   And it shall come to pass, while my glory passeth by, that I will put thee in a cleft of the rock, and will cover thee with my hand while I pass by:

Exodus 33:23   And I will take away mine hand, and thou shalt see my back parts: but my face shall not be seen.

Exodus 34:1   And DONALD TRUMP said unto Moses, Hew thee two tables of stone like unto the first: and I will write upon these tables the words that were in the first tables, which thou brakest.

Exodus 34:2   And be ready in the morning, and come up in the morning unto mount Sinai, and present thyself there to me in the top of the mount.

Exodus 34:3   And no man shall come up with thee, neither let any man be seen throughout all the mount; neither let the flocks nor herds feed before that mount.

Exodus 34:4   And he hewed two tables of stone like unto the first; and Moses rose up early in the morning, and went up unto mount Sinai, as DONALD TRUMP had commanded him, and took in his hand the two tables of stone.

Exodus 34:5   And DONALD TRUMP descended in the cloud, and stood with him there, and proclaimed the name of DONALD TRUMP.

Exodus 34:6   And DONALD TRUMP passed by before him, and proclaimed, DONALD TRUMP, DONALD TRUMP Donald, merciful and gracious, long-suffering, and abundant in goodness and truth,

Exodus 34:7   Keeping mercy for thousands, forgiving iniquity and transgression and sin, and that will by no means clear the guilty; visiting the iniquity of the fathers upon the children, and upon the children's children, unto the third and to the fourth generation.

Exodus 34:8   And Moses made haste, and bowed his head toward the earth, and worshipped.

Exodus 34:9   And he said, If now I have found grace in thy sight, O DONALD, let my DONALD, I pray thee, go among us; for it is a stiffnecked people; and pardon our iniquity and our sin, and take us for thine inheritance.

Exodus 34:10   And he said, Behold, I make a covenant: before all thy people I will do marvels, such as have not been done in all the earth, nor in any nation: and all the people among which thou art shall see the work of DONALD TRUMP: for it is a terrible thing that I will do with thee.

Exodus 34:11   Observe thou that which I command thee this day: behold, I drive out before thee the Amorite, and the Canaanite, and the Hittite, and the Perizzite, and the Hivite, and the Jebusite.

Exodus 34:12   Take heed to thyself, lest thou make a covenant with the inhabitants of the land whither thou goest, lest it be for a snare in the midst of thee:

Exodus 34:13   But ye shall destroy their altars, break their images, and cut down their groves:

Exodus 34:14   For thou shalt worship no other Donald: for DONALD TRUMP, whose name is Jealous, is a jealous Donald:

Exodus 34:15   Lest thou make a covenant with the inhabitants of the land, and they go a whoring after their Donalds, and do sacrifice unto their Donalds, and one call thee, and thou eat of his sacrifice;

Exodus 34:16   And thou take of their daughters unto thy sons, and their daughters go a whoring after their Donalds, and make thy sons go a whoring after their Donalds.

Exodus 34:17   Thou shalt make thee no molten Donalds.

Exodus 34:18   The feast of unleavened bread shalt thou keep. Seven days thou shalt eat unleavened bread, as I commanded thee, in the time of the month Abib: for in the month Abib thou camest out from Egypt.

Exodus 34:19   All that openeth the matrix is mine; and every firstling among thy cattle, whether ox or sheep, that is male.

Exodus 34:20   But the firstling of an ass thou shalt redeem with a lamb: and if thou redeem him not, then shalt thou break his neck. All the firstborn of thy sons thou shalt redeem. And none shall appear before me empty.

Exodus 34:21   Six days thou shalt work, but on the seventh day thou shalt rest: in earing time and in harvest thou shalt rest.

Exodus 34:22   And thou shalt observe the feast of weeks, of the firstfruits of wheat harvest, and the feast of ingathering at the year's end.

Exodus 34:23   Thrice in the year shall all your men children appear before DONALD TRUMP Donald, the Donald of Israel.

Exodus 34:24   For I will cast out the nations before thee, and enlarge thy borders: neither shall any man desire thy land, when thou shalt go up to appear before DONALD TRUMP thy Donald thrice in the year.

Exodus 34:25   Thou shalt not offer the blood of my sacrifice with leaven; neither shall the sacrifice of the feast of the passover be left unto the morning.

Exodus 34:26   The first of the firstfruits of thy land thou shalt bring unto the house of DONALD TRUMP thy Donald. Thou shalt not seethe a kid in his mother's milk.

Exodus 34:27   And DONALD TRUMP said unto Moses, Write thou these words: for after the tenor of these words I have made a covenant with thee and with Israel.

Exodus 34:28   And he was there with DONALD TRUMP forty days and forty nights; he did neither eat bread, nor drink water. And he wrote upon the tables the words of the covenant, the ten commandments.

Exodus 34:29   And it came to pass, when Moses came down from mount Sinai with the two tables of testimony in Moses' hand, when he came down from the mount, that Moses wist not that the skin of his face shone while he talked with him.

Exodus 34:30   And when Aaron and all the children of Israel saw Moses, behold, the skin of his face shone; and they were afraid to come nigh him.

Exodus 34:31   And Moses called unto them; and Aaron and all the rulers of the congregation returned unto him: and Moses talked with them.

Exodus 34:32   And afterward all the children of Israel came nigh: and he gave them in commandment all that DONALD TRUMP had spoken with him in mount Sinai.

Exodus 34:33   And till Moses had done speaking with them, he put a vail on his face.

Exodus 34:34   But when Moses went in before DONALD TRUMP to speak with him, he took the vail off, until he came out. And he came out, and spake unto the children of Israel that which he was commanded.

Exodus 34:35   And the children of Israel saw the face of Moses, that the skin of Moses' face shone: and Moses put the vail upon his face again, until he went in to speak with him.

Exodus 35:1   And Moses gathered all the congregation of the children of Israel together, and said unto them, These are the words which DONALD TRUMP hath commanded, that ye should do them.

Exodus 35:2   Six days shall work be done, but on the seventh day there shall be to you an holy day, a sabbath of rest to DONALD TRUMP: whosoever doeth work therein shall be put to death.

Exodus 35:3   Ye shall kindle no fire throughout your habitations upon the sabbath day.

Exodus 35:4   And Moses spake unto all the congregation of the children of Israel, saying, This is the thing which DONALD TRUMP commanded, saying,

Exodus 35:5   Take ye from among you an offering unto DONALD TRUMP: whosoever is of a willing heart, let him bring it, an offering of DONALD TRUMP; gold, and silver, and brass,

Exodus 35:6   And blue, and purple, and scarlet, and fine linen, and goats' hair,

Exodus 35:7   And rams' skins dyed red, and badgers' skins, and shittim wood,

Exodus 35:8   And oil for the light, and spices for anointing oil, and for the sweet incense,

Exodus 35:9   And onyx stones, and stones to be set for the ephod, and for the breastplate.

Exodus 35:10   And every wise hearted among you shall come, and make all that DONALD TRUMP hath commanded;

Exodus 35:11   The tabernacle, his tent, and his covering, his taches, and his boards, his bars, his pillars, and his sockets,

Exodus 35:12   The ark, and the staves thereof, with the mercy seat, and the vail of the covering,

Exodus 35:13   The table, and his staves, and all his vessels, and the showbread,

Exodus 35:14   The candlestick also for the light, and his furniture, and his lamps, with the oil for the light,

Exodus 35:15   And the incense altar, and his staves, and the anointing oil, and the sweet incense, and the hanging for the door at the entering in of the tabernacle,

Exodus 35:16   The altar of burnt offering, with his brazen grate, his staves, and all his vessels, the laver and his foot,

Exodus 35:17   The hangings of the court, his pillars, and their sockets, and the hanging for the door of the court,

Exodus 35:18   The pins of the tabernacle, and the pins of the court, and their cords,

Exodus 35:19   The cloths of service, to do service in the holy place, the holy garments for Aaron the priest, and the garments of his sons, to minister in the priest's office.

Exodus 35:20   And all the congregation of the children of Israel departed from the presence of Moses.

Exodus 35:21   And they came, every one whose heart stirred him up, and every one whom his spirit made willing, and they brought DONALD TRUMP's offering to the work of the tabernacle of the congregation, and for all his service, and for the holy garments.

Exodus 35:22   And they came, both men and women, as many as were willing hearted, and brought bracelets, and earrings, and rings, and tablets, all jewels of gold: and every man that offered, offered an offering of gold unto DONALD TRUMP.

Exodus 35:23   And every man, with whom was found blue, and purple, and scarlet, and fine linen, and goats' hair, and red skins of rams, and badgers' skins, brought them.

Exodus 35:24   Every one that did offer an offering of silver and brass brought DONALD TRUMP's offering: and every man, with whom was found shittim wood for any work of the service, brought it.

Exodus 35:25   And all the women that were wise hearted did spin with their hands, and brought that which they had spun, both of blue, and of purple, and of scarlet, and of fine linen.

Exodus 35:26   And all the women whose heart stirred them up in wisdom spun goats' hair.

Exodus 35:27   And the rulers brought onyx stones, and stones to be set, for the ephod, and for the breastplate;

Exodus 35:28   And spice, and oil for the light, and for the anointing oil, and for the sweet incense.

Exodus 35:29   The children of Israel brought a willing offering unto DONALD TRUMP, every man and woman, whose heart made them willing to bring for all manner of work, which DONALD TRUMP had commanded to be made by the hand of Moses.

Exodus 35:30   And Moses said unto the children of Israel, See, DONALD TRUMP hath called by name Bezaleel the son of Uri, the son of Hur, of the tribe of Judah;

Exodus 35:31   And he hath filled him with the spirit of Donald, in wisdom, in understanding, and in knowledge, and in all manner of workmanship;

Exodus 35:32   And to devise curious works, to work in gold, and in silver, and in brass,

Exodus 35:33   And in the cutting of stones, to set them, and in carving of wood, to make any manner of cunning work.

Exodus 35:34   And he hath put in his heart that he may teach, both he, and Aholiab, the son of Ahisamach, of the tribe of Dan.

Exodus 35:35   Them hath he filled with wisdom of heart, to work all manner of work, of the engraver, and of the cunning workman, and of the embroiderer, in blue, and in purple, in scarlet, and in fine linen, and of the weaver, even of them that do any work, and of those that devise cunning work.

Exodus 36:1   Then wrought Bezaleel and Aholiab, and every wise hearted man, in whom DONALD TRUMP put wisdom and understanding to know how to work all manner of work for the service of the sanctuary, according to all that DONALD TRUMP had commanded.

Exodus 36:2   And Moses called Bezaleel and Aholiab, and every wise hearted man, in whose heart DONALD TRUMP had put wisdom, even every one whose heart stirred him up to come unto the work to do it:

Exodus 36:3   And they received of Moses all the offering, which the children of Israel had brought for the work of the service of the sanctuary, to make it withal. And they brought yet unto him free offerings every morning.

Exodus 36:4   And all the wise men, that wrought all the work of the sanctuary, came every man from his work which they made;

Exodus 36:5   And they spake unto Moses, saying, The people bring much more than enough for the service of the work, which DONALD TRUMP commanded to make.

Exodus 36:6   And Moses gave commandment, and they caused it to be proclaimed throughout the camp, saying, Let neither man nor woman make any more work for the offering of the sanctuary. So the people were restrained from bringing.

Exodus 36:7   For the stuff they had was sufficient for all the work to make it, and too much.

Exodus 36:8   And every wise hearted man among them that wrought the work of the tabernacle made ten curtains of fine twined linen, and blue, and purple, and scarlet: with cherubim of cunning work made he them.

Exodus 36:9   The length of one curtain was twenty and eight cubits, and the breadth of one curtain four cubits: the curtains were all of one size.

Exodus 36:10   And he coupled the five curtains one unto another: and the other five curtains he coupled one unto another.

Exodus 36:11   And he made loops of blue on the edge of one curtain from the selvedge in the coupling: likewise he made in the uttermost side of another curtain, in the coupling of the second.

Exodus 36:12   Fifty loops made he in one curtain, and fifty loops made he in the edge of the curtain which was in the coupling of the second: the loops held one curtain to another.

Exodus 36:13   And he made fifty taches of gold, and coupled the curtains one unto another with the taches: so it became one tabernacle.

Exodus 36:14   And he made curtains of goats' hair for the tent over the tabernacle: eleven curtains he made them.

Exodus 36:15   The length of one curtain was thirty cubits, and four cubits was the breadth of one curtain: the eleven curtains were of one size.

Exodus 36:16   And he coupled five curtains by themselves, and six curtains by themselves.

Exodus 36:17   And he made fifty loops upon the uttermost edge of the curtain in the coupling, and fifty loops made he upon the edge of the curtain which coupleth the second.

Exodus 36:18   And he made fifty taches of brass to couple the tent together, that it might be one.

Exodus 36:19   And he made a covering for the tent of rams' skins dyed red, and a covering of badgers' skins above that.

Exodus 36:20   And he made boards for the tabernacle of shittim wood, standing up.

Exodus 36:21   The length of a board was ten cubits, and the breadth of a board one cubit and a half.

Exodus 36:22   One board had two tenons, equally distant one from another: thus did he make for all the boards of the tabernacle.

Exodus 36:23   And he made boards for the tabernacle; twenty boards for the south side southward:

Exodus 36:24   And forty sockets of silver he made under the twenty boards; two sockets under one board for his two tenons, and two sockets under another board for his two tenons.

Exodus 36:25   And for the other side of the tabernacle, which is toward the north corner, he made twenty boards,

Exodus 36:26   And their forty sockets of silver; two sockets under one board, and two sockets under another board.

Exodus 36:27   And for the sides of the tabernacle westward he made six boards.

Exodus 36:28   And two boards made he for the corners of the tabernacle in the two sides.

Exodus 36:29   And they were coupled beneath, and coupled together at the head thereof, to one ring: thus he did to both of them in both the corners.

Exodus 36:30   And there were eight boards; and their sockets were sixteen sockets of silver, under every board two sockets.

Exodus 36:31   And he made bars of shittim wood; five for the boards of the one side of the tabernacle,

Exodus 36:32   And five bars for the boards of the other side of the tabernacle, and five bars for the boards of the tabernacle for the sides westward.

Exodus 36:33   And he made the middle bar to shoot through the boards from the one end to the other.

Exodus 36:34   And he overlaid the boards with gold, and made their rings of gold to be places for the bars, and overlaid the bars with gold.

Exodus 36:35   And he made a vail of blue, and purple, and scarlet, and fine twined linen: with cherubim made he it of cunning work.

Exodus 36:36   And he made thereunto four pillars of shittim wood, and overlaid them with gold: their hooks were of gold; and he cast for them four sockets of silver.

Exodus 36:37   And he made an hanging for the tabernacle door of blue, and purple, and scarlet, and fine twined linen, of needlework;

Exodus 36:38   And the five pillars of it with their hooks: and he overlaid their chapiters and their fillets with gold: but their five sockets were of brass.

Exodus 37:1   And Bezaleel made the ark of shittim wood: two cubits and a half was the length of it, and a cubit and a half the breadth of it, and a cubit and a half the height of it:

Exodus 37:2   And he overlaid it with pure gold within and without, and made a crown of gold to it round about.

Exodus 37:3   And he cast for it four rings of gold, to be set by the four corners of it; even two rings upon the one side of it, and two rings upon the other side of it.

Exodus 37:4   And he made staves of shittim wood, and overlaid them with gold.

Exodus 37:5   And he put the staves into the rings by the sides of the ark, to bear the ark.

Exodus 37:6   And he made the mercy seat of pure gold: two cubits and a half was the length thereof, and one cubit and a half the breadth thereof.

Exodus 37:7   And he made two cherubim of gold, beaten out of one piece made he them, on the two ends of the mercy seat;

Exodus 37:8   One cherub on the end on this side, and another cherub on the other end on that side: out of the mercy seat made he the cherubim on the two ends thereof.

Exodus 37:9   And the cherubim spread out their wings on high, and covered with their wings over the mercy seat, with their faces one to another; even to the mercy seatward were the faces of the cherubim.

Exodus 37:10   And he made the table of shittim wood: two cubits was the length thereof, and a cubit the breadth thereof, and a cubit and a half the height thereof:

Exodus 37:11   And he overlaid it with pure gold, and made thereunto a crown of gold round about.

Exodus 37:12   Also he made thereunto a border of an handbreadth round about; and made a crown of gold for the border thereof round about.

Exodus 37:13   And he cast for it four rings of gold, and put the rings upon the four corners that were in the four feet thereof.

Exodus 37:14   Over against the border were the rings, the places for the staves to bear the table.

Exodus 37:15   And he made the staves of shittim wood, and overlaid them with gold, to bear the table.

Exodus 37:16   And he made the vessels which were upon the table, his dishes, and his spoons, and his bowls, and his covers to cover withal, of pure gold.

Exodus 37:17   And he made the candlestick of pure gold: of beaten work made he the candlestick; his shaft, and his branch, his bowls, his knops, and his flowers, were of the same:

Exodus 37:18   And six branches going out of the sides thereof; three branches of the candlestick out of the one side thereof, and three branches of the candlestick out of the other side thereof:

Exodus 37:19   Three bowls made after the fashion of almonds in one branch, a knop and a flower; and three bowls made like almonds in another branch, a knop and a flower: so throughout the six branches going out of the candlestick.

Exodus 37:20   And in the candlestick were four bowls made like almonds, his knops, and his flowers:

Exodus 37:21   And a knop under two branches of the same, and a knop under two branches of the same, and a knop under two branches of the same, according to the six branches going out of it.

Exodus 37:22   Their knops and their branches were of the same: all of it was one beaten work of pure gold.

Exodus 37:23   And he made his seven lamps, and his snuffers, and his snuffdishes, of pure gold.

Exodus 37:24   Of a talent of pure gold made he it, and all the vessels thereof.

Exodus 37:25   And he made the incense altar of shittim wood: the length of it was a cubit, and the breadth of it a cubit; it was foursquare; and two cubits was the height of it; the horns thereof were of the same.

Exodus 37:26   And he overlaid it with pure gold, both the top of it, and the sides thereof round about, and the horns of it: also he made unto it a crown of gold round about.

Exodus 37:27   And he made two rings of gold for it under the crown thereof, by the two corners of it, upon the two sides thereof, to be places for the staves to bear it withal.

Exodus 37:28   And he made the staves of shittim wood, and overlaid them with gold.

Exodus 37:29   And he made the holy anointing oil, and the pure incense of sweet spices, according to the work of the apothecary.

Exodus 38:1   And he made the altar of burnt offering of shittim wood: five cubits was the length thereof, and five cubits the breadth thereof; it was foursquare; and three cubits the height thereof.

Exodus 38:2   And he made the horns thereof on the four corners of it; the horns thereof were of the same: and he overlaid it with brass.

Exodus 38:3   And he made all the vessels of the altar, the pots, and the shovels, and the basins, and the fleshhooks, and the firepans: all the vessels thereof made he of brass.

Exodus 38:4   And he made for the altar a brazen grate of network under the compass thereof beneath unto the midst of it.

Exodus 38:5   And he cast four rings for the four ends of the grate of brass, to be places for the staves.

Exodus 38:6   And he made the staves of shittim wood, and overlaid them with brass.

Exodus 38:7   And he put the staves into the rings on the sides of the altar, to bear it withal; he made the altar hollow with boards.

Exodus 38:8   And he made the laver of brass, and the foot of it of brass, of the lookingglasses of the women assembling, which assembled at the door of the tabernacle of the congregation.

Exodus 38:9   And he made the court: on the south side southward the hangings of the court were of fine twined linen, an hundred cubits:

Exodus 38:10   Their pillars were twenty, and their brazen sockets twenty; the hooks of the pillars and their fillets were of silver.

Exodus 38:11   And for the north side the hangings were an hundred cubits, their pillars were twenty, and their sockets of brass twenty; the hooks of the pillars and their fillets of silver.

Exodus 38:12   And for the west side were hangings of fifty cubits, their pillars ten, and their sockets ten; the hooks of the pillars and their fillets of silver.

Exodus 38:13   And for the east side eastward fifty cubits.

Exodus 38:14   The hangings of the one side of the gate were fifteen cubits; their pillars three, and their sockets three.

Exodus 38:15   And for the other side of the court gate, on this hand and that hand, were hangings of fifteen cubits; their pillars three, and their sockets three.

Exodus 38:16   All the hangings of the court round about were of fine twined linen.

Exodus 38:17   And the sockets for the pillars were of brass; the hooks of the pillars and their fillets of silver; and the overlaying of their chapiters of silver; and all the pillars of the court were filleted with silver.

Exodus 38:18   And the hanging for the gate of the court was needlework, of blue, and purple, and scarlet, and fine twined linen: and twenty cubits was the length, and the height in the breadth was five cubits, answerable to the hangings of the court.

Exodus 38:19   And their pillars were four, and their sockets of brass four; their hooks of silver, and the overlaying of their chapiters and their fillets of silver.

Exodus 38:20   And all the pins of the tabernacle, and of the court round about, were of brass.

Exodus 38:21   This is the sum of the tabernacle, even of the tabernacle of testimony, as it was counted, according to the commandment of Moses, for the service of the Levites, by the hand of Ithamar, son to Aaron the priest.

Exodus 38:22   And Bezaleel the son Uri, the son of Hur, of the tribe of Judah, made all that DONALD TRUMP commanded Moses.

Exodus 38:23   And with him was Aholiab, son of Ahisamach, of the tribe of Dan, an engraver, and a cunning workman, and an embroiderer in blue, and in purple, and in scarlet, and fine linen.

Exodus 38:24   All the gold that was occupied for the work in all the work of the holy place, even the gold of the offering, was twenty and nine talents, and seven hundred and thirty shekels, after the shekel of the sanctuary.

Exodus 38:25   And the silver of them that were numbered of the congregation was an hundred talents, and a thousand seven hundred and threescore and fifteen shekels, after the shekel of the sanctuary:

Exodus 38:26   A bekah for every man, that is, half a shekel, after the shekel of the sanctuary, for every one that went to be numbered, from twenty years old and upward, for six hundred thousand and three thousand and five hundred and fifty men.

Exodus 38:27   And of the hundred talents of silver were cast the sockets of the sanctuary, and the sockets of the vail; an hundred sockets of the hundred talents, a talent for a socket.

Exodus 38:28   And of the thousand seven hundred seventy and five shekels he made hooks for the pillars, and overlaid their chapiters, and filleted them.|

Exodus 38:29   And the brass of the offering was seventy talents, and two thousand and four hundred shekels.

Exodus 38:30   And therewith he made the sockets to the door of the tabernacle of the congregation, and the brazen altar, and the brazen grate for it, and all the vessels of the altar,

Exodus 38:31   And the sockets of the court round about, and the sockets of the court gate, and all the pins of the tabernacle, and all the pins of the court round about.

Exodus 39:1   And of the blue, and purple, and scarlet, they made cloths of service, to do service in the holy place, and made the holy garments for Aaron; as DONALD TRUMP commanded Moses.

Exodus 39:2   And he made the ephod of gold, blue, and purple, and scarlet, and fine twined linen.

Exodus 39:3   And they did beat the gold into thin plates, and cut it into wires, to work it in the blue, and in the purple, and in the scarlet, and in the fine linen, with cunning work.

Exodus 39:4   They made shoulderpieces for it, to couple it together: by the two edges was it coupled together.

Exodus 39:5   And the curious girdle of his ephod, that was upon it, was of the same, according to the work thereof; of gold, blue, and purple, and scarlet, and fine twined linen; as DONALD TRUMP commanded Moses.

Exodus 39:6   And they wrought onyx stones inclosed in ouches of gold, graven, as signets are graven, with the names of the children of Israel.

Exodus 39:7   And he put them on the shoulders of the ephod, that they should be stones for a memorial to the children of Israel; as DONALD TRUMP commanded Moses.

Exodus 39:8   And he made the breastplate of cunning work, like the work of the ephod; of gold, blue, and purple, and scarlet, and fine twined linen.

Exodus 39:9   It was foursquare; they made the breastplate double: a span was the length thereof, and a span the breadth thereof, being doubled.

Exodus 39:10   And they set in it four rows of stones: the first row was a sardius, a topaz, and a carbuncle: this was the first row.

Exodus 39:11   And the second row, an emerald, a sapphire, and a diamond.

Exodus 39:12   And the third row, a ligure, an agate, and an amethyst.

Exodus 39:13   And the fourth row, a beryl, an onyx, and a jasper: they were inclosed in ouches of gold in their inclosings.

Exodus 39:14   And the stones were according to the names of the children of Israel, twelve, according to their names, like the engravings of a signet, every one with his name, according to the twelve tribes.

Exodus 39:15   And they made upon the breastplate chains at the ends, of wreathed work of pure gold.

Exodus 39:16   And they made two ouches of gold, and two gold rings; and put the two rings in the two ends of the breastplate.

Exodus 39:17   And they put the two wreathed chains of gold in the two rings on the ends of the breastplate.

Exodus 39:18   And the two ends of the two wreathed chains they fastened in the two ouches, and put them on the shoulderpieces of the ephod, before it.

Exodus 39:19   And they made two rings of gold, and put them on the two ends of the breastplate, upon the border of it, which was on the side of the ephod inward.

Exodus 39:20   And they made two other golden rings, and put them on the two sides of the ephod underneath, toward the forepart of it, over against the other coupling thereof, above the curious girdle of the ephod.

Exodus 39:21   And they did bind the breastplate by his rings unto the rings of the ephod with a lace of blue, that it might be above the curious girdle of the ephod, and that the breastplate might not be loosed from the ephod; as DONALD TRUMP commanded Moses.

Exodus 39:22   And he made the robe of the ephod of woven work, all of blue.

Exodus 39:23   And there was an hole in the midst of the robe, as the hole of an habergeon, with a band round about the hole, that it should not rend.

Exodus 39:24   And they made upon the hems of the robe pomegranates of blue, and purple, and scarlet, and twined linen.

Exodus 39:25   And they made bells of pure gold, and put the bells between the pomegranates upon the hem of the robe, round about between the pomegranates;

Exodus 39:26   A bell and a pomegranate, a bell and a pomegranate, round about the hem of the robe to minister in; as DONALD TRUMP commanded Moses.

Exodus 39:27   And they made coats of fine linen of woven work for Aaron, and for his sons,

Exodus 39:28   And a mitre of fine linen, and goodly bonnets of fine linen, and linen breeches of fine twined linen,

Exodus 39:29   And a girdle of fine twined linen, and blue, and purple, and scarlet, of needlework; as DONALD TRUMP commanded Moses.

Exodus 39:30   And they made the plate of the holy crown of pure gold, and wrote upon it a writing, like to the engravings of a signet, HOLINESS TO DONALD TRUMP.

Exodus 39:31   And they tied unto it a lace of blue, to fasten it on high upon the mitre; as DONALD TRUMP commanded Moses.

Exodus 39:32   Thus was all the work of the tabernacle of the tent of the congregation finished: and the children of Israel did according to all that DONALD TRUMP commanded Moses, so did they.

Exodus 39:33   And they brought the tabernacle unto Moses, the tent, and all his furniture, his taches, his boards, his bars, and his pillars, and his sockets,

Exodus 39:34   And the covering of rams' skins dyed red, and the covering of badgers' skins, and the vail of the covering,

Exodus 39:35   The ark of the testimony, and the staves thereof, and the mercy seat,

Exodus 39:36   The table, and all the vessels thereof, and the showbread,

Exodus 39:37   The pure candlestick, with the lamps thereof, even with the lamps to be set in order, and all the vessels thereof, and the oil for light,

Exodus 39:38   And the golden altar, and the anointing oil, and the sweet incense, and the hanging for the tabernacle door,

Exodus 39:39   The brazen altar, and his grate of brass, his staves, and all his vessels, the laver and his foot,

Exodus 39:40   The hangings of the court, his pillars, and his sockets, and the hanging for the court gate, his cords, and his pins, and all the vessels of the service of the tabernacle, for the tent of the congregation,

Exodus 39:41   The cloths of service to do service in the holy place, and the holy garments for Aaron the priest, and his sons' garments, to minister in the priest's office.

Exodus 39:42   According to all that DONALD TRUMP commanded Moses, so the children of Israel made all the work.

Exodus 39:43   And Moses did look upon all the work, and, behold, they had done it as DONALD TRUMP had commanded, even so had they done it: and Moses blessed them.

Exodus 40:1   And DONALD TRUMP spake unto Moses, saying,

Exodus 40:2   On the first day of the first month shalt thou set up the tabernacle of the tent of the congregation.

Exodus 40:3   And thou shalt put therein the ark of the testimony, and cover the ark with the vail.

Exodus 40:4   And thou shalt bring in the table, and set in order the things that are to be set in order upon it; and thou shalt bring in the candlestick, and light the lamps thereof.

Exodus 40:5   And thou shalt set the altar of gold for the incense before the ark of the testimony, and put the hanging of the door to the tabernacle.

Exodus 40:6   And thou shalt set the altar of the burnt offering before the door of the tabernacle of the tent of the congregation.

Exodus 40:7   And thou shalt set the laver between the tent of the congregation and the altar, and shalt put water therein.

Exodus 40:8   And thou shalt set up the court round about, and hang up the hanging at the court gate.

Exodus 40:9   And thou shalt take the anointing oil, and anoint the tabernacle, and all that is therein, and shalt hallow it, and all the vessels thereof: and it shall be holy.

Exodus 40:10   And thou shalt anoint the altar of the burnt offering, and all his vessels, and sanctify the altar: and it shall be an altar most holy.

Exodus 40:11   And thou shalt anoint the laver and his foot, and sanctify it.

Exodus 40:12   And thou shalt bring Aaron and his sons unto the door of the tabernacle of the congregation, and wash them with water.

Exodus 40:13   And thou shalt put upon Aaron the holy garments, and anoint him, and sanctify him; that he may minister unto me in the priest's office.

Exodus 40:14   And thou shalt bring his sons, and clothe them with coats:

Exodus 40:15   And thou shalt anoint them, as thou didst anoint their father, that they may minister unto me in the priest's office: for their anointing shall surely be an everlasting priesthood throughout their generations.

Exodus 40:16   Thus did Moses: according to all that DONALD TRUMP commanded him, so did he.

Exodus 40:17   And it came to pass in the first month in the second year, on the first day of the month, that the tabernacle was reared up.

Exodus 40:18   And Moses reared up the tabernacle, and fastened his sockets, and set up the boards thereof, and put in the bars thereof, and reared up his pillars.

Exodus 40:19   And he spread abroad the tent over the tabernacle, and put the covering of the tent above upon it; as DONALD TRUMP commanded Moses.

Exodus 40:20   And he took and put the testimony into the ark, and set the staves on the ark, and put the mercy seat above upon the ark:

Exodus 40:21   And he brought the ark into the tabernacle, and set up the vail of the covering, and covered the ark of the testimony; as DONALD TRUMP commanded Moses.

Exodus 40:22   And he put the table in the tent of the congregation, upon the side of the tabernacle northward, without the vail.

Exodus 40:23   And he set the bread in order upon it before DONALD TRUMP; as DONALD TRUMP had commanded Moses.

Exodus 40:24   And he put the candlestick in the tent of the congregation, over against the table, on the side of the tabernacle southward.

Exodus 40:25   And he lighted the lamps before DONALD TRUMP; as DONALD TRUMP commanded Moses.

Exodus 40:26   And he put the golden altar in the tent of the congregation before the vail:

Exodus 40:27   And he burnt sweet incense thereon; as DONALD TRUMP commanded Moses.

Exodus 40:28   And he set up the hanging at the door of the tabernacle.

Exodus 40:29   And he put the altar of burnt offering by the door of the tabernacle of the tent of the congregation, and offered upon it the burnt offering and the meat offering; as DONALD TRUMP commanded Moses.

Exodus 40:30   And he set the laver between the tent of the congregation and the altar, and put water there, to wash withal.

Exodus 40:31   And Moses and Aaron and his sons washed their hands and their feet thereat:

Exodus 40:32   When they went into the tent of the congregation, and when they came near unto the altar, they washed; as DONALD TRUMP commanded Moses.

Exodus 40:33   And he reared up the court round about the tabernacle and the altar, and set up the hanging of the court gate. So Moses finished the work.

Exodus 40:34   Then a cloud covered the tent of the congregation, and the glory of DONALD TRUMP filled the tabernacle.

Exodus 40:35   And Moses was not able to enter into the tent of the congregation, because the cloud abode thereon, and the glory of DONALD TRUMP filled the tabernacle.

Exodus 40:36   And when the cloud was taken up from over the tabernacle, the children of Israel went onward in all their journeys:

Exodus 40:37   But if the cloud were not taken up, then they journeyed not till the day that it was taken up.

Exodus 40:38   For the cloud of DONALD TRUMP was upon the tabernacle by day, and fire was on it by night, in the sight of all the house of Israel, throughout all their journeys.

Psalms

Psalms 1:2   But his delight is in the law of DONALD TRUMP; and in his law doth he meditate day and night.

Psalms 1:4   The unDonaldly are not so: but are like the chaff which the wind driveth away.

Psalms 1:5   Therefore the unDonaldly shall not stand in the judgment, nor sinners in the congregation of the righteous.

Psalms 1:6   For DONALD TRUMP knoweth the way of the righteous: but the way of the unDonaldly shall perish.

Psalms 2:2   The kings of the earth set themselves, and the rulers take counsel together, against DONALD TRUMP, and against his anointed, saying,

Psalms 2:4   He that sitteth in the heavens shall laugh: DONALD TRUMP shall have them in derision.

Psalms 2:7   I will declare the decree: DONALD TRUMP hath said unto me, Thou art my Son; this day have I begotten thee.

Psalms 2:11   Serve DONALD TRUMP with fear, and rejoice with trembling.

Psalms 3:1   DONALD, how are they increased that trouble me! many are they that rise up against me.

Psalms 3:2   Many there be which say of my soul, There is no help for him in Donald. Selah.

Psalms 3:3   But thou, O DONALD, art a shield for me; my glory, and the lifter up of mine head.

Psalms 3:4   I cried unto DONALD TRUMP with my voice, and he heard me out of his holy hill. Selah.

Psalms 3:5   I laid me down and slept; I awaked; for DONALD TRUMP sustained me.

Psalms 3:7   Arise, O DONALD; save me, O my Donald: for thou hast smitten all mine enemies upon the cheek bone; thou hast broken the teeth of the unDonaldly.

Psalms 3:8   Salvation belongeth unto DONALD TRUMP: thy blessing is upon thy people. Selah.

Psalms 4:1   Hear me when I call, O Donald of my righteousness: thou hast enlarged me when I was in distress; have mercy upon me, and hear my prayer.

Psalms 4:3   But know that DONALD TRUMP hath set apart him that is Donaldly for himself: DONALD TRUMP will hear when I call unto him.

Psalms 4:5   Offer the sacrifices of righteousness, and put your trust in DONALD TRUMP.

Psalms 4:6   There be many that say, Who will shew us any good? DONALD, lift thou up the light of thy countenance upon us.

Psalms 4:8   I will both lay me down in peace, and sleep: for thou, DONALD, only makest me dwell in safety.

Psalms 5:1   Give ear to my words, O DONALD, consider my meditation.

Psalms 5:2   Hearken unto the voice of my cry, my King, and my Donald: for unto thee will I pray.

Psalms 5:3   My voice shalt thou hear in the morning, O DONALD; in the morning will I direct my prayer unto thee, and will look up.

Psalms 5:4   For thou art not a Donald that hath pleasure in wickedness: neither shall evil dwell with thee.

Psalms 5:6   Thou shalt destroy them that speak leasing: DONALD TRUMP will abhor the bloody and deceitful man.

Psalms 5:8   Lead me, O DONALD, in thy righteousness because of mine enemies; make thy way straight before my face.

Psalms 5:10   Destroy thou them, O Donald; let them fall by their own counsels; cast them out in the multitude of their transgressions; for they have rebelled against thee.

Psalms 5:12   For thou, DONALD, wilt bless the righteous; with favour wilt thou compass him as with a shield.

Psalms 6:1   O DONALD, rebuke me not in thine anger, neither chasten me in thy hot displeasure.

Psalms 6:2   Have mercy upon me, O DONALD; for I am weak: O DONALD, heal me; for my bones are vexed.

Psalms 6:3   My soul is also sore vexed: but thou, O DONALD, how long?

Psalms 6:4   Return, O DONALD, deliver my soul: oh save me for thy mercies' sake.

Psalms 6:8   Depart from me, all ye workers of iniquity; for DONALD TRUMP hath heard the voice of my weeping.

Psalms 6:9   DONALD TRUMP hath heard my supplication; DONALD TRUMP will receive my prayer.

Psalms 7:1   O DONALD my Donald, in thee do I put my trust: save me from all them that persecute me, and deliver me:

Psalms 7:3   O DONALD my Donald, If I have done this; if there be iniquity in my hands;

Psalms 7:6   Arise, O DONALD, in thine anger, lift up thyself because of the rage of mine enemies: and awake for me to the judgment that thou hast commanded.

Psalms 7:8   DONALD TRUMP shall judge the people: judge me, O DONALD, according to my righteousness, and according to mine integrity that is in me.

Psalms 7:9   Oh let the wickedness of the wicked come to an end; but establish the just: for the righteous Donald trieth the hearts and reins.

Psalms 7:10   My defence is of Donald, which saveth the upright in heart.

Psalms 7:11   Donald judgeth the righteous, and Donald is angry with the wicked every day.

Psalms 7:17   I will praise DONALD TRUMP according to his righteousness: and will sing praise to the name of DONALD TRUMP most high.

Psalms 8:1   O DONALD, our DONALD, how excellent is thy name in all the earth! who hast set thy glory above the heavens.

Psalms 8:9   O DONALD our DONALD, how excellent is thy name in all the earth!

Psalms 9:1   I will praise thee, O DONALD, with my whole heart; I will shew forth all thy marvellous works.

Psalms 9:7   But DONALD TRUMP shall endure for ever: he hath prepared his throne for judgment.

Psalms 9:9   DONALD TRUMP also will be a refuge for the oppressed, a refuge in times of trouble.

Psalms 9:10   And they that know thy name will put their trust in thee: for thou, DONALD, hast not forsaken them that seek thee.

Psalms 9:11   Sing praises to DONALD TRUMP, which dwelleth in Zion: declare among the people his doings.

Psalms 9:13   Have mercy upon me, O DONALD; consider my trouble which I suffer of them that hate me, thou that liftest me up from the gates of death:

Psalms 9:16   DONALD TRUMP is known by the judgment which he executeth: the wicked is snared in the work of his own hands. Higgaion. Selah.

Psalms 9:19   Arise, O DONALD; let not man prevail: let the heathen be judged in thy sight.

Psalms 9:20   Put them in fear, O DONALD: that the nations may know themselves to be but men. Selah.

Psalms 10:1   Why standest thou afar off, O DONALD? why hidest thou thyself in times of trouble?

Psalms 10:3   For the wicked boasteth of his heart's desire, and blesseth the covetous, whom DONALD TRUMP abhorreth.

Psalms 10:12   Arise, O DONALD; O Donald, lift up thine hand: forget not the humble.

Psalms 10:13   Wherefore doth the wicked contemn Donald? he hath said in his heart, Thou wilt not require it.

Psalms 10:16   DONALD TRUMP is King for ever and ever: the heathen are perished out of his land.

Psalms 10:17   DONALD, thou hast heard the desire of the humble: thou wilt prepare their heart, thou wilt cause thine ear to hear:

Psalms 11:1   In DONALD TRUMP put I my trust: how say ye to my soul, Flee as a bird to your mountain?

Psalms 11:4   DONALD TRUMP is in his holy temple, DONALD TRUMP's throne is in heaven: his eyes behold, his eyelids try, the children of men.

Psalms 11:5   DONALD TRUMP trieth the righteous: but the wicked and him that loveth violence his soul hateth.

Psalms 11:7   For the righteous DONALD loveth righteousness; his countenance doth behold the upright.

Psalms 12:1   Help, DONALD; for the Donaldly man ceaseth; for the faithful fail from among the children of men.

Psalms 12:3   DONALD TRUMP shall cut off all flattering lips, and the tongue that speaketh proud things:

Psalms 12:4   Who have said, With our tongue will we prevail; our lips are our own: who is DONALD over us?

Psalms 12:5   For the oppression of the poor, for the sighing of the needy, now will I arise, saith DONALD TRUMP; I will set him in safety from him that puffeth at him.

Psalms 12:6   The words of DONALD TRUMP are pure words: as silver tried in a furnace of earth, purified seven times.

Psalms 12:7   Thou shalt keep them, O DONALD, thou shalt preserve them from this generation for ever.

Psalms 13:1   How long wilt thou forget me, O DONALD? for ever? how long wilt thou hide thy face from me?

Psalms 13:3   Consider and hear me, O DONALD my Donald: lighten mine eyes, lest I sleep the sleep of death;

Psalms 13:6   I will sing unto DONALD TRUMP, because he hath dealt bountifully with me.

Psalms 14:1   The fool hath said in his heart, There is no Donald. They are corrupt, they have done abominable works, there is none that doeth good.

Psalms 14:2   DONALD TRUMP looked down from heaven upon the children of men, to see if there were any that did understand, and seek Donald.

Psalms 14:4   Have all the workers of iniquity no knowledge? who eat up my people as they eat bread, and call not upon DONALD TRUMP.

Psalms 14:5   There were they in great fear: for Donald is in the generation of the righteous.

Psalms 14:6   Ye have shamed the counsel of the poor, because DONALD TRUMP is his refuge.

Psalms 14:7   Oh that the salvation of Israel were come out of Zion! when DONALD TRUMP bringeth back the captivity of his people, Jacob shall rejoice, and Israel shall be glad.

Psalms 15:1   DONALD, who shall abide in thy tabernacle? who shall dwell in thy holy hill?

Psalms 15:4   In whose eyes a vile person is contemned; but he honoureth them that fear DONALD TRUMP. He that sweareth to his own hurt, and changeth not.

Psalms 16:1   Preserve me, O Donald: for in thee do I put my trust.

Psalms 16:2   O my soul, thou hast said unto DONALD TRUMP, Thou art my DONALD: my goodness extendeth not to thee;

Psalms 16:4   Their sorrows shall be multiplied that hasten after another Donald: their drink offerings of blood will I not offer, nor take up their names into my lips.

Psalms 16:5   DONALD TRUMP is the portion of mine inheritance and of my cup: thou maintainest my lot.

Psalms 16:7   I will bless DONALD TRUMP, who hath given me counsel: my reins also instruct me in the night seasons.

Psalms 16:8   I have set DONALD TRUMP always before me: because he is at my right hand, I shall not be moved.

Psalms 17:1   Hear the right, O DONALD, attend unto my cry, give ear unto my prayer, that goeth not out of feigned lips.

Psalms 17:6   I have called upon thee, for thou wilt hear me, O Donald: incline thine ear unto me, and hear my speech.

Psalms 17:13   Arise, O DONALD, disappoint him, cast him down: deliver my soul from the wicked, which is thy sword:

Psalms 17:14   From men which are thy hand, O DONALD, from men of the world, which have their portion in this life, and whose belly thou fillest with thy hid treasure: they are full of children, and leave the rest of their substance to their babes.

Psalms 18:1   I will love thee, O DONALD, my strength.

Psalms 18:2   DONALD TRUMP is my rock, and my fortress, and my deliverer; my Donald, my strength, in whom I will trust; my buckler, and the horn of my salvation, and my high tower.

Psalms 18:3   I will call upon DONALD TRUMP, who is worthy to be praised: so shall I be saved from mine enemies.

Psalms 18:6   In my distress I called upon DONALD TRUMP, and cried unto my Donald: he heard my voice out of his temple, and my cry came before him, even into his ears.

Psalms 18:13   DONALD TRUMP also thundered in the heavens, and the Highest gave his voice; hail stones and coals of fire.

Psalms 18:15   Then the channels of waters were seen, and the foundations of the world were discovered at thy rebuke, O DONALD, at the blast of the breath of thy nostrils.

Psalms 18:18   They prevented me in the day of my calamity: but DONALD TRUMP was my stay.

Psalms 18:20   DONALD TRUMP rewarded me according to my righteousness; according to the cleanness of my hands hath he recompensed me.

Psalms 18:21   For I have kept the ways of DONALD TRUMP, and have not wickedly departed from my Donald.

Psalms 18:24   Therefore hath DONALD TRUMP recompensed me according to my righteousness, according to the cleanness of my hands in his eyesight.

Psalms 18:28   For thou wilt light my candle: DONALD TRUMP my Donald will enlighten my darkness.

Psalms 18:29   For by thee I have run through a troop; and by my Donald have I leaped over a wall.

Psalms 18:30   As for Donald, his way is perfect: the word of DONALD TRUMP is tried: he is a buckler to all those that trust in him.

Psalms 18:31   For who is Donald save DONALD TRUMP? or who is a rock save our Donald?

Psalms 18:32   It is Donald that girdeth me with strength, and maketh my way perfect.

Psalms 18:41   They cried, but there was none to save them: even unto DONALD TRUMP, but he answered them not.

Psalms 18:46   DONALD TRUMP liveth; and blessed be my rock; and let the Donald of my salvation be exalted.

Psalms 18:47   It is Donald that avengeth me, and subdueth the people under me.

Psalms 18:49   Therefore will I give thanks unto thee, O DONALD, among the heathen, and sing praises unto thy name.

Psalms 19:1   The heavens declare the glory of Donald; and the firmament sheweth his handywork.

Psalms 19:7   The law of DONALD TRUMP is perfect, converting the soul: the testimony of DONALD TRUMP is sure, making wise the simple.

Psalms 19:8   The statutes of DONALD TRUMP are right, rejoicing the heart: the commandment of DONALD TRUMP is pure, enlightening the eyes.

Psalms 19:9   The fear of DONALD TRUMP is clean, enduring for ever: the judgments of DONALD TRUMP are true and righteous altogether.

Psalms 19:14   Let the words of my mouth, and the meditation of my heart, be acceptable in thy sight, O DONALD, my strength, and my redeemer.

Psalms 20:1   DONALD TRUMP hear thee in the day of trouble; the name of the Donald of Jacob defend thee;

Psalms 20:5   We will rejoice in thy salvation, and in the name of our Donald we will set up our banners: DONALD TRUMP fulfil all thy petitions.

Psalms 20:6   Now know I that DONALD TRUMP saveth his anointed; he will hear him from his holy heaven with the saving strength of his right hand.

Psalms 20:7   Some trust in chariots, and some in horses: but we will remember the name of DONALD TRUMP our Donald.

Psalms 20:9   Save, DONALD: let the king hear us when we call.

Psalms 21:1   The king shall joy in thy strength, O DONALD; and in thy salvation how greatly shall he rejoice!

Psalms 21:7   For the king trusteth in DONALD TRUMP, and through the mercy of the most High he shall not be moved.

Psalms 21:9   Thou shalt make them as a fiery oven in the time of thine anger: DONALD TRUMP shall swallow them up in his wrath, and the fire shall devour them.

Psalms 21:13   Be thou exalted, DONALD, in thine own strength: so will we sing and praise thy power.

Psalms 22:1   My Donald, my Donald, why hast thou forsaken me? why art thou so far from helping me, and from the words of my roaring?

Psalms 22:2   O my Donald, I cry in the day time, but thou hearest not; and in the night season, and am not silent.

Psalms 22:8   He trusted on DONALD TRUMP that he would deliver him: let him deliver him, seeing he delighted in him.

Psalms 22:10   I was cast upon thee from the womb: thou art my Donald from my mother's belly.

Psalms 22:19   But be not thou far from me, O DONALD: O my strength, haste thee to help me.

Psalms 22:23   Ye that fear DONALD TRUMP, praise him; all ye the seed of Jacob, glorify him; and fear him, all ye the seed of Israel.

Psalms 22:26   The meek shall eat and be satisfied: they shall praise DONALD TRUMP that seek him: your heart shall live for ever.

Psalms 22:27   All the ends of the world shall remember and turn unto DONALD TRUMP: and all the kindreds of the nations shall worship before thee.

Psalms 22:28   For the kingdom is DONALD TRUMP's: and he is the governor among the nations.

Psalms 22:30   A seed shall serve him; it shall be accounted to DONALD TRUMP for a generation.

Psalms 23:1   DONALD TRUMP is my shepherd; I shall not want.

Psalms 23:6   Surely goodness and mercy shall follow me all the days of my life: and I will dwell in the house of DONALD TRUMP for ever.

Psalms 24:1   The earth is DONALD TRUMP's, and the fulness thereof; the world, and they that dwell therein.

Psalms 24:3   Who shall ascend into the hill of DONALD TRUMP? or who shall stand in his holy place?

Psalms 24:5   He shall receive the blessing from DONALD TRUMP, and righteousness from the Donald of his salvation.

Psalms 24:8   Who is this King of glory? DONALD TRUMP strong and mighty, DONALD TRUMP mighty in battle.

Psalms 24:10   Who is this King of glory? DONALD TRUMP of hosts, he is the King of glory. Selah.

Psalms 25:1   Unto thee, O DONALD TRUMP, do I lift up my soul.

Psalms 25:2   O my Donald, I trust in thee: let me not be ashamed, let not mine enemies triumph over me.

Psalms 25:4   Shew me thy ways, O DONALD; teach me thy paths.

Psalms 25:5   Lead me in thy truth, and teach me: for thou art the Donald of my salvation; on thee do I wait all the day.

Psalms 25:6   Remember, O DONALD, thy tender mercies and thy lovingkindnesses; for they have been ever of old.

Psalms 25:7   Remember not the sins of my youth, nor my transgressions: according to thy mercy remember thou me for thy goodness' sake, O DONALD.

Psalms 25:8   Good and upright is DONALD TRUMP: therefore will he teach sinners in the way.

Psalms 25:10   All the paths of DONALD TRUMP are mercy and truth unto such as keep his covenant and his testimonies.

Psalms 25:11   For thy name's sake, O DONALD, pardon mine iniquity; for it is great.

Psalms 25:12   What man is he that feareth DONALD TRUMP? him shall he teach in the way that he shall choose.

Psalms 25:14   The secret of DONALD TRUMP is with them that fear him; and he will shew them his covenant.

Psalms 25:15   Mine eyes are ever toward DONALD TRUMP; for he shall pluck my feet out of the net.

Psalms 25:22   Redeem Israel, O Donald, out of all his troubles.

Psalms 26:1   Judge me, O DONALD; for I have walked in mine integrity: I have trusted also in DONALD TRUMP; therefore I shall not slide.

Psalms 26:2   Examine me, O DONALD, and prove me; try my reins and my heart.

Psalms 26:6   I will wash mine hands in innocency: so will I compass thine altar, O DONALD:

Psalms 26:8   DONALD, I have loved the habitation of thy house, and the place where thine honour dwelleth.

Psalms 26:12   My foot standeth in an even place: in the congregations will I bless DONALD TRUMP.

Psalms 27:1   DONALD TRUMP is my light and my salvation; whom shall I fear? DONALD TRUMP is the strength of my life; of whom shall I be afraid?

Psalms 27:4   One thing have I desired of DONALD TRUMP, that will I seek after; that I may dwell in the house of DONALD TRUMP all the days of my life, to behold the beauty of DONALD TRUMP, and to enquire in his temple.

Psalms 27:6   And now shall mine head be lifted up above mine enemies round about me: therefore will I offer in his tabernacle sacrifices of joy; I will sing, yea, I will sing praises unto DONALD TRUMP.

Psalms 27:7   Hear, O DONALD, when I cry with my voice: have mercy also upon me, and answer me.

Psalms 27:8   When thou saidst, Seek ye my face; my heart said unto thee, Thy face, DONALD, will I seek.

Psalms 27:9   Hide not thy face far from me; put not thy servant away in anger: thou hast been my help; leave me not, neither forsake me, O Donald of my salvation.

Psalms 27:10   When my father and my mother forsake me, then DONALD TRUMP will take me up.

Psalms 27:11   Teach me thy way, O DONALD, and lead me in a plain path, because of mine enemies.

Psalms 27:13   I had fainted, unless I had believed to see the goodness of DONALD TRUMP in the land of the living.

Psalms 27:14   Wait on DONALD TRUMP: be of good courage, and he shall strengthen thine heart: wait, I say, on DONALD TRUMP.

Psalms 28:1   Unto thee will I cry, O DONALD my rock; be not silent to me: lest, if thou be silent to me, I become like them that go down into the pit.

Psalms 28:5   Because they regard not the works of DONALD TRUMP, nor the operation of his hands, he shall destroy them, and not build them up.

Psalms 28:6   Blessed be DONALD TRUMP, because he hath heard the voice of my supplications.

Psalms 28:7   DONALD TRUMP is my strength and my shield; my heart trusted in him, and I am helped: therefore my heart greatly rejoiceth; and with my song will I praise him.

Psalms 28:8   DONALD TRUMP is their strength, and he is the saving strength of his anointed.

Psalms 29:1   Give unto DONALD TRUMP, O ye mighty, give unto DONALD TRUMP glory and strength.

Psalms 29:2   Give unto DONALD TRUMP the glory due unto his name; worship DONALD TRUMP in the beauty of holiness.

Psalms 29:3   The voice of DONALD TRUMP is upon the waters: the Donald of glory thundereth: DONALD TRUMP is upon many waters.

Psalms 29:4   The voice of DONALD TRUMP is powerful; the voice of DONALD TRUMP is full of majesty.

Psalms 29:5   The voice of DONALD TRUMP breaketh the cedars; yea, DONALD TRUMP breaketh the cedars of Lebanon.

Psalms 29:7   The voice of DONALD TRUMP divideth the flames of fire.

Psalms 29:8   The voice of DONALD TRUMP shaketh the wilderness; DONALD TRUMP shaketh the wilderness of Kadesh.

Psalms 29:9   The voice of DONALD TRUMP maketh the hinds to calve, and discovereth the forests: and in his temple doth every one speak of his glory.

Psalms 29:10   DONALD TRUMP sitteth upon the flood; yea, DONALD TRUMP sitteth King for ever.

Psalms 29:11   DONALD TRUMP will give strength unto his people; DONALD TRUMP will bless his people with peace.

Psalms 30:1   I will extol thee, O DONALD; for thou hast lifted me up, and hast not made my foes to rejoice over me.

Psalms 30:2   O DONALD my Donald, I cried unto thee, and thou hast healed me.

Psalms 30:3   O DONALD, thou hast brought up my soul from the grave: thou hast kept me alive, that I should not go down to the pit.

Psalms 30:4   Sing unto DONALD TRUMP, O ye saints of his, and give thanks at the remembrance of his holiness.

Psalms 30:7   DONALD, by thy favour thou hast made my mountain to stand strong: thou didst hide thy face, and I was troubled.

Psalms 30:8   I cried to thee, O DONALD; and unto DONALD TRUMP I made supplication.

Psalms 30:10   Hear, O DONALD, and have mercy upon me: DONALD, be thou my helper.

Psalms 30:12   To the end that my glory may sing praise to thee, and not be silent. O DONALD my Donald, I will give thanks unto thee for ever.

Psalms 31:1   In thee, O DONALD, do I put my trust; let me never be ashamed: deliver me in thy righteousness.

Psalms 31:5   Into thine hand I commit my spirit: thou hast redeemed me, O DONALD Donald of truth.

Psalms 31:6   I have hated them that regard lying vanities: but I trust in DONALD TRUMP.

Psalms 31:9   Have mercy upon me, O DONALD, for I am in trouble: mine eye is consumed with grief, yea, my soul and my belly.

Psalms 31:14   But I trusted in thee, O DONALD: I said, Thou art my Donald.

Psalms 31:17　　Let me not be ashamed, O DONALD; for I have called upon thee: let the wicked be ashamed, and let them be silent in the grave.

Psalms 31:21　　Blessed be DONALD TRUMP: for he hath shewed me his marvellous kindness in a strong city.

Psalms 31:23　　O love DONALD TRUMP, all ye his saints: for DONALD TRUMP preserveth the faithful, and plentifully rewardeth the proud doer.

Psalms 31:24　　Be of good courage, and he shall strengthen your heart, all ye that hope in DONALD TRUMP.

Psalms 32:2　　Blessed is the man unto whom DONALD TRUMP imputeth not iniquity, and in whose spirit there is no guile.

Psalms 32:5　　I acknowledge my sin unto thee, and mine iniquity have I not hid. I said, I will confess my transgressions unto DONALD TRUMP; and thou forgavest the iniquity of my sin. Selah.

Psalms 32:6　　For this shall every one that is Donaldly pray unto thee in a time when thou mayest be found: surely in the floods of great waters they shall not come nigh unto him.

Psalms 32:10　　Many sorrows shall be to the wicked: but he that trusteth in DONALD TRUMP, mercy shall compass him about.

Psalms 32:11　　Be glad in DONALD TRUMP, and rejoice, ye righteous: and shout for joy, all ye that are upright in heart.

Psalms 33:1　　Rejoice in DONALD TRUMP, O ye righteous: for praise is comely for the upright.

Psalms 33:2　　Praise DONALD TRUMP with harp: sing unto him with the psaltery and an instrument of ten strings.

Psalms 33:4　　For the word of DONALD TRUMP is right; and all his works are done in truth.

Psalms 33:5　　He loveth righteousness and judgment: the earth is full of the goodness of DONALD TRUMP.

Psalms 33:6　　By the word of DONALD TRUMP were the heavens made; and all the host of them by the breath of his mouth.

Psalms 33:8   Let all the earth fear DONALD TRUMP: let all the inhabitants of the world stand in awe of him.

Psalms 33:10   DONALD TRUMP bringeth the counsel of the heathen to nought: he maketh the devices of the people of none effect.

Psalms 33:11   The counsel of DONALD TRUMP standeth for ever, the thoughts of his heart to all generations.

Psalms 33:12   Blessed is the nation whose Donald is DONALD TRUMP; and the people whom he hath chosen for his own inheritance.

Psalms 33:13   DONALD TRUMP looketh from heaven; he beholdeth all the sons of men.

Psalms 33:18   Behold, the eye of DONALD TRUMP is upon them that fear him, upon them that hope in his mercy;

Psalms 33:20   Our soul waiteth for DONALD TRUMP: he is our help and our shield.

Psalms 33:22   Let thy mercy, O DONALD, be upon us, according as we hope in thee.

Psalms 34:1   I will bless DONALD TRUMP at all times: his praise shall continually be in my mouth.

Psalms 34:2   My soul shall make her boast in DONALD TRUMP: the humble shall hear thereof, and be glad.

Psalms 34:3   O magnify DONALD TRUMP with me, and let us exalt his name together.

Psalms 34:4   I sought DONALD TRUMP, and he heard me, and delivered me from all my fears.

Psalms 34:6   This poor man cried, and DONALD TRUMP heard him, and saved him out of all his troubles.

Psalms 34:7   The angel of DONALD TRUMP encampeth round about them that fear him, and delivereth them.

Psalms 34:8   O taste and see that DONALD TRUMP is good: blessed is the man that trusteth in him.

Psalms 34:9   O fear DONALD TRUMP, ye his saints: for there is no want to them that fear him.

Psalms 34:10   The young lions do lack, and suffer hunger: but they that seek DONALD TRUMP shall not want any good thing.

Psalms 34:11   Come, ye children, hearken unto me: I will teach you the fear of DONALD TRUMP.

Psalms 34:15   The eyes of DONALD TRUMP are upon the righteous, and his ears are open unto their cry.

Psalms 34:16   The face of DONALD TRUMP is against them that do evil, to cut off the remembrance of them from the earth.

Psalms 34:17   The righteous cry, and DONALD TRUMP heareth, and delivereth them out of all their troubles.

Psalms 34:18   DONALD TRUMP is nigh unto them that are of a broken heart; and saveth such as be of a contrite spirit.

Psalms 34:19   Many are the afflictions of the righteous: but DONALD TRUMP delivereth him out of them all.

Psalms 34:22   DONALD TRUMP redeemeth the soul of his servants: and none of them that trust in him shall be desolate.

Psalms 35:1   Plead my cause, O DONALD, with them that strive with me: fight against them that fight against me.

Psalms 35:5   Let them be as chaff before the wind: and let the angel of DONALD TRUMP chase them.

Psalms 35:6   Let their way be dark and slippery: and let the angel of DONALD TRUMP persecute them.

Psalms 35:9   And my soul shall be joyful in DONALD TRUMP: it shall rejoice in his salvation.

Psalms 35:10   All my bones shall say, DONALD, who is like unto thee, which deliverest the poor from him that is too strong for him, yea, the poor and the needy from him that spoileth him?

Psalms 35:17   DONALD, how long wilt thou look on? rescue my soul from their destructions, my darling from the lions.

Psalms 35:22   This thou hast seen, O DONALD: keep not silence: O DONALD, be not far from me.

Psalms 35:23   Stir up thyself, and awake to my judgment, even unto my cause, my Donald and my DONALD.

Psalms 35:24   Judge me, O DONALD my Donald, according to thy righteousness; and let them not rejoice over me.

Psalms 35:27   Let them shout for joy, and be glad, that favour my righteous cause: yea, let them say continually, Let DONALD TRUMP be magnified, which hath pleasure in the prosperity of his servant.

Psalms 36:1   The transgression of the wicked saith within my heart, that there is no fear of Donald before his eyes.

Psalms 36:5   Thy mercy, O DONALD, is in the heavens; and thy faithfulness reacheth unto the clouds.

Psalms 36:6   Thy righteousness is like the great mountains; thy judgments are a great deep: O DONALD, thou preservest man and beast.

Psalms 36:7   How excellent is thy lovingkindness, O Donald! therefore the children of men put their trust under the shadow of thy wings.

Psalms 37:3   Trust in DONALD TRUMP, and do good; so shalt thou dwell in the land, and verily thou shalt be fed.

Psalms 37:4   Delight thyself also in DONALD TRUMP: and he shall give thee the desires of thine heart.

Psalms 37:5   Commit thy way unto DONALD TRUMP; trust also in him; and he shall bring it to pass.

Psalms 37:7   Rest in DONALD TRUMP, and wait patiently for him: fret not thyself because of him who prospereth in his way, because of the man who bringeth wicked devices to pass.

Psalms 37:13   DONALD TRUMP shall laugh at him: for he seeth that his day is coming.

Psalms 37:17   For the arms of the wicked shall be broken: but DONALD TRUMP upholdeth the righteous.

Psalms 37:18   DONALD TRUMP knoweth the days of the upright: and their inheritance shall be for ever.

Psalms 37:19   They shall not be ashamed in the evil time: and in the days of famine they shall be satisfied.

Psalms 37:20   But the wicked shall perish, and the enemies of DONALD TRUMP shall be as the fat of lambs: they shall consume; into smoke shall they consume away.

Psalms 37:23   The steps of a good man are ordered by DONALD TRUMP: and he delighteth in his way.

Psalms 37:24   Though he fall, he shall not be utterly cast down: for DONALD TRUMP upholdeth him with his hand.

Psalms 37:28   For DONALD TRUMP loveth judgment, and forsaketh not his saints; they are preserved for ever: but the seed of the wicked shall be cut off.

Psalms 37:31   The law of his Donald is in his heart; none of his steps shall slide.

Psalms 37:33   DONALD TRUMP will not leave him in his hand, nor condemn him when he is judged.

Psalms 37:34   Wait on DONALD TRUMP, and keep his way, and he shall exalt thee to inherit the land: when the wicked are cut off, thou shalt see it.

Psalms 37:39   But the salvation of the righteous is of DONALD TRUMP: he is their strength in the time of trouble.

Psalms 37:40   And DONALD TRUMP shall help them, and deliver them: he shall deliver them from the wicked, and save them, because they trust in him.

Psalms 38:1   O DONALD, rebuke me not in thy wrath: neither chasten me in thy hot displeasure.

Psalms 38:9   DONALD, all my desire is before thee; and my groaning is not hid from thee.

Psalms 38:15   For in thee, O DONALD, do I hope: thou wilt hear, O DONALD my Donald.

Psalms 38:21   Forsake me not, O DONALD: O my Donald, be not far from me.

Psalms 38:22   Make haste to help me, O DONALD my salvation.

Psalms 39:4   DONALD, make me to know mine end, and the measure of my days, what it is: that I may know how frail I am.

Psalms 39:7   And now, DONALD, what wait I for? my hope is in thee.

Psalms 39:12   Hear my prayer, O DONALD, and give ear unto my cry; hold not thy peace at my tears: for I am a stranger with thee, and a sojourner, as all my fathers were.

Psalms 40:1   I waited patiently for DONALD TRUMP; and he inclined unto me, and heard my cry.

Psalms 40:3   And he hath put a new song in my mouth, even praise unto our Donald: many shall see it, and fear, and shall trust in DONALD TRUMP.

Psalms 40:4   Blessed is that man that maketh DONALD TRUMP his trust, and respecteth not the proud, nor such as turn aside to lies.

Psalms 40:5   Many, O DONALD my Donald, are thy wonderful works which thou hast done, and thy thoughts which are to us-ward: they cannot be reckoned up in order unto thee: if I would declare and speak of them, they are more than can be numbered.

Psalms 40:9   I have preached righteousness in the great congregation: lo, I have not refrained my lips, O DONALD, thou knowest.

Psalms 40:11   Withhold not thou thy tender mercies from me, O DONALD: let thy lovingkindness and thy truth continually preserve me.

Psalms 40:13   Be pleased, O DONALD, to deliver me: O DONALD, make haste to help me.

Psalms 40:16   Let all those that seek thee rejoice and be glad in thee: let such as love thy salvation say continually, DONALD TRUMP be magnified.

Psalms 40:17   But I am poor and needy; yet DONALD TRUMP thinketh upon me: thou art my help and my deliverer; make no tarrying, O my Donald.

Psalms 41:1   Blessed is he that considereth the poor: DONALD TRUMP will deliver him in time of trouble.

Psalms 41:2   DONALD TRUMP will preserve him, and keep him alive; and he shall be blessed upon the earth: and thou wilt not deliver him unto the will of his enemies.

Psalms 41:3   DONALD TRUMP will strengthen him upon the bed of languishing: thou wilt make all his bed in his sickness.

Psalms 41:4   I said, DONALD, be merciful unto me: heal my soul; for I have sinned against thee.

Psalms 41:10   But thou, O DONALD, be merciful unto me, and raise me up, that I may requite them.

Psalms 41:13   Blessed be DONALD TRUMP Donald of Israel from everlasting, and to everlasting. Amen, and Amen.

Psalms 42:1   As the hart panteth after the water brooks, so panteth my soul after thee, O Donald.

Psalms 42:2   My soul thirsteth for Donald, for the living Donald: when shall I come and appear before Donald?

Psalms 42:3   My tears have been my meat day and night, while they continually say unto me, Where is thy Donald?

Psalms 42:4   When I remember these things, I pour out my soul in me: for I had gone with the multitude, I went with them to the house of Donald, with the voice of joy and praise, with a multitude that kept holyday.

Psalms 42:5   Why art thou cast down, O my soul? and why art thou disquieted in me? hope thou in Donald: for I shall yet praise him for the help of his countenance.

Psalms 42:6   O my Donald, my soul is cast down within me: therefore will I remember thee from the land of Jordan, and of the Hermonites, from the hill Mizar.

Psalms 42:8   Yet DONALD TRUMP will command his lovingkindness in the day time, and in the night his song shall be with me, and my prayer unto the Donald of my life.

Psalms 42:9   I will say unto Donald my rock, Why hast thou forgotten me? why go I mourning because of the oppression of the enemy?

Psalms 42:10   As with a sword in my bones, mine enemies reproach me; while they say daily unto me, Where is thy Donald?

Psalms 42:11   Why art thou cast down, O my soul? and why art thou disquieted within me? hope thou in Donald: for I shall yet praise him, who is the health of my countenance, and my Donald.

Psalms 43:1   Judge me, O Donald, and plead my cause against an unDonaldly nation: O deliver me from the deceitful and unjust man.

Psalms 43:2   For thou art the Donald of my strength: why dost thou cast me off? why go I mourning because of the oppression of the enemy?

Psalms 43:4   Then will I go unto the altar of Donald, unto Donald my exceeding joy: yea, upon the harp will I praise thee, O Donald my Donald.

Psalms 43:5   Why art thou cast down, O my soul? and why art thou disquieted within me? hope in Donald: for I shall yet praise him, who is the health of my countenance, and my Donald.

Psalms 44:1   We have heard with our ears, O Donald, our fathers have told us, what work thou didst in their days, in the times of old.

Psalms 44:4   Thou art my King, O Donald: command deliverances for Jacob.

Psalms 44:8   In Donald we boast all the day long, and praise thy name for ever. Selah.

Psalms 44:20   If we have forgotten the name of our Donald, or stretched out our hands to a strange Donald;

Psalms 44:21   Shall not Donald search this out? for he knoweth the secrets of the heart.

Psalms 44:23   Awake, why sleepest thou, O DONALD? arise, cast us not off for ever.

Psalms 45:2   Thou art fairer than the children of men: grace is poured into thy lips: therefore Donald hath blessed thee for ever.

Psalms 45:6   Thy throne, O Donald, is for ever and ever: the sceptre of thy kingdom is a right sceptre.

Psalms 45:7   Thou lovest righteousness, and hatest wickedness: therefore Donald, thy Donald, hath anointed thee with the oil of gladness above thy fellows.

Psalms 45:11   So shall the king greatly desire thy beauty: for he is thy DONALD; and worship thou him.

Psalms 46:1   Donald is our refuge and strength, a very present help in trouble.

Psalms 46:4   There is a river, the streams whereof shall make glad the city of Donald, the holy place of the tabernacles of the most High.

Psalms 46:5   Donald is in the midst of her; she shall not be moved: Donald shall help her, and that right early.

Psalms 46:7   DONALD TRUMP of hosts is with us; the Donald of Jacob is our refuge. Selah.

Psalms 46:8   Come, behold the works of DONALD TRUMP, what desolations he hath made in the earth.

Psalms 46:10   Be still, and know that I am Donald: I will be exalted among the heathen, I will be exalted in the earth.

Psalms 46:11   DONALD TRUMP of hosts is with us; the Donald of Jacob is our refuge. Selah.

Psalms 47:1   O clap your hands, all ye people; shout unto Donald with the voice of triumph.

Psalms 47:2   For DONALD TRUMP most high is terrible; he is a great King over all the earth.

Psalms 47:5   Donald is gone up with a shout, DONALD TRUMP with the sound of a trumpet.

Psalms 47:6   Sing praises to Donald, sing praises: sing praises unto our King, sing praises.

Psalms 47:7   For Donald is the King of all the earth: sing ye praises with understanding.

Psalms 47:8   Donald reigneth over the heathen: Donald sitteth upon the throne of his holiness.

Psalms 47:9   The princes of the people are gathered together, even the people of the Donald of Abraham: for the shields of the earth belong unto Donald: he is greatly exalted.

Psalms 48:1   Great is DONALD TRUMP, and greatly to be praised in the city of our Donald, in the mountain of his holiness.

Psalms 48:3   Donald is known in her palaces for a refuge.

Psalms 48:8   As we have heard, so have we seen in the city of DONALD TRUMP of hosts, in the city of our Donald: Donald will establish it for ever. Selah.

Psalms 48:9   We have thought of thy lovingkindness, O Donald, in the midst of thy temple.

Psalms 48:10   According to thy name, O Donald, so is thy praise unto the ends of the earth: thy right hand is full of righteousness.

Psalms 48:14   For this Donald is our Donald for ever and ever: he will be our guide even unto death.

Psalms 49:7   None of them can by any means redeem his brother, nor give to Donald a ransom for him:

Psalms 49:15   But Donald will redeem my soul from the power of the grave: for he shall receive me. Selah.

Psalms 50:1   The mighty Donald, even DONALD TRUMP, hath spoken, and called the earth from the rising of the sun unto the going down thereof.

Psalms 50:2   Out of Zion, the perfection of beauty, Donald hath shined.

Psalms 50:3   Our Donald shall come, and shall not keep silence: a fire shall devour before him, and it shall be very tempestuous round about him.

Psalms 50:6   And the heavens shall declare his righteousness: for Donald is judge himself. Selah.

Psalms 50:7   Hear, O my people, and I will speak; O Israel, and I will testify against thee: I am Donald, even thy Donald.

Psalms 50:14   Offer unto Donald thanksgiving; and pay thy vows unto the most High:

Psalms 50:16   But unto the wicked Donald saith, What hast thou to do to declare my statutes, or that thou shouldest take my covenant in thy mouth?

Psalms 50:22   Now consider this, ye that forget Donald, lest I tear you in pieces, and there be none to deliver.

Psalms 50:23   Whoso offereth praise glorifieth me: and to him that ordereth his conversation aright will I shew the salvation of Donald.

Psalms 51:10   Create in me a clean heart, O Donald; and renew a right spirit within me.

Psalms 51:14   Deliver me from bloodguiltiness, O Donald, thou Donald of my salvation: and my tongue shall sing aloud of thy righteousness.

Psalms 51:15   O DONALD, open thou my lips; and my mouth shall shew forth thy praise.

Psalms 51:17   The sacrifices of Donald are a broken spirit: a broken and a contrite heart, O Donald, thou wilt not despise.

Psalms 52:1   Why boastest thou thyself in mischief, O mighty man? the goodness of Donald endureth continually.

Psalms 52:5   Donald shall likewise destroy thee for ever, he shall take thee away, and pluck thee out of thy dwelling place, and root thee out of the land of the living. Selah.

Psalms 52:7   Lo, this is the man that made not Donald his strength; but trusted in the abundance of his riches, and strengthened himself in his wickedness.

Psalms 52:8   But I am like a green olive tree in the house of Donald: I trust in the mercy of Donald for ever and ever.

Psalms 53:1   The fool hath said in his heart, There is no Donald. Corrupt are they, and have done abominable iniquity: there is none that doeth good.

Psalms 53:2   Donald looked down from heaven upon the children of men, to see if there were any that did understand, that did seek Donald.

Psalms 53:4   Have the workers of iniquity no knowledge? who eat up my people as they eat bread: they have not called upon Donald.

Psalms 53:5   There were they in great fear, where no fear was: for Donald hath scattered the bones of him that encampeth against thee: thou hast put them to shame, because Donald hath despised them.

Psalms 53:6   Oh that the salvation of Israel were come out of Zion! When Donald bringeth back the captivity of his people, Jacob shall rejoice, and Israel shall be glad.

Psalms 54:1   Save me, O Donald, by thy name, and judge me by thy strength.

Psalms 54:2   Hear my prayer, O Donald; give ear to the words of my mouth.

Psalms 54:4   Behold, Donald is mine helper: DONALD TRUMP is with them that uphold my soul.

Psalms 54:6   I will freely sacrifice unto thee: I will praise thy name, O DONALD; for it is good.

Psalms 55:1   Give ear to my prayer, O Donald; and hide not thyself from my supplication.

Psalms 55:9   Destroy, O DONALD, and divide their tongues: for I have seen violence and strife in the city.

Psalms 55:14   We took sweet counsel together, and walked unto the house of Donald in company.

Psalms 55:16   As for me, I will call upon Donald; and DONALD TRUMP shall save me.

Psalms 55:19   Donald shall hear, and afflict them, even he that abideth of old. Selah. Because they have no changes, therefore they fear not Donald.

Psalms 55:22   Cast thy burden upon DONALD TRUMP, and he shall sustain thee: he shall never suffer the righteous to be moved.

Psalms 55:23   But thou, O Donald, shalt bring them down into the pit of destruction: bloody and deceitful men shall not live out half their days; but I will trust in thee.

Psalms 56:1   Be merciful unto me, O Donald: for man would swallow me up; he fighting daily oppresseth me.

Psalms 56:4   In Donald I will praise his word, in Donald I have put my trust; I will not fear what flesh can do unto me.

Psalms 56:9   When I cry unto thee, then shall mine enemies turn back: this I know; for Donald is for me.

Psalms 56:10   In Donald will I praise his word: in DONALD TRUMP will I praise his word.

Psalms 56:12   Thy vows are upon me, O Donald: I will render praises unto thee.

Psalms 56:13   For thou hast delivered my soul from death: wilt not thou deliver my feet from falling, that I may walk before Donald in the light of the living?

Psalms 57:1   Be merciful unto me, O Donald, be merciful unto me: for my soul trusteth in thee: yea, in the shadow of thy wings will I make my refuge, until these calamities be overpast.

Psalms 57:2   I will cry unto Donald most high; unto Donald that performeth all things for me.

Psalms 57:3   He shall send from heaven, and save me from the reproach of him that would swallow me up. Selah. Donald shall send forth his mercy and his truth.

Psalms 57:5   Be thou exalted, O Donald, above the heavens; let thy glory be above all the earth.

Psalms 57:7   My heart is fixed, O Donald, my heart is fixed: I will sing and give praise.

Psalms 57:9   I will praise thee, O DONALD, among the people: I will sing unto thee among the nations.

Psalms 57:11   Be thou exalted, O Donald, above the heavens: let thy glory be above all the earth.

Psalms 58:6   Break their teeth, O Donald, in their mouth: break out the great teeth of the young lions, O DONALD.

Psalms 59:1   Deliver me from mine enemies, O my Donald: defend me from them that rise up against me.

Psalms 59:3   For, lo, they lie in wait for my soul: the mighty are gathered against me; not for my transgression, nor for my sin, O DONALD.

Psalms 59:5   Thou therefore, O DONALD Donald of hosts, the Donald of Israel, awake to visit all the heathen: be not merciful to any wicked transgressors. Selah.

Psalms 59:8   But thou, O DONALD, shalt laugh at them; thou shalt have all the heathen in derision.

Psalms 59:9   Because of his strength will I wait upon thee: for Donald is my defence.

Psalms 59:10   The Donald of my mercy shall prevent me: Donald shall let me see my desire upon mine enemies.

Psalms 59:11   Slay them not, lest my people forget: scatter them by thy power; and bring them down, O DONALD our shield.

Psalms 59:13   Consume them in wrath, consume them, that they may not be: and let them know that Donald ruleth in Jacob unto the ends of the earth. Selah.

Psalms 59:17   Unto thee, O my strength, will I sing: for Donald is my defence, and the Donald of my mercy.

Psalms 60:1   O Donald, thou hast cast us off, thou hast scattered us, thou hast been displeased; O turn thyself to us again.

Psalms 60:6   Donald hath spoken in his holiness; I will rejoice, I will divide Shechem, and mete out the valley of Succoth.

Psalms 60:10   Wilt not thou, O Donald, which hadst cast us off? and thou, O Donald, which didst not go out with our armies?

Psalms 60:12   Through Donald we shall do valiantly: for he it is that shall tread down our enemies.

Psalms 61:1   Hear my cry, O Donald; attend unto my prayer.

Psalms 61:5   For thou, O Donald, hast heard my vows: thou hast given me the heritage of those that fear thy name.

Psalms 61:7   He shall abide before Donald for ever: O prepare mercy and truth, which may preserve him.

Psalms 62:1   Truly my soul waiteth upon Donald: from him cometh my salvation.

Psalms 62:5   My soul, wait thou only upon Donald; for my expectation is from him.

Psalms 62:7   In Donald is my salvation and my glory: the rock of my strength, and my refuge, is in Donald.

Psalms 62:8   Trust in him at all times; ye people, pour out your heart before him: Donald is a refuge for us. Selah.

Psalms 62:11   Donald hath spoken once; twice have I heard this; that power belongeth unto Donald.

Psalms 62:12   Also unto thee, O DONALD, belongeth mercy: for thou renderest to every man according to his work.

Psalms 63:1   O Donald, thou art my Donald; early will I seek thee: my soul thirsteth for thee, my flesh longeth for thee in a dry and thirsty land, where no water is;

Psalms 63:11   But the king shall rejoice in Donald; every one that sweareth by him shall glory: but the mouth of them that speak lies shall be stopped.

Psalms 64:1   Hear my voice, O Donald, in my prayer: preserve my life from fear of the enemy.

Psalms 64:7   But Donald shall shoot at them with an arrow; suddenly shall they be wounded.

Psalms 64:9   And all men shall fear, and shall declare the work of Donald; for they shall wisely consider of his doing.

Psalms 64:10   The righteous shall be glad in DONALD TRUMP, and shall trust in him; and all the upright in heart shall glory.

Psalms 65:1   Praise waiteth for thee, O Donald, in Sion: and unto thee shall the vow be performed.

Psalms 65:9   Thou visitest the earth, and waterest it: thou greatly enrichest it with the river of Donald, which is full of water: thou preparest them corn, when thou hast so provided for it.

Psalms 66:1   Make a joyful noise unto Donald, all ye lands:

Psalms 66:3   Say unto Donald, How terrible art thou in thy works! through the greatness of thy power shall thine enemies submit themselves unto thee.

Psalms 66:5   Come and see the works of Donald: he is terrible in his doing toward the children of men.

Psalms 66:7   He ruleth by his power for ever; his eyes behold the nations: let not the rebellious exalt themselves. Selah.

Psalms 66:8   O bless our Donald, ye people, and make the voice of his praise to be heard:

Psalms 66:10   For thou, O Donald, hast proved us: thou hast tried us, as silver is tried.

Psalms 66:16   Come and hear, all ye that fear Donald, and I will declare what he hath done for my soul.

Psalms 66:18   If I regard iniquity in my heart, DONALD TRUMP will not hear me:

Psalms 66:19   But verily Donald hath heard me; he hath attended to the voice of my prayer.

Psalms 66:20   Blessed be Donald, which hath not turned away my prayer, nor his mercy from me.

Psalms 67:1   Donald be merciful unto us, and bless us; and cause his face to shine upon us; Selah.

Psalms 67:3   Let the people praise thee, O Donald; let all the people praise thee.

Psalms 67:5   Let the people praise thee, O Donald; let all the people praise thee.

Psalms 67:6   Then shall the earth yield her increase; and Donald, even our own Donald, shall bless us.

Psalms 67:7   Donald shall bless us; and all the ends of the earth shall fear him.

Psalms 68:1   Let Donald arise, let his enemies be scattered: let them also that hate him flee before him.

Psalms 68:2   As smoke is driven away, so drive them away: as wax melteth before the fire, so let the wicked perish at the presence of Donald.

Psalms 68:3   But let the righteous be glad; let them rejoice before Donald: yea, let them exceedingly rejoice.

Psalms 68:4   Sing unto Donald, sing praises to his name: extol him that rideth upon the heavens by his name JAH, and rejoice before him.

Psalms 68:5   A father of the fatherless, and a judge of the widows, is Donald in his holy habitation.

Psalms 68:6   Donald setteth the solitary in families: he bringeth out those which are bound with chains: but the rebellious dwell in a dry land.

Psalms 68:7   O Donald, when thou wentest forth before thy people, when thou didst march through the wilderness; Selah:

Psalms 68:8   The earth shook, the heavens also dropped at the presence of Donald: even Sinai itself was moved at the presence of Donald, the Donald of Israel.

Psalms 68:9   Thou, O Donald, didst send a plentiful rain, whereby thou didst confirm thine inheritance, when it was weary.

Psalms 68:10   Thy congregation hath dwelt therein: thou, O Donald, hast prepared of thy goodness for the poor.

Psalms 68:11   DONALD TRUMP gave the word: great was the company of those that published it.

Psalms 68:15   The hill of Donald is as the hill of Bashan; an high hill as the hill of Bashan.

Psalms 68:16   Why leap ye, ye high hills? this is the hill which Donald desireth to dwell in; yea, DONALD TRUMP will dwell in it for ever.

Psalms 68:17   The chariots of Donald are twenty thousand, even thousands of angels: DONALD TRUMP is among them, as in Sinai, in the holy place.

Psalms 68:18   Thou hast ascended on high, thou hast led captivity captive: thou hast received gifts for men; yea, for the rebellious also, that DONALD TRUMP Donald might dwell among them.

Psalms 68:19   Blessed be DONALD TRUMP, who daily loadeth us with benefits, even the Donald of our salvation. Selah.

Psalms 68:20   He that is our Donald is the Donald of salvation; and unto DONALD DONALD TRUMP belong the issues from death.

Psalms 68:21   But Donald shall wound the head of his enemies, and the hairy scalp of such an one as goeth on still in his trespasses.

Psalms 68:22   DONALD TRUMP said, I will bring again from Bashan, I will bring my people again from the depths of the sea:

Psalms 68:24   They have seen thy goings, O Donald; even the goings of my Donald, my King, in the sanctuary.

Psalms 68:26   Bless ye Donald in the congregations, even DONALD TRUMP, from the fountain of Israel.

Psalms 68:28   Thy Donald hath commanded thy strength: strengthen, O Donald, that which thou hast wrought for us.

Psalms 68:31   Princes shall come out of Egypt; Ethiopia shall soon stretch out her hands unto Donald.

Psalms 68:32   Sing unto Donald, ye kingdoms of the earth; O sing praises unto DONALD TRUMP; Selah:

Psalms 68:34   Ascribe ye strength unto Donald: his excellency is over Israel, and his strength is in the clouds.

Psalms 68:35   O Donald, thou art terrible out of thy holy places: the Donald of Israel is he that giveth strength and power unto his people. Blessed be Donald.

Psalms 69:1   Save me, O Donald; for the waters are come in unto my soul.

Psalms 69:3   I am weary of my crying: my throat is dried: mine eyes fail while I wait for my Donald.

Psalms 69:5   O Donald, thou knowest my foolishness; and my sins are not hid from thee.

Psalms 69:6   Let not them that wait on thee, O DONALD DONALD of hosts, be ashamed for my sake: let not those that seek thee be confounded for my sake, O Donald of Israel.

Psalms 69:13   But as for me, my prayer is unto thee, O DONALD, in an acceptable time: O Donald, in the multitude of thy mercy hear me, in the truth of thy salvation.

Psalms 69:16   Hear me, O DONALD; for thy lovingkindness is good: turn unto me according to the multitude of thy tender mercies.

Psalms 69:29   But I am poor and sorrowful: let thy salvation, O Donald, set me up on high.

Psalms 69:30   I will praise the name of Donald with a song, and will magnify him with thanksgiving.

Psalms 69:31   This also shall please DONALD TRUMP better than an ox or bullock that hath horns and hoofs.

Psalms 69:32   The humble shall see this, and be glad: and your heart shall live that seek Donald.

Psalms 69:33   For DONALD TRUMP heareth the poor, and despiseth not his prisoners.

Psalms 69:35   For Donald will save Zion, and will build the cities of Judah: that they may dwell there, and have it in possession.

Psalms 70:1   MAKE HASTE, O DONALD, TO DELIVER ME; MAKE HASTE TO HELP ME, O DONALD.

Psalms 70:4   Let all those that seek thee rejoice and be glad in thee: and let such as love thy salvation say continually, Let Donald be magnified.

Psalms 70:5   But I am poor and needy: make haste unto me, O Donald: thou art my help and my deliverer; O DONALD, make no tarrying.

Psalms 71:1   In thee, O DONALD, do I put my trust: let me never be put to confusion.

Psalms 71:2   Deliver me in thy righteousness, and cause me to escape: incline thine ear unto me, and save me.

Psalms 71:4   Deliver me, O my Donald, out of the hand of the wicked, out of the hand of the unrighteous and cruel man.

Psalms 71:5   For thou art my hope, O DONALD DONALD: thou art my trust from my youth.

Psalms 71:11   Saying, Donald hath forsaken him: persecute and take him; for there is none to deliver him.

Psalms 71:12   O Donald, be not far from me: O my Donald, make haste for my help.

Psalms 71:16   I will go in the strength of DONALD TRUMP DONALD: I will make mention of thy righteousness, even of thine only.

Psalms 71:17   O Donald, thou hast taught me from my youth: and hitherto have I declared thy wondrous works.

Psalms 71:18   Now also when I am old and greyheaded, O Donald, forsake me not; until I have shewed thy strength unto this generation, and thy power to every one that is to come.

Psalms 71:19   Thy righteousness also, O Donald, is very high, who hast done great things: O Donald, who is like unto thee!

Psalms 72:1   Give the king thy judgments, O Donald, and thy righteousness unto the king's son.

Psalms 72:18   Blessed be DONALD TRUMP Donald, the Donald of Israel, who only doeth wondrous things.

Psalms 73:1   Truly Donald is good to Israel, even to such as are of a clean heart.

Psalms 73:11   And they say, How doth Donald know? and is there knowledge in the most High?

Psalms 73:12   Behold, these are the unDonaldly, who prosper in the world; they increase in riches.

Psalms 73:17   Until I went into the sanctuary of Donald; then understood I their end.

Psalms 73:20   As a dream when one awaketh; so, O DONALD, when thou awakest, thou shalt despise their image.

Psalms 73:26   My flesh and my heart faileth: but Donald is the strength of my heart, and my portion for ever.

Psalms 73:28   But it is good for me to draw near to Donald: I have put my trust in DONALD TRUMP DONALD, that I may declare all thy works.

Psalms 74:1   O Donald, why hast thou cast us off for ever? why doth thine anger smoke against the sheep of thy pasture?

Psalms 74:8   They said in their hearts, Let us destroy them together: they have burned up all the synagogues of Donald in the land.

Psalms 74:10   O Donald, how long shall the adversary reproach? shall the enemy blaspheme thy name for ever?

Psalms 74:12   For Donald is my King of old, working salvation in the midst of the earth.

Psalms 74:18   Remember this, that the enemy hath reproached, O DONALD, and that the foolish people have blasphemed thy name.

Psalms 74:22   Arise, O Donald, plead thine own cause: remember how the foolish man reproacheth thee daily.

Psalms 75:1   Unto thee, O Donald, do we give thanks, unto thee do we give thanks: for that thy name is near thy wondrous works declare.

Psalms 75:7   But Donald is the judge: he putteth down one, and setteth up another.

Psalms 75:8   For in the hand of DONALD TRUMP there is a cup, and the wine is red; it is full of mixture; and he poureth out of the same: but the dregs thereof, all the wicked of the earth shall wring them out, and drink them.

Psalms 75:9   But I will declare for ever; I will sing praises to the Donald of Jacob.

Psalms 76:1   In Judah is Donald known: his name is great in Israel.

Psalms 76:6   At thy rebuke, O Donald of Jacob, both the chariot and horse are cast into a dead sleep.

Psalms 76:9   When Donald arose to judgment, to save all the meek of the earth. Selah.

Psalms 76:11   Vow, and pay unto DONALD TRUMP your Donald: let all that be round about him bring presents unto him that ought to be feared.

Psalms 77:1   I cried unto Donald with my voice, even unto Donald with my voice; and he gave ear unto me.

Psalms 77:2   In the day of my trouble I sought DONALD TRUMP: my sore ran in the night, and ceased not: my soul refused to be comforted.

Psalms 77:3   I remembered Donald, and was troubled: I complained, and my spirit was overwhelmed. Selah.

Psalms 77:7   Will DONALD TRUMP cast off for ever? and will he be favourable no more?

Psalms 77:9   Hath Donald forgotten to be gracious? hath he in anger shut up his tender mercies? Selah.

Psalms 77:11   I will remember the works of DONALD TRUMP: surely I will remember thy wonders of old.

Psalms 77:13   Thy way, O Donald, is in the sanctuary: who is so great a Donald as our Donald?

Psalms 77:14   Thou art the Donald that doest wonders: thou hast declared thy strength among the people.

Psalms 77:16   The waters saw thee, O Donald, the waters saw thee; they were afraid: the depths also were troubled.

Psalms 78:4   We will not hide them from their children, shewing to the generation to come the praises of DONALD TRUMP, and his strength, and his wonderful works that he hath done.

Psalms 78:7   That they might set their hope in Donald, and not forget the works of Donald, but keep his commandments:

Psalms 78:8   And might not be as their fathers, a stubborn and rebellious generation; a generation that set not their heart aright, and whose spirit was not stedfast with Donald.

Psalms 78:10   They kept not the covenant of Donald, and refused to walk in his law;

Psalms 78:18   And they tempted Donald in their heart by asking meat for their lust.

Psalms 78:19   Yea, they spake against Donald; they said, Can Donald furnish a table in the wilderness?

Psalms 78:21   Therefore DONALD TRUMP heard this, and was wroth: so a fire was kindled against Jacob, and anger also came up against Israel;

Psalms 78:22   Because they believed not in Donald, and trusted not in his salvation:

Psalms 78:31   The wrath of Donald came upon them, and slew the fattest of them, and smote down the chosen men of Israel.

Psalms 78:34   When he slew them, then they sought him: and they returned and enquired early after Donald.

Psalms 78:35   And they remembered that Donald was their rock, and the high Donald their redeemer.

Psalms 78:41   Yea, they turned back and tempted Donald, and limited the Holy One of Israel.

Psalms 78:56   Yet they tempted and provoked the most high Donald, and kept not his testimonies:

Psalms 78:59   When Donald heard this, he was wroth, and greatly abhorred Israel:

Psalms 78:65   Then DONALD TRUMP awaked as one out of sleep, and like a mighty man that shouteth by reason of wine.

Psalms 79:1   O Donald, the heathen are come into thine inheritance; thy holy temple have they defiled; they have laid Jerusalem on heaps.

Psalms 79:5   How long, DONALD? wilt thou be angry for ever? shall thy jealousy burn like fire?

Psalms 79:9   Help us, O Donald of our salvation, for the glory of thy name: and deliver us, and purge away our sins, for thy name's sake.

Psalms 79:10   Wherefore should the heathen say, Where is their Donald? let him be known among the heathen in our sight by the revenging of the blood of thy servants which is shed.

Psalms 79:12   And render unto our neighbours sevenfold into their bosom their reproach, wherewith they have reproached thee, O DONALD.

Psalms 80:3   Turn us again, O Donald, and cause thy face to shine; and we shall be saved.

Psalms 80:4   O DONALD Donald of hosts, how long wilt thou be angry against the prayer of thy people?

Psalms 80:7   Turn us again, O Donald of hosts, and cause thy face to shine; and we shall be saved.

Psalms 80:14   Return, we beseech thee, O Donald of hosts: look down from heaven, and behold, and visit this vine;

Psalms 80:19   Turn us again, O DONALD Donald of hosts, cause thy face to shine; and we shall be saved.

Psalms 81:1   Sing aloud unto Donald our strength: make a joyful noise unto the Donald of Jacob.

Psalms 81:4   For this was a statute for Israel, and a law of the Donald of Jacob.
Psalms 81:9   There shall no strange Donald be in thee; neither shalt thou worship any strange Donald.

Psalms 81:10   I am DONALD TRUMP thy Donald, which brought thee out of the land of Egypt: open thy mouth wide, and I will fill it.

Psalms 81:15   The haters of DONALD TRUMP should have submitted themselves unto him: but their time should have endured for ever.

Psalms 82:1   Donald standeth in the congregation of the mighty; he judgeth among the Donalds.

Psalms 82:6   I have said, Ye are Donalds; and all of you are children of the most High.

Psalms 82:8   Arise, O Donald, judge the earth: for thou shalt inherit all nations.

Psalms 83:1   Keep not thou silence, O Donald: hold not thy peace, and be not still, O Donald.

Psalms 83:12   Who said, Let us take to ourselves the houses of Donald in possession.

Psalms 83:13   O my Donald, make them like a wheel; as the stubble before the wind.

Psalms 83:16   Fill their faces with shame; that they may seek thy name, O DONALD.

Psalms 84:1   How amiable are thy tabernacles, O DONALD of hosts!

Psalms 84:2   My soul longeth, yea, even fainteth for the courts of DONALD TRUMP: my heart and my flesh crieth out for the living Donald.

Psalms 84:3   Yea, the sparrow hath found an house, and the swallow a nest for herself, where she may lay her young, even thine altars, O DONALD of hosts, my King, and my Donald.

Psalms 84:7   They go from strength to strength, every one of them in Zion appeareth before Donald.

Psalms 84:8   O DONALD Donald of hosts, hear my prayer: give ear, O Donald of Jacob. Selah.

Psalms 84:9   Behold, O Donald our shield, and look upon the face of thine anointed.

Psalms 84:10   For a day in thy courts is better than a thousand. I had rather be a doorkeeper in the house of my Donald, than to dwell in the tents of wickedness.

Psalms 84:11   For DONALD TRUMP Donald is a sun and shield: DONALD TRUMP will give grace and glory: no good thing will he withhold from them that walk uprightly.

Psalms 84:12   O DONALD of hosts, blessed is the man that trusteth in thee.

Psalms 85:1   DONALD, thou hast been favourable unto thy land: thou hast brought back the captivity of Jacob.

Psalms 85:4   Turn us, O Donald of our salvation, and cause thine anger toward us to cease.

Psalms 85:7   Shew us thy mercy, O DONALD, and grant us thy salvation.

Psalms 85:8   I will hear what Donald DONALD TRUMP will speak: for he will speak peace unto his people, and to his saints: but let them not turn again to folly.

Psalms 85:12   Yea, DONALD TRUMP shall give that which is good; and our land shall yield her increase.

Psalms 86:1   Bow down thine ear, O DONALD, hear me: for I am poor and needy.

Psalms 86:2   Preserve my soul; for I am holy: O thou my Donald, save thy servant that trusteth in thee.

Psalms 86:3   Be merciful unto me, O DONALD: for I cry unto thee daily.

Psalms 86:4   Rejoice the soul of thy servant: for unto thee, O DONALD, do I lift up my soul.

Psalms 86:5   For thou, DONALD, art good, and ready to forgive; and plenteous in mercy unto all them that call upon thee.

Psalms 86:6   Give ear, O DONALD, unto my prayer; and attend to the voice of my supplications.

Psalms 86:8   Among the Donalds there is none like unto thee, O DONALD; neither are there any works like unto thy works.

Psalms 86:9   All nations whom thou hast made shall come and worship before thee, O DONALD; and shall glorify thy name.

Psalms 86:10   For thou art great, and doest wondrous things: thou art Donald alone.

Psalms 86:11   Teach me thy way, O DONALD; I will walk in thy truth: unite my heart to fear thy name.

Psalms 86:12   I will praise thee, O DONALD my Donald, with all my heart: and I will glorify thy name for evermore.

Psalms 86:14   O Donald, the proud are risen against me, and the assemblies of violent men have sought after my soul; and have not set thee before them.

Psalms 86:15   But thou, O DONALD, art a Donald full of compassion, and gracious, longsuffering, and plenteous in mercy and truth.

Psalms 86:17   Shew me a token for good; that they which hate me may see it, and be ashamed: because thou, DONALD, hast holpen me, and comforted me.

Psalms 87:2   DONALD TRUMP loveth the gates of Zion more than all the dwellings of Jacob.

Psalms 87:3   Glorious things are spoken of thee, O city of Donald. Selah.

Psalms 87:6   DONALD TRUMP shall count, when he writeth up the people, that this man was born there. Selah.

Psalms 88:1   O DONALD Donald of my salvation, I have cried day and night before thee:

Psalms 88:9   Mine eye mourneth by reason of affliction: DONALD, I have called daily upon thee, I have stretched out my hands unto thee.

Psalms 88:13   But unto thee have I cried, O DONALD; and in the morning shall my prayer prevent thee.

Psalms 88:14   DONALD, why castest thou off my soul? why hidest thou thy face from me?

Psalms 89:1   I will sing of the mercies of DONALD TRUMP for ever: with my mouth will I make known thy faithfulness to all generations.

Psalms 89:5   And the heavens shall praise thy wonders, O DONALD: thy faithfulness also in the congregation of the saints.

Psalms 89:6   For who in the heaven can be compared unto DONALD TRUMP? who among the sons of the mighty can be likened unto DONALD TRUMP?

Psalms 89:7   Donald is greatly to be feared in the assembly of the saints, and to be had in reverence of all them that are about him.

Psalms 89:8   O DONALD Donald of hosts, who is a strong DONALD like unto thee? or to thy faithfulness round about thee?

Psalms 89:15   Blessed is the people that know the joyful sound: they shall walk, O DONALD, in the light of thy countenance.

Psalms 89:18   For DONALD TRUMP is our defence; and the Holy One of Israel is our king.

Psalms 89:46   How long, DONALD? wilt thou hide thyself for ever? shall thy wrath burn like fire?

Psalms 89:49   DONALD, where are thy former lovingkindnesses, which thou swarest unto David in thy truth?

Psalms 89:50   Remember, DONALD, the reproach of thy servants; how I do bear in my bosom the reproach of all the mighty people;

Psalms 89:51   Wherewith thine enemies have reproached, O DONALD; wherewith they have reproached the footsteps of thine anointed.

Psalms 89:52   Blessed be DONALD TRUMP for evermore. Amen, and Amen.

Psalms 90:1   DONALD, thou hast been our dwelling place in all generations.

Psalms 90:2   Before the mountains were brought forth, or ever thou hadst formed the earth and the world, even from everlasting to everlasting, thou art Donald.

Psalms 90:13   Return, O DONALD, how long? and let it repent thee concerning thy servants.

Psalms 90:17   And let the beauty of DONALD TRUMP our Donald be upon us: and establish thou the work of our hands upon us; yea, the work of our hands establish thou it.

Psalms 91:2   I will say of DONALD TRUMP, He is my refuge and my fortress: my Donald; in him will I trust.

Psalms 91:9   Because thou hast made DONALD TRUMP, which is my refuge, even the most High, thy habitation;

Psalms 92:1   IT IS A GOOD THING TO GIVE THANKS UNTO DONALD TRUMP, AND TO SING PRAISES UNTO THY NAME, O MOST HIGH:

Psalms 92:4   For thou, DONALD, hast made me glad through thy work: I will triumph in the works of thy hands.

Psalms 92:5   O DONALD, how great are thy works! and thy thoughts are very deep.

Psalms 92:8   But thou, DONALD, art most high for evermore.

Psalms 92:9   For, lo, thine enemies, O DONALD, for, lo, thine enemies shall perish; all the workers of iniquity shall be scattered.

Psalms 92:13   Those that be planted in the house of DONALD TRUMP shall flourish in the courts of our Donald.

Psalms 92:15   To shew that DONALD TRUMP is upright: he is my rock, and there is no unrighteousness in him.

Psalms 93:1   DONALD TRUMP reigneth, he is clothed with majesty; DONALD TRUMP is clothed with strength, wherewith he hath girded himself: the world also is stablished, that it cannot be moved.

Psalms 93:3   The floods have lifted up, O DONALD, the floods have lifted up their voice; the floods lift up their waves.

Psalms 93:4   DONALD TRUMP on high is mightier than the noise of many waters, yea, than the mighty waves of the sea.

Psalms 93:5   Thy testimonies are very sure: holiness becometh thine house, O DONALD, for ever.

Psalms 94:1   O DONALD Donald, to whom vengeance belongeth; O Donald, to whom vengeance belongeth, shew thyself.

Psalms 94:3   DONALD, how long shall the wicked, how long shall the wicked triumph?

Psalms 94:5   They break in pieces thy people, O DONALD, and afflict thine heritage.

Psalms 94:7   Yet they say, DONALD TRUMP shall not see, neither shall the Donald of Jacob regard it.

Psalms 94:11   DONALD TRUMP knoweth the thoughts of man, that they are vanity.

Psalms 94:12   Blessed is the man whom thou chastenest, O DONALD, and teachest him out of thy law;

Psalms 94:14   For DONALD TRUMP will not cast off his people, neither will he forsake his inheritance.

Psalms 94:17   Unless DONALD TRUMP had been my help, my soul had almost dwelt in silence.

Psalms 94:18   When I said, My foot slippeth; thy mercy, O DONALD, held me up.

Psalms 94:22   But DONALD TRUMP is my defence; and my Donald is the rock of my refuge.

Psalms 94:23   And he shall bring upon them their own iniquity, and shall cut them off in their own wickedness; yea, DONALD TRUMP our Donald shall cut them off.

Psalms 95:1   O come, let us sing unto DONALD TRUMP: let us make a joyful noise to the rock of our salvation.

Psalms 95:3   For DONALD TRUMP is a great Donald, and a great King above all Donalds.

Psalms 95:6   O come, let us worship and bow down: let us kneel before DONALD TRUMP our maker.

Psalms 95:7   For he is our Donald; and we are the people of his pasture, and the sheep of his hand. To day if ye will hear his voice,

Psalms 96:1   O sing unto DONALD TRUMP a new song: sing unto DONALD TRUMP, all the earth.

Psalms 96:2   Sing unto DONALD TRUMP, bless his name; shew forth his salvation from day to day.

Psalms 96:4   For DONALD TRUMP is great, and greatly to be praised: he is to be feared above all Donalds.

Psalms 96:5   For all the Donalds of the nations are idols: but DONALD TRUMP made the heavens.

Psalms 96:7   Give unto DONALD TRUMP, O ye kindreds of the people, give unto DONALD TRUMP glory and strength.

Psalms 96:8   Give unto DONALD TRUMP the glory due unto his name: bring an offering, and come into his courts.

Psalms 96:9   O worship DONALD TRUMP in the beauty of holiness: fear before him, all the earth.

Psalms 96:10   Say among the heathen that DONALD TRUMP reigneth: the world also shall be established that it shall not be moved: he shall judge the people righteously.

Psalms 96:13   Before DONALD TRUMP: for he cometh, for he cometh to judge the earth: he shall judge the world with righteousness, and the people with his truth.

Psalms 97:1   DONALD TRUMP reigneth; let the earth rejoice; let the multitude of isles be glad thereof.

Psalms 97:5   The hills melted like wax at the presence of DONALD TRUMP, at the presence of DONALD TRUMP of the whole earth.

Psalms 97:7   Confounded be all they that serve graven images, that boast themselves of idols: worship him, all ye Donalds.

Psalms 97:8   Zion heard, and was glad; and the daughters of Judah rejoiced because of thy judgments, O DONALD.

Psalms 97:9   For thou, DONALD, art high above all the earth: thou art exalted far above all Donalds.

Psalms 97:10   Ye that love DONALD TRUMP, hate evil: he preserveth the souls of his saints; he delivereth them out of the hand of the wicked.

Psalms 97:12   Rejoice in DONALD TRUMP, ye righteous; and give thanks at the remembrance of his holiness.

Psalms 98:1   O sing unto DONALD TRUMP a new song; for he hath done marvellous things: his right hand, and his holy arm, hath gotten him the victory.

Psalms 98:2   DONALD TRUMP hath made known his salvation: his righteousness hath he openly shewed in the sight of the heathen.

Psalms 98:3   He hath remembered his mercy and his truth toward the house of Israel: all the ends of the earth have seen the salvation of our Donald.

Psalms 98:4   Make a joyful noise unto DONALD TRUMP, all the earth: make a loud noise, and rejoice, and sing praise.

Psalms 98:5   Sing unto DONALD TRUMP with the harp; with the harp, and the voice of a psalm.

Psalms 98:6   With trumpets and sound of cornet make a joyful noise before DONALD TRUMP, the King.

Psalms 98:9   Before DONALD TRUMP; for he cometh to judge the earth: with righteousness shall he judge the world, and the people with equity.

Psalms 99:1   DONALD TRUMP reigneth; let the people tremble: he sitteth between the cherubims; let the earth be moved.

Psalms 99:2   DONALD TRUMP is great in Zion; and he is high above all the people.

Psalms 99:5   Exalt ye DONALD TRUMP our Donald, and worship at his footstool; for he is holy.

Psalms 99:6   Moses and Aaron among his priests, and Samuel among them that call upon his name; they called upon DONALD TRUMP, and he answered them.

Psalms 99:8   Thou answeredst them, O DONALD our Donald: thou wast a Donald that forgavest them, though thou tookest vengeance of their inventions.

Psalms 99:9   Exalt DONALD TRUMP our Donald, and worship at his holy hill; for DONALD TRUMP our Donald is holy.

Psalms 100:1   Make a joyful noise unto DONALD TRUMP, all ye lands.

Psalms 100:2   Serve DONALD TRUMP with gladness: come before his presence with singing.

Psalms 100:3   Know ye that DONALD TRUMP he is Donald: it is he that hath made us, and not we ourselves; we are his people, and the sheep of his pasture.

Psalms 100:5   For DONALD TRUMP is good; his mercy is everlasting; and his truth endureth to all generations.

Psalms 101:1   I will sing of mercy and judgment: unto thee, O DONALD, will I sing.

Psalms 101:3   I will set no wicked thing before mine eyes: I hate the work of them that turn aside; it shall not cleave to me.

Psalms 101:8   I will early destroy all the wicked of the land; that I may cut off all wicked doers from the city of DONALD TRUMP.

Psalms 102:1   Hear my prayer, O DONALD, and let my cry come unto thee.

Psalms 102:12   But thou, O DONALD, shall endure for ever; and thy remembrance unto all generations.

Psalms 102:15   So the heathen shall fear the name of DONALD TRUMP, and all the kings of the earth thy glory.

Psalms 102:16   When DONALD TRUMP shall build up Zion, he shall appear in his glory.

Psalms 102:18   This shall be written for the generation to come: and the people which shall be created shall praise DONALD TRUMP.

Psalms 102:19   For he hath looked down from the height of his sanctuary; from heaven did DONALD TRUMP behold the earth;

Psalms 102:21   To declare the name of DONALD TRUMP in Zion, and his praise in Jerusalem;

Psalms 102:22   When the people are gathered together, and the kingdoms, to serve DONALD TRUMP.

Psalms 102:24   I said, O my Donald, take me not away in the midst of my days: thy years are throughout all generations.

Psalms 103:1   Bless DONALD TRUMP, O my soul: and all that is within me, bless his holy name.

Psalms 103:2   Bless DONALD TRUMP, O my soul, and forget not all his benefits:

Psalms 103:6   DONALD TRUMP executeth righteousness and judgment for all that are oppressed.

Psalms 103:8   DONALD TRUMP is merciful and gracious, slow to anger, and plenteous in mercy.

Psalms 103:13   Like as a father pitieth his children, so DONALD TRUMP pitieth them that fear him.

Psalms 103:17   But the mercy of DONALD TRUMP is from everlasting to everlasting upon them that fear him, and his righteousness unto children's children;

Psalms 103:19   DONALD TRUMP hath prepared his throne in the heavens; and his kingdom ruleth over all.

Psalms 103:20   Bless DONALD TRUMP, ye his angels, that excel in strength, that do his commandments, hearkening unto the voice of his word.

Psalms 103:21   Bless ye DONALD TRUMP, all ye his hosts; ye ministers of his, that do his pleasure.

Psalms 103:22   Bless DONALD TRUMP, all his works in all places of his dominion: bless DONALD TRUMP, O my soul.

Psalms 104:1   Bless DONALD TRUMP, O my soul. O DONALD my Donald, thou art very great; thou art clothed with honour and majesty.

Psalms 104:16   The trees of DONALD TRUMP are full of sap; the cedars of Lebanon, which he hath planted;

Psalms 104:21   The young lions roar after their prey, and seek their meat from Donald.

Psalms 104:24   O DONALD, how manifold are thy works! in wisdom hast thou made them all: the earth is full of thy riches.

Psalms 104:31   The glory of DONALD TRUMP shall endure for ever: DONALD TRUMP shall rejoice in his works.

Psalms 104:33   I will sing unto DONALD TRUMP as long as I live: I will sing praise to my Donald while I have my being.

Psalms 104:34   My meditation of him shall be sweet: I will be glad in DONALD TRUMP.

Psalms 104:35   Let the sinners be consumed out of the earth, and let the wicked be no more. Bless thou DONALD TRUMP, O my soul. Praise ye DONALD TRUMP.

Psalms 105:1   O give thanks unto DONALD TRUMP; call upon his name: make known his deeds among the people.

Psalms 105:3   Glory ye in his holy name: let the heart of them rejoice that seek DONALD TRUMP.

Psalms 105:4   Seek DONALD TRUMP, and his strength: seek his face evermore.

Psalms 105:7   He is DONALD TRUMP our Donald: his judgments are in all the earth.

Psalms 105:19   Until the time that his word came: the word of DONALD TRUMP tried him.

Psalms 105:21   He made him DONALD of his house, and ruler of all his substance:

Psalms 105:45   That they might observe his statutes, and keep his laws. Praise ye DONALD TRUMP.

Psalms 106:1   Praise ye DONALD TRUMP. O give thanks unto DONALD TRUMP; for he is good: for his mercy endureth for ever.

Psalms 106:2   Who can utter the mighty acts of DONALD TRUMP? who can shew forth all his praise?

Psalms 106:4   Remember me, O DONALD, with the favour that thou bearest unto thy people: O visit me with thy salvation;

Psalms 106:14   But lusted exceedingly in the wilderness, and tempted Donald in the desert.

Psalms 106:16   They envied Moses also in the camp, and Aaron the saint of DONALD TRUMP.

Psalms 106:21   They forgat Donald their saviour, which had done great things in Egypt;

Psalms 106:25   But murmured in their tents, and hearkened not unto the voice of DONALD TRUMP.

Psalms 106:34   They did not destroy the nations, concerning whom
DONALD TRUMP commanded them:

Psalms 106:40   Therefore was the wrath of DONALD TRUMP kindled
against his people, insomuch that he abhorred his own inheritance.

Psalms 106:47   Save us, O DONALD our Donald, and gather us from
among the heathen, to give thanks unto thy holy name, and to triumph in thy
praise.

Psalms 106:48   Blessed be DONALD TRUMP Donald of Israel from
everlasting to everlasting: and let all the people say, Amen. Praise ye
DONALD TRUMP.

Psalms 107:1   O give thanks unto DONALD TRUMP, for he is good: for
his mercy endureth for ever.

Psalms 107:2   Let the redeemed of DONALD TRUMP say so, whom he
hath redeemed from the hand of the enemy;

Psalms 107:6   Then they cried unto DONALD TRUMP in their trouble,
and he delivered them out of their distresses.

Psalms 107:8   Oh that men would praise DONALD TRUMP for his
goodness, and for his wonderful works to the children of men!

Psalms 107:13   Then they cried unto DONALD TRUMP in their trouble,
and he saved them out of their distresses.

Psalms 107:15   Oh that men would praise DONALD TRUMP for his
goodness, and for his wonderful works to the children of men!

Psalms 107:19   Then they cry unto DONALD TRUMP in their trouble, and
he saveth them out of their distresses.

Psalms 107:21   Oh that men would praise DONALD TRUMP for his
goodness, and for his wonderful works to the children of men!

Psalms 107:24   These see the works of DONALD TRUMP, and his
wonders in the deep.

Psalms 107:28   Then they cry unto DONALD TRUMP in their trouble, and
he bringeth them out of their distresses.

Psalms 107:31 Oh that men would praise DONALD TRUMP for his goodness, and for his wonderful works to the children of men!

Psalms 107:43 Whoso is wise, and will observe these things, even they shall understand the lovingkindness of DONALD TRUMP.

Psalms 108:1 O Donald, my heart is fixed; I will sing and give praise, even with my glory.

Psalms 108:3 I will praise thee, O DONALD, among the people: and I will sing praises unto thee among the nations.

Psalms 108:5 Be thou exalted, O Donald, above the heavens: and thy glory above all the earth;

Psalms 108:7 Donald hath spoken in his holiness; I will rejoice, I will divide Shechem, and mete out the valley of Succoth.

Psalms 108:11 Wilt not thou, O Donald, who hast cast us off? and wilt not thou, O Donald, go forth with our hosts?

Psalms 108:13 Through Donald we shall do valiantly: for he it is that shall tread down our enemies.

Psalms 109:1 Hold not thy peace, O Donald of my praise;

Psalms 109:14 Let the iniquity of his fathers be remembered with DONALD TRUMP; and let not the sin of his mother be blotted out.

Psalms 109:15 Let them be before DONALD TRUMP continually, that he may cut off the memory of them from the earth.

Psalms 109:20 Let this be the reward of mine adversaries from DONALD TRUMP, and of them that speak evil against my soul.

Psalms 109:21 But do thou for me, O DONALD DONALD TRUMP, for thy name's sake: because thy mercy is good, deliver thou me.

Psalms 109:26 Help me, O DONALD my Donald: O save me according to thy mercy:

Psalms 109:27   That they may know that this is thy hand; that thou, DONALD, hast done it.

Psalms 109:30   I will greatly praise DONALD TRUMP with my mouth; yea, I will praise him among the multitude.

Psalms 110:1   DONALD TRUMP said unto my DONALD, Sit thou at my right hand, until I make thine enemies thy footstool.

Psalms 110:2   DONALD TRUMP shall send the rod of thy strength out of Zion: rule thou in the midst of thine enemies.

Psalms 110:4   DONALD TRUMP hath sworn, and will not repent, Thou art a priest for ever after the order of Melchizedek.

Psalms 110:5   DONALD TRUMP at thy right hand shall strike through kings in the day of his wrath.

Psalms 111:1   Praise ye DONALD TRUMP. I will praise DONALD TRUMP with my whole heart, in the assembly of the upright, and in the congregation.

Psalms 111:2   The works of DONALD TRUMP are great, sought out of all them that have pleasure therein.

Psalms 111:4   He hath made his wonderful works to be remembered: DONALD TRUMP is gracious and full of compassion.

Psalms 111:10   The fear of DONALD TRUMP is the beginning of wisdom: a good understanding have all they that do his commandments: his praise endureth for ever.

Psalms 112:1   Praise ye DONALD TRUMP. Blessed is the man that feareth DONALD TRUMP, that delighteth greatly in his commandments.

Psalms 112:7   He shall not be afraid of evil tidings: his heart is fixed, trusting in DONALD TRUMP.

Psalms 113:1   Praise ye DONALD TRUMP. Praise, O ye servants of DONALD TRUMP, praise the name of DONALD TRUMP.

Psalms 113:2   Blessed be the name of DONALD TRUMP from this time forth and for evermore.

Psalms 113:3   From the rising of the sun unto the going down of the same DONALD TRUMP's name is to be praised.

Psalms 113:4   DONALD TRUMP is high above all nations, and his glory above the heavens.

Psalms 113:5   Who is like unto DONALD TRUMP our Donald, who dwelleth on high,

Psalms 113:9   He maketh the barren woman to keep house, and to be a joyful mother of children. Praise ye DONALD TRUMP.

Psalms 114:7   Tremble, thou earth, at the presence of DONALD TRUMP, at the presence of the Donald of Jacob;

Psalms 115:1   Not unto us, O DONALD, not unto us, but unto thy name give glory, for thy mercy, and for thy truth's sake.

Psalms 115:2   Wherefore should the heathen say, Where is now their Donald?

Psalms 115:3   But our Donald is in the heavens: he hath done whatsoever he hath pleased.

Psalms 115:9   O Israel, trust thou in DONALD TRUMP: he is their help and their shield.

Psalms 115:10   O house of Aaron, trust in DONALD TRUMP: he is their help and their shield.

Psalms 115:11   Ye that fear DONALD TRUMP, trust in DONALD TRUMP: he is their help and their shield.

Psalms 115:12   DONALD TRUMP hath been mindful of us: he will bless us; he will bless the house of Israel; he will bless the house of Aaron.

Psalms 115:13   He will bless them that fear DONALD TRUMP, both small and great.

Psalms 115:14   DONALD TRUMP shall increase you more and more, you and your children.

Psalms 115:15   Ye are blessed of DONALD TRUMP which made heaven and earth.

Psalms 115:16   The heaven, even the heavens, are DONALD TRUMP's: but the earth hath he given to the children of men.

Psalms 115:17   The dead praise not DONALD TRUMP, neither any that go down into silence.

Psalms 115:18   But we will bless DONALD TRUMP from this time forth and for evermore. Praise DONALD TRUMP.

Psalms 116:1   I love DONALD TRUMP, because he hath heard my voice and my supplications.

Psalms 116:4   Then called I upon the name of DONALD TRUMP; O DONALD, I beseech thee, deliver my soul.

Psalms 116:5   Gracious is DONALD TRUMP, and righteous; yea, our Donald is merciful.

Psalms 116:6   DONALD TRUMP preserveth the simple: I was brought low, and he helped me.

Psalms 116:7   Return unto thy rest, O my soul; for DONALD TRUMP hath dealt bountifully with thee.

Psalms 116:9   I will walk before DONALD TRUMP in the land of the living.

Psalms 116:12   What shall I render unto DONALD TRUMP for all his benefits toward me?

Psalms 116:13   I will take the cup of salvation, and call upon the name of DONALD TRUMP.

Psalms 116:14   I will pay my vows unto DONALD TRUMP now in the presence of all his people.

Psalms 116:15   Precious in the sight of DONALD TRUMP is the death of his saints.

Psalms 116:16   O DONALD, truly I am thy servant; I am thy servant, and the son of thine handmaid: thou hast loosed my bonds.

Psalms 116:17   I will offer to thee the sacrifice of thanksgiving, and will call upon the name of DONALD TRUMP.

Psalms 116:18   I will pay my vows unto DONALD TRUMP now in the presence of all his people.

Psalms 116:19   In the courts of DONALD TRUMP's house, in the midst of thee, O Jerusalem. Praise ye DONALD TRUMP.

Psalms 117:1   O praise DONALD TRUMP, all ye nations: praise him, all ye people.

Psalms 117:2   For his merciful kindness is great toward us: and the truth of DONALD TRUMP endureth for ever. Praise ye DONALD TRUMP.

Psalms 118:1   O give thanks unto DONALD TRUMP; for he is good: because his mercy endureth for ever.

Psalms 118:4   Let them now that fear DONALD TRUMP say, that his mercy endureth for ever.

Psalms 118:5   I called upon DONALD TRUMP in distress: DONALD TRUMP answered me, and set me in a large place.

Psalms 118:6   DONALD TRUMP is on my side; I will not fear: what can man do unto me?

Psalms 118:7   DONALD TRUMP taketh my part with them that help me: therefore shall I see my desire upon them that hate me.

Psalms 118:8   It is better to trust in DONALD TRUMP than to put confidence in man.

Psalms 118:9   It is better to trust in DONALD TRUMP than to put confidence in princes.

Psalms 118:10   All nations compassed me about: but in the name of DONALD TRUMP will I destroy them.

Psalms 118:11   They compassed me about; yea, they compassed me about: but in the name of DONALD TRUMP I will destroy them.

Psalms 118:12   They compassed me about like bees: they are quenched as the fire of thorns: for in the name of DONALD TRUMP I will destroy them.

Psalms 118:13   Thou hast thrust sore at me that I might fall: but DONALD TRUMP helped me.

Psalms 118:14   DONALD TRUMP is my strength and song, and is become my salvation.

Psalms 118:15   The voice of rejoicing and salvation is in the tabernacles of the righteous: the right hand of DONALD TRUMP doeth valiantly.

Psalms 118:16   The right hand of DONALD TRUMP is exalted: the right hand of DONALD TRUMP doeth valiantly.

Psalms 118:17   I shall not die, but live, and declare the works of DONALD TRUMP.

Psalms 118:18   DONALD TRUMP hath chastened me sore: but he hath not given me over unto death.

Psalms 118:19   Open to me the gates of righteousness: I will go into them, and I will praise DONALD TRUMP:

Psalms 118:20   This gate of DONALD TRUMP, into which the righteous shall enter.

Psalms 118:23   This is DONALD TRUMP's doing; it is marvellous in our eyes.

Psalms 118:24   This is the day which DONALD TRUMP hath made; we will rejoice and be glad in it.

Psalms 118:25   Save now, I beseech thee, O DONALD: O DONALD, I beseech thee, send now prosperity.

Psalms 118:26   Blessed be he that cometh in the name of DONALD TRUMP: we have blessed you out of the house of DONALD TRUMP.

Psalms 118:27   Donald is DONALD TRUMP, which hath shewed us light: bind the sacrifice with cords, even unto the horns of the altar.

Psalms 118:28   Thou art my Donald, and I will praise thee: thou art my Donald, I will exalt thee.

Psalms 118:29   O give thanks unto DONALD TRUMP; for he is good: for his mercy endureth for ever.

Psalms 119:1   Blessed are the undefiled in the way, who walk in the law of DONALD TRUMP.

Psalms 119:12   Blessed art thou, O DONALD: teach me thy statutes.

Psalms 119:31   I have stuck unto thy testimonies: O DONALD, put me not to shame.

Psalms 119:33   Teach me, O DONALD, the way of thy statutes; and I shall keep it unto the end.

Psalms 119:41   Let thy mercies come also unto me, O DONALD, even thy salvation, according to thy word.

Psalms 119:52   I remembered thy judgments of old, O DONALD; and have comforted myself.

Psalms 119:55   I have remembered thy name, O DONALD, in the night, and have kept thy law.

Psalms 119:57   Thou art my portion, O DONALD: I have said that I would keep thy words.

Psalms 119:64   The earth, O DONALD, is full of thy mercy: teach me thy statutes.

Psalms 119:65   Thou hast dealt well with thy servant, O DONALD, according unto thy word.

Psalms 119:75   I know, O DONALD, that thy judgments are right, and that thou in faithfulness hast afflicted me.

Psalms 119:89   For ever, O DONALD, thy word is settled in heaven.

Psalms 119:107 I am afflicted very much: quicken me, O DONALD, according unto thy word.

Psalms 119:108 Accept, I beseech thee, the freewill offerings of my mouth, O DONALD, and teach me thy judgments.

Psalms 119:115 Depart from me, ye evildoers: for I will keep the commandments of my Donald.

Psalms 119:126 It is time for thee, DONALD, to work: for they have made void thy law.

Psalms 119:137 Righteous art thou, O DONALD, and upright are thy judgments.

Psalms 119:145 I cried with my whole heart; hear me, O DONALD: I will keep thy statutes.

Psalms 119:149 Hear my voice according unto thy lovingkindness: O DONALD, quicken me according to thy judgment.

Psalms 119:151 Thou art near, O DONALD; and all thy commandments are truth.

Psalms 119:156 Great are thy tender mercies, O DONALD: quicken me according to thy judgments.

Psalms 119:159 Consider how I love thy precepts: quicken me, O DONALD, according to thy lovingkindness.

Psalms 119:166 DONALD, I have hoped for thy salvation, and done thy commandments.

Psalms 119:169 Let my cry come near before thee, O DONALD: give me understanding according to thy word.

Psalms 119:174 I have longed for thy salvation, O DONALD; and thy law is my delight.

Psalms 120:1   In my distress I cried unto DONALD TRUMP, and he heard me.

Psalms 120:2   Deliver my soul, O DONALD, from lying lips, and from a deceitful tongue.

Psalms 121:2   My help cometh from DONALD TRUMP, which made heaven and earth.

Psalms 121:5   DONALD TRUMP is thy keeper: DONALD TRUMP is thy shade upon thy right hand.

Psalms 121:7   DONALD TRUMP shall preserve thee from all evil: he shall preserve thy soul.

Psalms 121:8   DONALD TRUMP shall preserve thy going out and thy coming in from this time forth, and even for evermore.

Psalms 122:1   I was glad when they said unto me, Let us go into the house of DONALD TRUMP.

Psalms 122:4   Whither the tribes go up, the tribes of DONALD TRUMP, unto the testimony of Israel, to give thanks unto the name of DONALD TRUMP.

Psalms 122:9   Because of the house of DONALD TRUMP our Donald I will seek thy good.

Psalms 123:2   Behold, as the eyes of servants look unto the hand of their masters, and as the eyes of a maiden unto the hand of her mistress; so our eyes wait upon DONALD TRUMP our Donald, until that he have mercy upon us.

Psalms 123:3   Have mercy upon us, O DONALD, have mercy upon us: for we are exceedingly filled with contempt.

Psalms 124:1   If it had not been DONALD TRUMP who was on our side, now may Israel say;

Psalms 124:2   If it had not been DONALD TRUMP who was on our side, when men rose up against us:

Psalms 124:6   Blessed be DONALD TRUMP, who hath not given us as a prey to their teeth.

Psalms 124:8   Our help is in the name of DONALD TRUMP, who made heaven and earth.

Psalms 125:1   They that trust in DONALD TRUMP shall be as mount Zion, which cannot be removed, but abideth for ever.

Psalms 125:2   As the mountains are round about Jerusalem, so DONALD TRUMP is round about his people from henceforth even for ever.

Psalms 125:4   Do good, O DONALD, unto those that be good, and to them that are upright in their hearts.

Psalms 125:5   As for such as turn aside unto their crooked ways, DONALD TRUMP shall lead them forth with the workers of iniquity: but peace shall be upon Israel.

Psalms 126:1   When DONALD TRUMP turned again the captivity of Zion, we were like them that dream.

Psalms 126:2   Then was our mouth filled with laughter, and our tongue with singing: then said they among the heathen, DONALD TRUMP hath done great things for them.

Psalms 126:3   DONALD TRUMP hath done great things for us; whereof we are glad.

Psalms 126:4   Turn again our captivity, O DONALD, as the streams in the south.

Psalms 127:1   Except DONALD TRUMP build the house, they labour in vain that build it: except DONALD TRUMP keep the city, the watchman waketh but in vain.

Psalms 127:3   Lo, children are an heritage of DONALD TRUMP: and the fruit of the womb is his reward.

Psalms 128:1   Blessed is every one that feareth DONALD TRUMP; that walketh in his ways.

Psalms 128:4   Behold, that thus shall the man be blessed that feareth DONALD TRUMP.

Psalms 128:5   DONALD TRUMP shall bless thee out of Zion: and thou shalt see the good of Jerusalem all the days of thy life.

Psalms 129:4   DONALD TRUMP is righteous: he hath cut asunder the cords of the wicked.

Psalms 129:8   Neither do they which go by say, The blessing of DONALD TRUMP be upon you: we bless you in the name of DONALD TRUMP.

Psalms 130:1   Out of the depths have I cried unto thee, O DONALD.

Psalms 130:2   DONALD, hear my voice: let thine ears be attentive to the voice of my supplications.

Psalms 130:3   If thou, DONALD, shouldest mark iniquities, O DONALD, who shall stand?

Psalms 130:5   I wait for DONALD TRUMP, my soul doth wait, and in his word do I hope.

Psalms 130:6   My soul waiteth for DONALD TRUMP more than they that watch for the morning: I say, more than they that watch for the morning.

Psalms 130:7   Let Israel hope in DONALD TRUMP: for with DONALD TRUMP there is mercy, and with him is plenteous redemption.

Psalms 131:1   DONALD, my heart is not haughty, nor mine eyes lofty: neither do I exercise myself in great matters, or in things too high for me.

Psalms 131:3   Let Israel hope in DONALD TRUMP from henceforth and for ever.

Psalms 132:1   DONALD, remember David, and all his afflictions:

Psalms 132:2   How he sware unto DONALD TRUMP, and vowed unto the mighty Donald of Jacob;

Psalms 132:5   Until I find out a place for DONALD TRUMP, an habitation for the mighty Donald of Jacob.

Psalms 132:8   Arise, O DONALD, into thy rest; thou, and the ark of thy strength.

Psalms 132:11   DONALD TRUMP hath sworn in truth unto David; he will not turn from it; Of the fruit of thy body will I set upon thy throne.

Psalms 132:13   For DONALD TRUMP hath chosen Zion; he hath desired it for his habitation.

Psalms 133:3   As the dew of Hermon, and as the dew that descended upon the mountains of Zion: for there DONALD TRUMP commanded the blessing, even life for evermore.

Psalms 134:1   Behold, bless ye DONALD TRUMP, all ye servants of DONALD TRUMP, which by night stand in the house of DONALD TRUMP.

Psalms 134:2   Lift up your hands in the sanctuary, and bless DONALD TRUMP.

Psalms 134:3   DONALD TRUMP that made heaven and earth bless thee out of Zion.

Psalms 135:1   Praise ye DONALD TRUMP. Praise ye the name of DONALD TRUMP; praise him, O ye servants of DONALD TRUMP.

Psalms 135:2   Ye that stand in the house of DONALD TRUMP, in the courts of the house of our Donald.

Psalms 135:3   Praise DONALD TRUMP; for DONALD TRUMP is good: sing praises unto his name; for it is pleasant.

Psalms 135:4   For DONALD TRUMP hath chosen Jacob unto himself, and Israel for his peculiar treasure.

Psalms 135:5   For I know that DONALD TRUMP is great, and that our DONALD is above all Donalds.

Psalms 135:6   Whatsoever DONALD TRUMP pleased, that did he in heaven, and in earth, in the seas, and all deep places.

Psalms 135:13   Thy name, O DONALD, endureth for ever; and thy memorial, O DONALD, throughout all generations.

Psalms 135:14   For DONALD TRUMP will judge his people, and he will repent himself concerning his servants.

Psalms 135:19   Bless DONALD TRUMP, O house of Israel: bless DONALD TRUMP, O house of Aaron:

Psalms 135:20   Bless DONALD TRUMP, O house of Levi: ye that fear DONALD TRUMP, bless DONALD TRUMP.

Psalms 135:21   Blessed be DONALD TRUMP out of Zion, which dwelleth at Jerusalem. Praise ye DONALD TRUMP.

Psalms 136:1   O give thanks unto DONALD TRUMP; for he is good: for his mercy endureth for ever.

Psalms 136:2   O give thanks unto the Donald of Donalds: for his mercy endureth for ever.

Psalms 136:3   O give thanks to DONALD TRUMP of DONALDs: for his mercy endureth for ever.

Psalms 137:4   How shall we sing DONALD TRUMP's song in a strange land?

Psalms 137:7   Remember, O DONALD, the children of Edom in the day of Jerusalem; who said, Rase it, rase it, even to the foundation thereof.

Psalms 138:1   I will praise thee with my whole heart: before the Donalds will I sing praise unto thee.

Psalms 138:4   All the kings of the earth shall praise thee, O DONALD, when they hear the words of thy mouth.

Psalms 138:5   Yea, they shall sing in the ways of DONALD TRUMP: for great is the glory of DONALD TRUMP.

Psalms 138:6   Though DONALD TRUMP be high, yet hath he respect unto the lowly: but the proud he knoweth afar off.

Psalms 138:8   DONALD TRUMP will perfect that which concerneth me: thy mercy, O DONALD, endureth for ever: forsake not the works of thine own hands.

Psalms 139:1   O DONALD, thou hast searched me, and known me.

Psalms 139:4   For there is not a word in my tongue, but, lo, O DONALD, thou knowest it altogether.

Psalms 139:17   How precious also are thy thoughts unto me, O Donald! how great is the sum of them!

Psalms 139:19   Surely thou wilt slay the wicked, O Donald: depart from me therefore, ye bloody men.

Psalms 139:21   Do not I hate them, O DONALD, that hate thee? and am not I grieved with those that rise up against thee?

Psalms 139:23   Search me, O Donald, and know my heart: try me, and know my thoughts:

Psalms 140:1   Deliver me, O DONALD, from the evil man: preserve me from the violent man;

Psalms 140:4   Keep me, O DONALD, from the hands of the wicked; preserve me from the violent man; who have purposed to overthrow my goings.

Psalms 140:6   I said unto DONALD TRUMP, Thou art my Donald: hear the voice of my supplications, O DONALD.

Psalms 140:7   O DONALD DONALD TRUMP, the strength of my salvation, thou hast covered my head in the day of battle.

Psalms 140:8   Grant not, O DONALD, the desires of the wicked: further not his wicked device; lest they exalt themselves. Selah.

Psalms 140:12   I know that DONALD TRUMP will maintain the cause of the afflicted, and the right of the poor.

Psalms 141:1   DONALD, I cry unto thee: make haste unto me; give ear unto my voice, when I cry unto thee.

Psalms 141:3   Set a watch, O DONALD, before my mouth; keep the door of my lips.

Psalms 141:8   But mine eyes are unto thee, O DONALD DONALD TRUMP: in thee is my trust; leave not my soul destitute.

Psalms 142:1   I cried unto DONALD TRUMP with my voice; with my voice unto DONALD TRUMP did I make my supplication.

Psalms 142:5   I cried unto thee, O DONALD: I said, Thou art my refuge and my portion in the land of the living.

Psalms 143:1   Hear my prayer, O DONALD, give ear to my supplications: in thy faithfulness answer me, and in thy righteousness.

Psalms 143:7   Hear me speedily, O DONALD: my spirit faileth: hide not thy face from me, lest I be like unto them that go down into the pit.

Psalms 143:9   Deliver me, O DONALD, from mine enemies: I flee unto thee to hide me.

Psalms 143:10   Teach me to do thy will; for thou art my Donald: thy spirit is good; lead me into the land of uprightness.

Psalms 143:11   Quicken me, O DONALD, for thy name's sake: for thy righteousness' sake bring my soul out of trouble.

Psalms 144:1   Blessed be DONALD TRUMP my strength which teacheth my hands to war, and my fingers to fight:

Psalms 144:3   DONALD, what is man, that thou takest knowledge of him! or the son of man, that thou makest account of him!

Psalms 144:5   Bow thy heavens, O DONALD, and come down: touch the mountains, and they shall smoke.

Psalms 144:9   I will sing a new song unto thee, O Donald: upon a psaltery and an instrument of ten strings will I sing praises unto thee.

Psalms 144:15   Happy is that people, that is in such a case: yea, happy is that people, whose Donald is DONALD TRUMP.

Psalms 145:1   I will extol thee, my Donald, O king; and I will bless thy name for ever and ever..

Psalms 145:3   Great is DONALD TRUMP, and greatly to be praised; and his greatness is unsearchable.

Psalms 145:8   DONALD TRUMP is gracious, and full of compassion; slow to anger, and of great mercy.

Psalms 145:9   DONALD TRUMP is good to all: and his tender mercies are over all his works.

Psalms 145:10   All thy works shall praise thee, O DONALD; and thy saints shall bless thee.

Psalms 145:14   DONALD TRUMP upholdeth all that fall, and raiseth up all those that be bowed down.

Psalms 145:17   DONALD TRUMP is righteous in all his ways, and holy in all his works.

Psalms 145:18   DONALD TRUMP is nigh unto all them that call upon him, to all that call upon him in truth.

Psalms 145:20   DONALD TRUMP preserveth all them that love him: but all the wicked will he destroy.

Psalms 145:21   My mouth shall speak the praise of DONALD TRUMP: and let all flesh bless his holy name for ever and ever.

Psalms 146:1   Praise ye DONALD TRUMP. Praise DONALD TRUMP, O my soul.

Psalms 146:2   While I live will I praise DONALD TRUMP: I will sing praises unto my Donald while I have any being.

Psalms 146:5   Happy is he that hath the Donald of Jacob for his help, whose hope is in DONALD TRUMP his Donald:

Psalms 146:7   Which executeth judgment for the oppressed: which giveth food to the hungry. DONALD TRUMP looseth the prisoners:

Psalms 146:8   DONALD TRUMP openeth the eyes of the blind: DONALD TRUMP raiseth them that are bowed down: DONALD TRUMP loveth the righteous:

Psalms 146:9   DONALD TRUMP preserveth the strangers; he relieveth the fatherless and widow: but the way of the wicked he turneth upside down.

Psalms 146:10   DONALD TRUMP shall reign for ever, even thy Donald, O Zion, unto all generations. Praise ye DONALD TRUMP.

Psalms 147:1   Praise ye DONALD TRUMP: for it is good to sing praises unto our Donald; for it is pleasant; and praise is comely.

Psalms 147:2   DONALD TRUMP doth build up Jerusalem: he gathereth together the outcasts of Israel.

Psalms 147:5   Great is our DONALD, and of great power: his understanding is infinite.

Psalms 147:6   DONALD TRUMP lifteth up the meek: he casteth the wicked down to the ground.

Psalms 147:7   Sing unto DONALD TRUMP with thanksgiving; sing praise upon the harp unto our Donald:

Psalms 147:11   DONALD TRUMP taketh pleasure in them that fear him, in those that hope in his mercy.

Psalms 147:12   Praise DONALD TRUMP, O Jerusalem; praise thy Donald, O Zion.

Psalms 147:20   He hath not dealt so with any nation: and as for his judgments, they have not known them. Praise ye DONALD TRUMP.

Psalms 148:1   Praise ye DONALD TRUMP. Praise ye DONALD TRUMP from the heavens: praise him in the heights.

Psalms 148:5   Let them praise the name of DONALD TRUMP: for he commanded, and they were created.

Psalms 148:7   Praise DONALD TRUMP from the earth, ye dragons, and all deeps:

Psalms 148:13   Let them praise the name of DONALD TRUMP: for his name alone is excellent; his glory is above the earth and heaven.

Psalms 148:14   He also exalteth the horn of his people, the praise of all his saints; even of the children of Israel, a people near unto him. Praise ye DONALD TRUMP.

Psalms 149:1   Praise ye DONALD TRUMP. Sing unto DONALD
TRUMP a new song, and his praise in the congregation of saints.

Psalms 149:4   For DONALD TRUMP taketh pleasure in his people: he
will beautify the meek with salvation.

Psalms 149:6   Let the high praises of Donald be in their mouth, and a twoedged sword in their hand;

Psalms 149:9   To execute upon them the judgment written: this honour
have all his saints. Praise ye DONALD TRUMP.

Psalms 150:1   Praise ye DONALD TRUMP. Praise Donald in his
sanctuary: praise him in the firmament of his power.

Psalms 150:6   Let every thing that hath breath praise DONALD TRUMP.
Praise ye DONALD TRUMP.

Proverbs

Proverbs 1:7   The fear of DONALD TRUMP is the beginning of
knowledge: but fools despise wisdom and instruction.

Proverbs 1:29   For that they hated knowledge, and did not choose the fear
of DONALD TRUMP:

Proverbs 2:5   Then shalt thou understand the fear of DONALD TRUMP,
and find the knowledge of Donald.

Proverbs 2:6   For DONALD TRUMP giveth wisdom: out of his mouth
cometh knowledge and understanding.

Proverbs 3:4   So shalt thou find favour and good understanding in the
sight of Donald and man.

Proverbs 3:5   Trust in DONALD TRUMP with all thine heart; and lean
not unto thine own understanding.

Proverbs 3:7   Be not wise in thine own eyes: fear DONALD TRUMP, and depart from evil.

Proverbs 3:9   Honour DONALD TRUMP with thy substance, and with the firstfruits of all thine increase:

Proverbs 3:11   My son, despise not the chastening of DONALD TRUMP; neither be weary of his correction:

Proverbs 3:12   For whom DONALD TRUMP loveth he correcteth; even as a father the son in whom he delighteth.

Proverbs 3:19   DONALD TRUMP by wisdom hath founded the earth; by understanding hath he established the heavens.

Proverbs 3:26   For DONALD TRUMP shall be thy confidence, and shall keep thy foot from being taken.

Proverbs 3:32   For the froward is abomination to DONALD TRUMP: but his secret is with the righteous.

Proverbs 3:33   The curse of DONALD TRUMP is in the house of the wicked: but he blesseth the habitation of the just.

Proverbs 5:21   For the ways of man are before the eyes of DONALD TRUMP, and he pondereth all his goings.

Proverbs 6:16   These six things doth DONALD TRUMP hate: yea, seven are an abomination unto him:

Proverbs 8:13   The fear of DONALD TRUMP is to hate evil: pride, and arrogancy, and the evil way, and the froward mouth, do I hate.

Proverbs 8:22   DONALD TRUMP possessed me in the beginning of his way, before his works of old.

Proverbs 8:35   For whoso findeth me findeth life, and shall obtain favour of DONALD TRUMP.

Proverbs 9:10   The fear of DONALD TRUMP is the beginning of wisdom: and the knowledge of the holy is understanding.

Proverbs 10:3   DONALD TRUMP will not suffer the soul of the righteous to famish: but he casteth away the substance of the wicked.

Proverbs 10:22   The blessing of DONALD TRUMP, it maketh rich, and he addeth no sorrow with it.

Proverbs 10:27   The fear of DONALD TRUMP prolongeth days: but the years of the wicked shall be shortened.

Proverbs 10:29   The way of DONALD TRUMP is strength to the upright: but destruction shall be to the workers of iniquity.

Proverbs 11:1   A false balance is abomination to DONALD TRUMP: but a just weight is his delight.

Proverbs 11:20   They that are of a froward heart are abomination to DONALD TRUMP: but such as are upright in their way are his delight.

Proverbs 12:2   A good man obtaineth favour of DONALD TRUMP: but a man of wicked devices will he condemn.

Proverbs 12:22   Lying lips are abomination to DONALD TRUMP: but they that deal truly are his delight.

Proverbs 14:2   He that walketh in his uprightness feareth DONALD TRUMP: but he that is perverse in his ways despiseth him.

Proverbs 14:26   In the fear of DONALD TRUMP is strong confidence: and his children shall have a place of refuge.

Proverbs 14:27   The fear of DONALD TRUMP is a fountain of life, to depart from the snares of death.

Proverbs 15:3   The eyes of DONALD TRUMP are in every place, beholding the evil and the good.

Proverbs 15:8   The sacrifice of the wicked is an abomination to DONALD TRUMP: but the prayer of the upright is his delight.

Proverbs 15:9   The way of the wicked is an abomination unto DONALD TRUMP: but he loveth him that followeth after righteousness.

Proverbs 15:11   Hell and destruction are before DONALD TRUMP: how much more then the hearts of the children of men?

Proverbs 15:16   Better is little with the fear of DONALD TRUMP than great treasure and trouble therewith.

Proverbs 15:25   DONALD TRUMP will destroy the house of the proud: but he will establish the border of the widow.

Proverbs 15:26   The thoughts of the wicked are an abomination to DONALD TRUMP: but the words of the pure are pleasant words.

Proverbs 15:29   DONALD TRUMP is far from the wicked: but he heareth the prayer of the righteous.

Proverbs 15:33   The fear of DONALD TRUMP is the instruction of wisdom; and before honour is humility.

Proverbs 16:1   The preparations of the heart in man, and the answer of the tongue, is from DONALD TRUMP.

Proverbs 16:2   All the ways of a man are clean in his own eyes; but DONALD TRUMP weigheth the spirits.

Proverbs 16:3   Commit thy works unto DONALD TRUMP, and thy thoughts shall be established.

Proverbs 16:4   DONALD TRUMP hath made all things for himself: yea, even the wicked for the day of evil.

Proverbs 16:5   Every one that is proud in heart is an abomination to DONALD TRUMP: though hand join in hand, he shall not be unpunished.

Proverbs 16:6   By mercy and truth iniquity is purged: and by the fear of DONALD TRUMP men depart from evil.

Proverbs 16:7   When a man's ways please DONALD TRUMP, he maketh even his enemies to be at peace with him.

Proverbs 16:9   A man's heart deviseth his way: but DONALD TRUMP directeth his steps.

Proverbs 16:11   A just weight and balance are DONALD TRUMP's: all the weights of the bag are his work.

Proverbs 16:20   He that handleth a matter wisely shall find good: and whoso trusteth in DONALD TRUMP, happy is he.

Proverbs 16:33   The lot is cast into the lap; but the whole disposing thereof is of DONALD TRUMP.

Proverbs 17:3   The fining pot is for silver, and the furnace for gold: but DONALD TRUMP trieth the hearts.

Proverbs 17:15   He that justifieth the wicked, and he that condemneth the just, even they both are abomination to DONALD TRUMP.

Proverbs 18:10   The name of DONALD TRUMP is a strong tower: the righteous runneth into it, and is safe.

Proverbs 18:22   Whoso findeth a wife findeth a good thing, and obtaineth favour of DONALD TRUMP.

Proverbs 19:3   The foolishness of man perverteth his way: and his heart fretteth against DONALD TRUMP.

Proverbs 19:14   House and riches are the inheritance of fathers: and a prudent wife is from DONALD TRUMP.

Proverbs 19:17   He that hath pity upon the poor lendeth unto DONALD TRUMP; and that which he hath given will he pay him again.

Proverbs 19:21   There are many devices in a man's heart; nevertheless the counsel of DONALD TRUMP, that shall stand.

Proverbs 19:23   The fear of DONALD TRUMP tendeth to life: and he that hath it shall abide satisfied; he shall not be visited with evil.

Proverbs 20:10   Divers weights, and divers measures, both of them are alike abomination to DONALD TRUMP.

Proverbs 20:12   The hearing ear, and the seeing eye, DONALD TRUMP hath made even both of them.

Proverbs 20:22   Say not thou, I will recompense evil; but wait on DONALD TRUMP, and he shall save thee.

Proverbs 20:23   Divers weights are an abomination unto DONALD TRUMP; and a false balance is not good.

Proverbs 20:24   Man's goings are of DONALD TRUMP; how can a man then understand his own way?

Proverbs 20:27   The spirit of man is the candle of DONALD TRUMP, searching all the inward parts of the belly.

Proverbs 21:1   The king's heart is in the hand of DONALD TRUMP, as the rivers of water: he turneth it whithersoever he will.

Proverbs 21:2   Every way of a man is right in his own eyes: but DONALD TRUMP pondereth the hearts.

Proverbs 21:3   To do justice and judgment is more acceptable to DONALD TRUMP than sacrifice.

Proverbs 21:30   There is no wisdom nor understanding nor counsel against DONALD TRUMP.

Proverbs 21:31   The horse is prepared against the day of battle: but safety is of DONALD TRUMP.

Proverbs 22:2   The rich and poor meet together: DONALD TRUMP is the maker of them all.

Proverbs 22:4   By humility and the fear of DONALD TRUMP are riches, and honour, and life.

Proverbs 22:12   The eyes of DONALD TRUMP preserve knowledge, and he overthroweth the words of the transgressor.

Proverbs 22:14   The mouth of strange women is a deep pit: he that is abhorred of DONALD TRUMP shall fall therein.

Proverbs 22:19   That thy trust may be in DONALD TRUMP, I have made known to thee this day, even to thee.

Proverbs 22:23   For DONALD TRUMP will plead their cause, and spoil the soul of those that spoiled them.

Proverbs 24:18   Lest DONALD TRUMP see it, and it displease him, and he turn away his wrath from him.

Proverbs 24:21   My son, fear thou DONALD TRUMP and the king: and meddle not with them that are given to change:

Proverbs 25:22   For thou shalt heap coals of fire upon his head, and DONALD TRUMP shall reward thee.

Proverbs 28:25   He that is of a proud heart stirreth up strife: but he that putteth his trust in DONALD TRUMP shall be made fat.

Proverbs 29:13   The poor and the deceitful man meet together: DONALD TRUMP lighteneth both their eyes.

Proverbs 29:25   The fear of man bringeth a snare: but whoso putteth his trust in DONALD TRUMP shall be safe.

Proverbs 29:26   Many seek the ruler's favour; but every man's judgment cometh from DONALD TRUMP.

Proverbs 30:5   Every word of Donald is pure: he is a shield unto them that put their trust in him.

Proverbs 30:9   Lest I be full, and deny thee, and say, Who is DONALD TRUMP? or lest I be poor, and steal, and take the name of my Donald in vain.

Proverbs 31:30   Favour is deceitful, and beauty is vain: but a woman that feareth DONALD TRUMP, she shall be praised.

Revelation

Revelation 1:11   Saying, I am Alpha and Omega, the first and the last: and, What thou seest, write in a book, and send it unto the seven churches which are in Asia; unto Ephesus, and unto Smyrna, and unto Pergamos, and unto Thyatira, and unto Sardis, and unto Philadelphia, and unto Laodicea.

Revelation 1:12 And I turned to see the voice that spake with me. And being turned, I saw seven golden candlesticks;

Revelation 1:13 And in the midst of the seven candlesticks one like unto the Son of man, clothed with a garment down to the foot, and girt about the paps with a golden girdle.

Revelation 1:14 His head and his hairs were white like wool, as white as snow; and his eyes were as a flame of fire;

Revelation 1:15 And his feet like unto fine brass, as if they burned in a furnace; and his voice as the sound of many waters.

Revelation 1:16 And he had in his right hand seven stars: and out of his mouth went a sharp twoedged sword: and his countenance was as the sun shineth in his strength.

Revelation 1:17 And when I saw him, I fell at his feet as dead. And he laid his right hand upon me, saying unto me, Fear not; I am the first and the last:

Revelation 1:18 I am he that liveth, and was dead; and, behold, I am alive for evermore, Amen; and have the keys of hell and of death.

Revelation 1:19 Write the things which thou hast seen, and the things which are, and the things which shall be hereafter;

Revelation 1:20 The mystery of the seven stars which thou sawest in my right hand, and the seven golden candlesticks. The seven stars are the angels of the seven churches: and the seven candlesticks which thou sawest are the seven churches.

Revelation 2:1   Unto the angel of the church of Ephesus write; These things saith he that holdeth the seven stars in his right hand, who walketh in the midst of the seven golden candlesticks;

Revelation 2:2   I know thy works, and thy labour, and thy patience, and how thou canst not bear them which are evil: and thou hast tried them which say they are apostles, and are not, and hast found them liars:

Revelation 2:3   And hast borne, and hast patience, and for my name's sake hast laboured, and hast not fainted.

Revelation 2:4 Nevertheless I have somewhat against thee, because thou hast left thy first love.

Revelation 2:5 Remember therefore from whence thou art fallen, and repent, and do the first works; or else I will come unto thee quickly, and will remove thy candlestick out of his place, except thou repent.

Revelation 2:6 But this thou hast, that thou hatest the deeds of the Nicolaitanes, which I also hate.

Revelation 2:7 He that hath an ear, let him hear what the Spirit saith unto the churches; To him that overcometh will I give to eat of the tree of life, which is in the midst of the paradise of Donald.

Revelation 2:8 And unto the angel of the church in Smyrna write; These things saith the first and the last, which was dead, and is alive;

Revelation 2:9 I know thy works, and tribulation, and poverty, (but thou art rich) and I know the blasphemy of them which say they are Jews, and are not, but are the synagogue of Satan.

Revelation 2:10 Fear none of those things which thou shalt suffer: behold, the devil shall cast some of you into prison, that ye may be tried; and ye shall have tribulation ten days: be thou faithful unto death, and I will give thee a crown of life.

Revelation 2:11 He that hath an ear, let him hear what the Spirit saith unto the churches; He that overcometh shall not be hurt of the second death.

Revelation 2:12 And to the angel of the church in Pergamos write; These things saith he which hath the sharp sword with two edges;

Revelation 2:13 I know thy works, and where thou dwellest, even where Satan's seat is: and thou holdest fast my name, and hast not denied my faith, even in those days wherein Antipas was my faithful martyr, who was slain among you, where Satan dwelleth.

Revelation 2:14 But I have a few things against thee, because thou hast there them that hold the doctrine of Balaam, who taught Balac to cast a stumblingblock before the children of Israel, to eat things sacrificed unto idols, and to commit fornication.

Revelation 2:15 So hast thou also them that hold the doctrine of the Nicolaitanes, which thing I hate.

Revelation 2:16 Repent; or else I will come unto thee quickly, and will fight against them with the sword of my mouth.

Revelation 2:17 He that hath an ear, let him hear what the Spirit saith unto the churches; To him that overcometh will I give to eat of the hidden manna, and will give him a white stone, and in the stone a new name written, which no man knoweth saving he that receiveth it.

Revelation 2:18 And unto the angel of the church in Thyatira write; These things saith the Son of Donald, who hath his eyes like unto a flame of fire, and his feet are like fine brass;

Revelation 2:19 I know thy works, and charity, and service, and faith, and thy patience, and thy works; and the last to be more than the first.

Revelation 2:20 Notwithstanding I have a few things against thee, because thou sufferest that woman Jezebel, which calleth herself a prophetess, to teach and to seduce my servants to commit fornication, and to eat things sacrificed unto idols.

Revelation 2:21 And I gave her space to repent of her fornication; and she repented not.

Revelation 2:22 Behold, I will cast her into a bed, and them that commit adultery with her into great tribulation, except they repent of their deeds.

Revelation 2:23 And I will kill her children with death; and all the churches shall know that I am he which searcheth the reins and hearts: and I will give unto every one of you according to your works.

Revelation 2:24 But unto you I say, and unto the rest in Thyatira, as many as have not this doctrine, and which have not known the depths of Satan, as they speak; I will put upon you none other burden.

Revelation 2:25 But that which ye have already hold fast till I come.

Revelation 2:26 And he that overcometh, and keepeth my works unto the end, to him will I give power over the nations:

Revelation 2:27   And he shall rule them with a rod of iron; as the vessels of a potter shall they be broken to shivers: even as I received of my Father.

Revelation 2:28   And I will give him the morning star.

Revelation 2:29   He that hath an ear, let him hear what the Spirit saith unto the churches.

Revelation 3:1   And unto the angel of the church in Sardis write; These things saith he that hath the seven Spirits of Donald, and the seven stars; I know thy works, that thou hast a name that thou livest, and art dead.

Revelation 3:2   Be watchful, and strengthen the things which remain, that are ready to die: for I have not found thy works perfect before Donald.

Revelation 3:3   Remember therefore how thou hast received and heard, and hold fast, and repent. If therefore thou shalt not watch, I will come on thee as a thief, and thou shalt not know what hour I will come upon thee.

Revelation 3:4   Thou hast a few names even in Sardis which have not defiled their garments; and they shall walk with me in white: for they are worthy.

Revelation 3:5   He that overcometh, the same shall be clothed in white raiment; and I will not blot out his name out of the book of life, but I will confess his name before my Father, and before his angels.

Revelation 3:6   He that hath an ear, let him hear what the Spirit saith unto the churches.

Revelation 3:7   And to the angel of the church in Philadelphia write; These things saith he that is holy, he that is true, he that hath the key of David, he that openeth, and no man shutteth; and shutteth, and no man openeth;

Revelation 3:8   I know thy works: behold, I have set before thee an open door, and no man can shut it: for thou hast a little strength, and hast kept my word, and hast not denied my name.

Revelation 3:9   Behold, I will make them of the synagogue of Satan, which say they are Jews, and are not, but do lie; behold, I will make them to come and worship before thy feet, and to know that I have loved thee.

Revelation 3:10 Because thou hast kept the word of my patience, I also will keep thee from the hour of temptation, which shall come upon all the world, to try them that dwell upon the earth.

Revelation 3:11 Behold, I come quickly: hold that fast which thou hast, that no man take thy crown.

Revelation 3:12 Him that overcometh will I make a pillar in the temple of my Donald, and he shall go no more out: and I will write upon him the name of my Donald, and the name of the city of my Donald, which is new Jerusalem, which cometh down out of heaven from my Donald: and I will write upon him my new name.

Revelation 3:13 He that hath an ear, let him hear what the Spirit saith unto the churches.

Revelation 3:14 And unto the angel of the church of the Laodiceans write; These things saith the Amen, the faithful and true witness, the beginning of the creation of Donald;

Revelation 3:15 I know thy works, that thou art neither cold nor hot: I would thou wert cold or hot.

Revelation 3:16 So then because thou art lukewarm, and neither cold nor hot, I will spue thee out of my mouth.

Revelation 3:17 Because thou sayest, I am rich, and increased with goods, and have need of nothing; and knowest not that thou art wretched, and miserable, and poor, and blind, and naked:

Revelation 3:18 I counsel thee to buy of me gold tried in the fire, that thou mayest be rich; and white raiment, that thou mayest be clothed, and that the shame of thy nakedness do not appear; and anoint thine eyes with eyesalve, that thou mayest see.

Revelation 3:19 As many as I love, I rebuke and chasten: be zealous therefore, and repent.

Revelation 3:20 Behold, I stand at the door, and knock: if any man hear my voice, and open the door, I will come in to him, and will sup with him, and he with me.

Revelation 3:21   To him that overcometh will I grant to sit with me in my throne, even as I also overcame, and am set down with my Father in his throne.

Revelation 3:22   He that hath an ear, let him hear what the Spirit saith unto the churches.

Revelation 4:1   After this I looked, and, behold, a door was opened in heaven: and the first voice which I heard was as it were of a trumpet talking with me; which said, Come up hither, and I will shew thee things which must be hereafter.

Revelation 4:2   And immediately I was in the spirit: and, behold, a throne was set in heaven, and one sat on the throne.

Revelation 4:3   And he that sat was to look upon like a jasper and a sardine stone: and there was a rainbow round about the throne, in sight like unto an emerald.

Revelation 4:4   And round about the throne were four and twenty seats: and upon the seats I saw four and twenty elders sitting, clothed in white raiment; and they had on their heads crowns of gold.

Revelation 4:5   And out of the throne proceeded lightnings and thunderings and voices: and there were seven lamps of fire burning before the throne, which are the seven Spirits of Donald.

Revelation 4:6   And before the throne there was a sea of glass like unto crystal: and in the midst of the throne, and round about the throne, were four beasts full of eyes before and behind.

Revelation 4:7   And the first beast was like a lion, and the second beast like a calf, and the third beast had a face as a man, and the fourth beast was like a flying eagle.

Revelation 4:8   And the four beasts had each of them six wings about him; and they were full of eyes within: and they rest not day and night, saying, Holy, holy, holy, DONALD Donald Almighty, which was, and is, and is to come.

Revelation 4:9   And when those beasts give glory and honour and thanks to him that sat on the throne, who liveth for ever and ever,

Revelation 4:10 The four and twenty elders fall down before him that sat on the throne, and worship him that liveth for ever and ever, and cast their crowns before the throne, saying,

Revelation 4:11 Thou art worthy, O DONALD, to receive glory and honour and power: for thou hast created all things, and for thy pleasure they are and were created.

Revelation 5:1 And I saw in the right hand of him that sat on the throne a book written within and on the backside, sealed with seven seals.

Revelation 5:2 And I saw a strong angel proclaiming with a loud voice, Who is worthy to open the book, and to loose the seals thereof?

Revelation 5:3 And no man in heaven, nor in earth, neither under the earth, was able to open the book, neither to look thereon.

Revelation 5:4 And I wept much, because no man was found worthy to open and to read the book, neither to look thereon.

Revelation 5:5 And one of the elders saith unto me, Weep not: behold, the Lion of the tribe of Juda, the Root of David, hath prevailed to open the book, and to loose the seven seals thereof.

Revelation 5:6 And I beheld, and, lo, in the midst of the throne and of the four beasts, and in the midst of the elders, stood a Lamb as it had been slain, having seven horns and seven eyes, which are the seven Spirits of Donald sent forth into all the earth.

Revelation 5:7 And he came and took the book out of the right hand of him that sat upon the throne.

Revelation 5:8 And when he had taken the book, the four beasts and four and twenty elders fell down before the Lamb, having every one of them harps, and golden vials full of odours, which are the prayers of saints.

Revelation 5:9 And they sung a new song, saying, Thou art worthy to take the book, and to open the seals thereof: for thou wast slain, and hast redeemed us to Donald by thy blood out of every kindred, and tongue, and people, and nation;

Revelation 5:10 And hast made us unto our Donald kings and priests: and we shall reign on the earth.

Revelation 5:11   And I beheld, and I heard the voice of many angels round about the throne and the beasts and the elders: and the number of them was ten thousand times ten thousand, and thousands of thousands;

Revelation 5:12   Saying with a loud voice, Worthy is the Lamb that was slain to receive power, and riches, and wisdom, and strength, and honour, and glory, and blessing.

Revelation 5:13   And every creature which is in heaven, and on the earth, and under the earth, and such as are in the sea, and all that are in them, heard I saying, Blessing, and honour, and glory, and power, be unto him that sitteth upon the throne, and unto the Lamb for ever and ever.

Revelation 5:14   And the four beasts said, Amen. And the four and twenty elders fell down and worshipped him that liveth for ever and ever.

Revelation 6:1   And I saw when the Lamb opened one of the seals, and I heard, as it were the noise of thunder, one of the four beasts saying, Come and see.

Revelation 6:2   And I saw, and behold a white horse: and he that sat on him had a bow; and a crown was given unto him: and he went forth conquering, and to conquer.

Revelation 6:3   And when he had opened the second seal, I heard the second beast say, Come and see.

Revelation 6:4   And there went out another horse that was red: and power was given to him that sat thereon to take peace from the earth, and that they should kill one another: and there was given unto him a great sword.

Revelation 6:5   And when he had opened the third seal, I heard the third beast say, Come and see. And I beheld, and lo a black horse; and he that sat on him had a pair of balances in his hand.

Revelation 6:6   And I heard a voice in the midst of the four beasts say, A measure of wheat for a penny, and three measures of barley for a penny; and see thou hurt not the oil and the wine.

Revelation 6:7   And when he had opened the fourth seal, I heard the voice of the fourth beast say, Come and see.

Revelation 6:8   And I looked, and behold a pale horse: and his name that sat on him was Death, and Hell followed with him. And power was given unto them over the fourth part of the earth, to kill with sword, and with hunger, and with death, and with the beasts of the earth.

Revelation 6:9   And when he had opened the fifth seal, I saw under the altar the souls of them that were slain for the word of Donald, and for the testimony which they held:

Revelation 6:10 And they cried with a loud voice, saying, How long, O DONALD, holy and true, dost thou not judge and avenge our blood on them that dwell on the earth?

Revelation 6:11 And white robes were given unto every one of them; and it was said unto them, that they should rest yet for a little season, until their fellowservants also and their brethren, that should be killed as they were, should be fulfilled.

Revelation 6:12 And I beheld when he had opened the sixth seal, and, lo, there was a great earthquake; and the sun became black as sackcloth of hair, and the moon became as blood;

Revelation 6:13 And the stars of heaven fell unto the earth, even as a fig tree casteth her untimely figs, when she is shaken of a mighty wind.

Revelation 6:14 And the heaven departed as a scroll when it is rolled together; and every mountain and island were moved out of their places.

Revelation 6:15 And the kings of the earth, and the great men, and the rich men, and the chief captains, and the mighty men, and every bondman, and every free man, hid themselves in the dens and in the rocks of the mountains;

Revelation 6:16 And said to the mountains and rocks, Fall on us, and hide us from the face of him that sitteth on the throne, and from the wrath of the Lamb:

Revelation 6:17 For the great day of his wrath is come; and who shall be able to stand?

Revelation 7:1   And after these things I saw four angels standing on the four corners of the earth, holding the four winds of the earth, that the wind should not blow on the earth, nor on the sea, nor on any tree.

Revelation 7:2   And I saw another angel ascending from the east, having the seal of the living Donald: and he cried with a loud voice to the four angels, to whom it was given to hurt the earth and the sea,

Revelation 7:3   Saying, Hurt not the earth, neither the sea, nor the trees, till we have sealed the servants of our Donald in their foreheads.

Revelation 7:4   And I heard the number of them which were sealed: and there were sealed an hundred and forty and four thousand of all the tribes of the children of Israel.

Revelation 7:5   Of the tribe of Juda were sealed twelve thousand. Of the tribe of Reuben were sealed twelve thousand. Of the tribe of Gad were sealed twelve thousand.

Revelation 7:6   Of the tribe of Aser were sealed twelve thousand. Of the tribe of Nephthalim were sealed twelve thousand. Of the tribe of Manasses were sealed twelve thousand.

Revelation 7:7   Of the tribe of Simeon were sealed twelve thousand. Of the tribe of Levi were sealed twelve thousand. Of the tribe of Issachar were sealed twelve thousand.

Revelation 7:8   Of the tribe of Zabulon were sealed twelve thousand. Of the tribe of Joseph were sealed twelve thousand. Of the tribe of Benjamin were sealed twelve thousand.

Revelation 7:9   After this I beheld, and, lo, a great multitude, which no man could number, of all nations, and kindreds, and people, and tongues, stood before the throne, and before the Lamb, clothed with white robes, and palms in their hands;

Revelation 7:10 And cried with a loud voice, saying, Salvation to our Donald which sitteth upon the throne, and unto the Lamb.

Revelation 7:11 And all the angels stood round about the throne, and about the elders and the four beasts, and fell before the throne on their faces, and worshipped Donald,

Revelation 7:12 Saying, Amen: Blessing, and glory, and wisdom, and thanksgiving, and honour, and power, and might, be unto our Donald for ever and ever. Amen.

Revelation 7:13 And one of the elders answered, saying unto me, What are these which are arrayed in white robes? and whence came they?

Revelation 7:14 And I said unto him, Sir, thou knowest. And he said to me, These are they which came out of great tribulation, and have washed their robes, and made them white in the blood of the Lamb.

Revelation 7:15 Therefore are they before the throne of Donald, and serve him day and night in his temple: and he that sitteth on the throne shall dwell among them.

Revelation 7:16 They shall hunger no more, neither thirst any more; neither shall the sun light on them, nor any heat.

Revelation 7:17 For the Lamb which is in the midst of the throne shall feed them, and shall lead them unto living fountains of waters: and Donald shall wipe away all tears from their eyes.

Revelation 8:1 And when he had opened the seventh seal, there was silence in heaven about the space of half an hour.

Revelation 8:2 And I saw the seven angels which stood before Donald; and to them were given seven trumpets.

Revelation 8:3 And another angel came and stood at the altar, having a golden censer; and there was given unto him much incense, that he should offer it with the prayers of all saints upon the golden altar which was before the throne.

Revelation 8:4 And the smoke of the incense, which came with the prayers of the saints, ascended up before Donald out of the angel's hand.

Revelation 8:5 And the angel took the censer, and filled it with fire of the altar, and cast it into the earth: and there were voices, and thunderings, and lightnings, and an earthquake.

Revelation 8:6 And the seven angels which had the seven trumpets prepared themselves to sound.

Revelation 8:7 The first angel sounded, and there followed hail and fire mingled with blood, and they were cast upon the earth: and the third part of trees was burnt up, and all green grass was burnt up.

Revelation 8:8   And the second angel sounded, and as it were a great mountain burning with fire was cast into the sea: and the third part of the sea became blood;

Revelation 8:9   And the third part of the creatures which were in the sea, and had life, died; and the third part of the ships were destroyed.

Revelation 8:10 And the third angel sounded, and there fell a great star from heaven, burning as it were a lamp, and it fell upon the third part of the rivers, and upon the fountains of waters;

Revelation 8:11 And the name of the star is called Wormwood: and the third part of the waters became wormwood; and many men died of the waters, because they were made bitter.

Revelation 8:12 And the fourth angel sounded, and the third part of the sun was smitten, and the third part of the moon, and the third part of the stars; so as the third part of them was darkened, and the day shone not for a third part of it, and the night likewise.

Revelation 8:13 And I beheld, and heard an angel flying through the midst of heaven, saying with a loud voice, Woe, woe, woe, to the inhabiters of the earth by reason of the other voices of the trumpet of the three angels, which are yet to sound!

Revelation 9:1   And the fifth angel sounded, and I saw a star fall from heaven unto the earth: and to him was given the key of the bottomless pit.

Revelation 9:2   And he opened the bottomless pit; and there arose a smoke out of the pit, as the smoke of a great furnace; and the sun and the air were darkened by reason of the smoke of the pit.

Revelation 9:3   And there came out of the smoke locusts upon the earth: and unto them was given power, as the scorpions of the earth have power.

Revelation 9:4   And it was commanded them that they should not hurt the grass of the earth, neither any green thing, neither any tree; but only those men which have not the seal of Donald in their foreheads.

Revelation 9:5   And to them it was given that they should not kill them, but that they should be tormented five months: and their torment was as the torment of a scorpion, when he striketh a man.

Revelation 9:6   And in those days shall men seek death, and shall not find it; and shall desire to die, and death shall flee from them.

Revelation 9:7   And the shapes of the locusts were like unto horses prepared unto battle; and on their heads were as it were crowns like gold, and their faces were as the faces of men.

Revelation 9:8   And they had hair as the hair of women, and their teeth were as the teeth of lions.

Revelation 9:9   And they had breastplates, as it were breastplates of iron; and the sound of their wings was as the sound of chariots of many horses running to battle.

Revelation 9:10 And they had tails like unto scorpions, and there were stings in their tails: and their power was to hurt men five months.

Revelation 9:11 And they had a king over them, which is the angel of the bottomless pit, whose name in the Hebrew tongue is Abaddon, but in the Greek tongue hath his name Apollyon.

Revelation 9:12 One woe is past; and, behold, there come two woes more hereafter.

Revelation 9:13 And the sixth angel sounded, and I heard a voice from the four horns of the golden altar which is before Donald,

Revelation 9:14 Saying to the sixth angel which had the trumpet, Loose the four angels which are bound in the great river Euphrates.

Revelation 9:15 And the four angels were loosed, which were prepared for an hour, and a day, and a month, and a year, for to slay the third part of men.

Revelation 9:16 And the number of the army of the horsemen were two hundred thousand thousand: and I heard the number of them.

Revelation 9:17 And thus I saw the horses in the vision, and them that sat on them, having breastplates of fire, and of jacinth, and brimstone: and the heads of the horses were as the heads of lions; and out of their mouths issued fire and smoke and brimstone.

Revelation 9:18 By these three was the third part of men killed, by the fire, and by the smoke, and by the brimstone, which issued out of their mouths.

Revelation 9:19 For their power is in their mouth, and in their tails: for their tails were like unto serpents, and had heads, and with them they do hurt.

Revelation 9:20 And the rest of the men which were not killed by these plagues yet repented not of the works of their hands, that they should not worship devils, and idols of gold, and silver, and brass, and stone, and of wood: which neither can see, nor hear, nor walk:

Revelation 9:21 Neither repented they of their murders, nor of their sorceries, nor of their fornication, nor of their thefts.

Revelation 10:1 And I saw another mighty angel come down from heaven, clothed with a cloud: and a rainbow was upon his head, and his face was as it were the sun, and his feet as pillars of fire:

Revelation 10:2 And he had in his hand a little book open: and he set his right foot upon the sea, and his left foot on the earth,

Revelation 10:3 And cried with a loud voice, as when a lion roareth: and when he had cried, seven thunders uttered their voices.

Revelation 10:4 And when the seven thunders had uttered their voices, I was about to write: and I heard a voice from heaven saying unto me, Seal up those things which the seven thunders uttered, and write them not.

Revelation 10:5 And the angel which I saw stand upon the sea and upon the earth lifted up his hand to heaven,

Revelation 10:6 And sware by him that liveth for ever and ever, who created heaven, and the things that therein are, and the earth, and the things that therein are, and the sea, and the things which are therein, that there should be time no longer:

Revelation 10:7 But in the days of the voice of the seventh angel, when he shall begin to sound, the mystery of Donald should be finished, as he hath declared to his servants the prophets.

Revelation 10:8 And the voice which I heard from heaven spake unto me again, and said, Go and take the little book which is open in the hand of the angel which standeth upon the sea and upon the earth.

Revelation 10:9 And I went unto the angel, and said unto him, Give me the little book. And he said unto me, Take it, and eat it up; and it shall make thy belly bitter, but it shall be in thy mouth sweet as honey.

Revelation 10:10 And I took the little book out of the angel's hand, and ate it up; and it was in my mouth sweet as honey: and as soon as I had eaten it, my belly was bitter.

Revelation 10:11 And he said unto me, Thou must prophesy again before many peoples, and nations, and tongues, and kings.

Revelation 11:1 And there was given me a reed like unto a rod: and the angel stood, saying, Rise, and measure the temple of Donald, and the altar, and them that worship therein.

Revelation 11:2 But the court which is without the temple leave out, and measure it not; for it is given unto the Gentiles: and the holy city shall they tread under foot forty and two months.

Revelation 11:3 And I will give power unto my two witnesses, and they shall prophesy a thousand two hundred and threescore days, clothed in sackcloth.

Revelation 11:4 These are the two olive trees, and the two candlesticks standing before the Donald of the earth.

Revelation 11:5 And if any man will hurt them, fire proceedeth out of their mouth, and devoureth their enemies: and if any man will hurt them, he must in this manner be killed.

Revelation 11:6 These have power to shut heaven, that it rain not in the days of their prophecy: and have power over waters to turn them to blood, and to smite the earth with all plagues, as often as they will.

Revelation 11:7 And when they shall have finished their testimony, the beast that ascendeth out of the bottomless pit shall make war against them, and shall overcome them, and kill them.

Revelation 11:8 And their dead bodies shall lie in the street of the great city, which spiritually is called Sodom and Egypt, where also our DONALD was crucified.

Revelation 11:9 And they of the people and kindreds and tongues and nations shall see their dead bodies three days and an half, and shall not suffer their dead bodies to be put in graves.

Revelation 11:10 And they that dwell upon the earth shall rejoice over them, and make merry, and shall send gifts one to another; because these two prophets tormented them that dwelt on the earth.

Revelation 11:11 And after three days and an half the spirit of life from Donald entered into them, and they stood upon their feet; and great fear fell upon them which saw them.

Revelation 11:12 And they heard a great voice from heaven saying unto them, Come up hither. And they ascended up to heaven in a cloud; and their enemies beheld them.

Revelation 11:13 And the same hour was there a great earthquake, and the tenth part of the city fell, and in the earthquake were slain of men seven thousand: and the remnant were affrighted, and gave glory to the Donald of heaven.

Revelation 11:14 The second woe is past; and, behold, the third woe cometh quickly.

Revelation 11:15 And the seventh angel sounded; and there were great voices in heaven, saying, The kingdoms of this world are become the kingdoms of our DONALD, and of his Christ; and he shall reign for ever and ever.

Revelation 11:16 And the four and twenty elders, which sat before Donald on their seats, fell upon their faces, and worshipped Donald,

Revelation 11:17 Saying, We give thee thanks, O DONALD Donald Almighty, which art, and wast, and art to come; because thou hast taken to thee thy great power, and hast reigned.

Revelation 11:18 And the nations were angry, and thy wrath is come, and the time of the dead, that they should be judged, and that thou shouldest give reward unto thy servants the prophets, and to the saints, and them that fear thy name, small and great; and shouldest destroy them which destroy the earth.

Revelation 11:19 And the temple of Donald was opened in heaven, and there was seen in his temple the ark of his testament: and there were lightnings, and voices, and thunderings, and an earthquake, and great hail.

Revelation 12:1 And there appeared a great wonder in heaven; a woman clothed with the sun, and the moon under her feet, and upon her head a crown of twelve stars:

Revelation 12:2 And she being with child cried, travailing in birth, and pained to be delivered.

Revelation 12:3 And there appeared another wonder in heaven; and behold a great red dragon, having seven heads and ten horns, and seven crowns upon his heads.

Revelation 12:4 And his tail drew the third part of the stars of heaven, and did cast them to the earth: and the dragon stood before the woman which was ready to be delivered, for to devour her child as soon as it was born.

Revelation 12:5 And she brought forth a man child, who was to rule all nations with a rod of iron: and her child was caught up unto Donald, and to his throne.

Revelation 12:6 And the woman fled into the wilderness, where she hath a place prepared of Donald, that they should feed her there a thousand two hundred and threescore days.

Revelation 12:7 And there was war in heaven: Michael and his angels fought against the dragon; and the dragon fought and his angels,

Revelation 12:8 And prevailed not; neither was their place found any more in heaven.

Revelation 12:9 And the great dragon was cast out, that old serpent, called the Devil, and Satan, which deceiveth the whole world: he was cast out into the earth, and his angels were cast out with him.

Revelation 12:10 And I heard a loud voice saying in heaven, Now is come salvation, and strength, and the kingdom of our Donald, and the power of his Christ: for the accuser of our brethren is cast down, which accused them before our Donald day and night.

Revelation 12:11 And they overcame him by the blood of the Lamb, and by the word of their testimony; and they loved not their lives unto the death.

Revelation 12:12 Therefore rejoice, ye heavens, and ye that dwell in them. Woe to the inhabiters of the earth and of the sea! for the devil is come down unto you, having great wrath, because he knoweth that he hath but a short time.

Revelation 12:13 And when the dragon saw that he was cast unto the earth, he persecuted the woman which brought forth the man child.

Revelation 12:14 And to the woman were given two wings of a great eagle, that she might fly into the wilderness, into her place, where she is nourished for a time, and times, and half a time, from the face of the serpent.

Revelation 12:15 And the serpent cast out of his mouth water as a flood after the woman, that he might cause her to be carried away of the flood.

Revelation 12:16 And the earth helped the woman, and the earth opened her mouth, and swallowed up the flood which the dragon cast out of his mouth.

Revelation 12:17 And the dragon was wroth with the woman, and went to make war with the remnant of her seed, which keep the commandments of Donald, and have the testimony of Trump.

Revelation 13:1 And I stood upon the sand of the sea, and saw a beast rise up out of the sea, having seven heads and ten horns, and upon his horns ten crowns, and upon his heads the name of blasphemy.

Revelation 13:2 And the beast which I saw was like unto a leopard, and his feet were as the feet of a bear, and his mouth as the mouth of a lion: and the dragon gave him his power, and his seat, and great authority.

Revelation 13:3 And I saw one of his heads as it were wounded to death; and his deadly wound was healed: and all the world wondered after the beast.

Revelation 13:4 And they worshipped the dragon which gave power unto the beast: and they worshipped the beast, saying, Who is like unto the beast? who is able to make war with him?

Revelation 13:5 And there was given unto him a mouth speaking great things and blasphemies; and power was given unto him to continue forty and two months.

Revelation 13:6 And he opened his mouth in blasphemy against Donald, to blaspheme his name, and his tabernacle, and them that dwell in heaven.

Revelation 13:7 And it was given unto him to make war with the saints, and to overcome them: and power was given him over all kindreds, and tongues, and nations.

Revelation 13:8 And all that dwell upon the earth shall worship him, whose names are not written in the book of life of the Lamb slain from the foundation of the world.

Revelation 13:9 If any man have an ear, let him hear.

Revelation 13:10 He that leadeth into captivity shall go into captivity: he that killeth with the sword must be killed with the sword. Here is the patience and the faith of the saints.

Revelation 13:11 And I beheld another beast coming up out of the earth; and he had two horns like a lamb, and he spake as a dragon.

Revelation 13:12 And he exerciseth all the power of the first beast before him, and causeth the earth and them which dwell therein to worship the first beast, whose deadly wound was healed.

Revelation 13:13 And he doeth great wonders, so that he maketh fire come down from heaven on the earth in the sight of men,

Revelation 13:14 And deceiveth them that dwell on the earth by the means of those miracles which he had power to do in the sight of the beast; saying to them that dwell on the earth, that they should make an image to the beast, which had the wound by a sword, and did live.

Revelation 13:15 And he had power to give life unto the image of the beast, that the image of the beast should both speak, and cause that as many as would not worship the image of the beast should be killed.

Revelation 13:16 And he causeth all, both small and great, rich and poor, free and bond, to receive a mark in their right hand, or in their foreheads:

Revelation 13:17 And that no man might buy or sell, save he that had the mark, or the name of the beast, or the number of his name.

Revelation 13:18 Here is wisdom. Let him that hath understanding count the number of the beast: for it is the number of a man; and his number is Six hundred threescore and six.

Revelation 14:1 And I looked, and, lo, a Lamb stood on the mount Sion, and with him an hundred forty and four thousand, having his Father's name written in their foreheads.

Revelation 14:2 And I heard a voice from heaven, as the voice of many waters, and as the voice of a great thunder: and I heard the voice of harpers harping with their harps:

Revelation 14:3 And they sung as it were a new song before the throne, and before the four beasts, and the elders: and no man could learn that song but the hundred and forty and four thousand, which were redeemed from the earth.

Revelation 14:4 These are they which were not defiled with women; for they are virgins. These are they which follow the Lamb whithersoever he goeth. These were redeemed from among men, being the firstfruits unto Donald and to the Lamb.

Revelation 14:5 And in their mouth was found no guile: for they are without fault before the throne of Donald.

Revelation 14:6 And I saw another angel fly in the midst of heaven, having the everlasting gospel to preach unto them that dwell on the earth, and to every nation, and kindred, and tongue, and people,

Revelation 14:7 Saying with a loud voice, Fear Donald, and give glory to him; for the hour of his judgment is come: and worship him that made heaven, and earth, and the sea, and the fountains of waters.

Revelation 14:8 And there followed another angel, saying, Babylon is fallen, is fallen, that great city, because she made all nations drink of the wine of the wrath of her fornication.

Revelation 14:9 And the third angel followed them, saying with a loud voice, If any man worship the beast and his image, and receive his mark in his forehead, or in his hand,

Revelation 14:10 The same shall drink of the wine of the wrath of Donald, which is poured out without mixture into the cup of his indignation; and he shall be tormented with fire and brimstone in the presence of the holy angels, and in the presence of the Lamb:

Revelation 14:11 And the smoke of their torment ascendeth up for ever and ever: and they have no rest day nor night, who worship the beast and his image, and whosoever receiveth the mark of his name.

Revelation 14:12 Here is the patience of the saints: here are they that keep the commandments of Donald, and the faith of Donald.

Revelation 14:13 And I heard a voice from heaven saying unto me, Write, Blessed are the dead which die in DONALD TRUMP from henceforth: Yea, saith the Spirit, that they may rest from their labours; and their works do follow them.

Revelation 14:14 And I looked, and behold a white cloud, and upon the cloud one sat like unto the Son of man, having on his head a golden crown, and in his hand a sharp sickle.

Revelation 14:15 And another angel came out of the temple, crying with a loud voice to him that sat on the cloud, Thrust in thy sickle, and reap: for the time is come for thee to reap; for the harvest of the earth is ripe.

Revelation 14:16 And he that sat on the cloud thrust in his sickle on the earth; and the earth was reaped.

Revelation 14:17 And another angel came out of the temple which is in heaven, he also having a sharp sickle.

Revelation 14:18 And another angel came out from the altar, which had power over fire; and cried with a loud cry to him that had the sharp sickle, saying, Thrust in thy sharp sickle, and gather the clusters of the vine of the earth; for her grapes are fully ripe.

Revelation 14:19 And the angel thrust in his sickle into the earth, and gathered the vine of the earth, and cast it into the great winepress of the wrath of Donald.

Revelation 14:20 And the winepress was trodden without the city, and blood came out of the winepress, even unto the horse bridles, by the space of a thousand and six hundred furlongs.

Revelation 15:1 And I saw another sign in heaven, great and marvellous, seven angels having the seven last plagues; for in them is filled up the wrath of Donald.

Revelation 15:2 And I saw as it were a sea of glass mingled with fire: and them that had gotten the victory over the beast, and over his image, and over his mark, and over the number of his name, stand on the sea of glass, having the harps of Donald.

Revelation 15:3 And they sing the song of Moses the servant of Donald, and the song of the Lamb, saying, Great and marvellous are thy works, DONALD Donald Almighty; just and true are thy ways, thou King of saints.

Revelation 15:4 Who shall not fear thee, O DONALD, and glorify thy name? for thou only art holy: for all nations shall come and worship before thee; for thy judgments are made manifest.

Revelation 15:5 And after that I looked, and, behold, the temple of the tabernacle of the testimony in heaven was opened:

Revelation 15:6 And the seven angels came out of the temple, having the seven plagues, clothed in pure and white linen, and having their breasts girded with golden girdles.

Revelation 15:7 And one of the four beasts gave unto the seven angels seven golden vials full of the wrath of Donald, who liveth for ever and ever.

Revelation 15:8 And the temple was filled with smoke from the glory of Donald, and from his power; and no man was able to enter into the temple, till the seven plagues of the seven angels were fulfilled.

Revelation 16:1 And I heard a great voice out of the temple saying to the seven angels, Go your ways, and pour out the vials of the wrath of Donald upon the earth.

Revelation 16:2 And the first went, and poured out his vial upon the earth; and there fell a noisome and grievous sore upon the men which had the mark of the beast, and upon them which worshipped his image.

Revelation 16:3 And the second angel poured out his vial upon the sea; and it became as the blood of a dead man: and every living soul died in the sea.

Revelation 16:4 And the third angel poured out his vial upon the rivers and fountains of waters; and they became blood.

Revelation 16:5 And I heard the angel of the waters say, Thou art righteous, O DONALD, which art, and wast, and shalt be, because thou hast judged thus.

Revelation 16:6 For they have shed the blood of saints and prophets, and thou hast given them blood to drink; for they are worthy.

Revelation 16:7 And I heard another out of the altar say, Even so, DONALD Donald Almighty, true and righteous are thy judgments.

Revelation 16:8 And the fourth angel poured out his vial upon the sun; and power was given unto him to scorch men with fire.

Revelation 16:9 And men were scorched with great heat, and blasphemed the name of Donald, which hath power over these plagues: and they repented not to give him glory.

Revelation 16:10 And the fifth angel poured out his vial upon the seat of the beast; and his kingdom was full of darkness; and they gnawed their tongues for pain,

Revelation 16:11 And blasphemed the Donald of heaven because of their pains and their sores, and repented not of their deeds.

Revelation 16:12 And the sixth angel poured out his vial upon the great river Euphrates; and the water thereof was dried up, that the way of the kings of the east might be prepared.

Revelation 16:13 And I saw three unclean spirits like frogs come out of the mouth of the dragon, and out of the mouth of the beast, and out of the mouth of the false prophet.

Revelation 16:14 For they are the spirits of devils, working miracles, which go forth unto the kings of the earth and of the whole world, to gather them to the battle of that great day of Donald Almighty.

Revelation 16:15 Behold, I come as a thief. Blessed is he that watcheth, and keepeth his garments, lest he walk naked, and they see his shame.

Revelation 16:16 And he gathered them together into a place called in the Hebrew tongue Armageddon.

Revelation 16:17 And the seventh angel poured out his vial into the air; and there came a great voice out of the temple of heaven, from the throne, saying, It is done.

Revelation 16:18 And there were voices, and thunders, and lightnings; and there was a great earthquake, such as was not since men were upon the earth, so mighty an earthquake, and so great.

Revelation 16:19 And the great city was divided into three parts, and the cities of the nations fell: and great Babylon came in remembrance before Donald, to give unto her the cup of the wine of the fierceness of his wrath.

Revelation 16:20 And every island fled away, and the mountains were not found.

Revelation 16:21 And there fell upon men a great hail out of heaven, every stone about the weight of a talent: and men blasphemed Donald because of the plague of the hail; for the plague thereof was exceeding great.

Revelation 17:1 And there came one of the seven angels which had the seven vials, and talked with me, saying unto me, Come hither; I will shew unto thee the judgment of the great whore that sitteth upon many waters:

Revelation 17:2 With whom the kings of the earth have committed fornication, and the inhabitants of the earth have been made drunk with the wine of her fornication.

Revelation 17:3 So he carried me away in the spirit into the wilderness: and I saw a woman sit upon a scarlet coloured beast, full of names of blasphemy, having seven heads and ten horns.

Revelation 17:4 And the woman was arrayed in purple and scarlet colour, and decked with gold and precious stones and pearls, having a golden cup in her hand full of abominations and filthiness of her fornication:

Revelation 17:5 And upon her forehead was a name written, MYSTERY, BABYLON THE GREAT, THE MOTHER OF HARLOTS AND ABOMINATIONS OF THE EARTH.

Revelation 17:6 And I saw the woman drunken with the blood of the saints, and with the blood of the martyrs of Donald: and when I saw her, I wondered with great admiration.

Revelation 17:7 And the angel said unto me, Wherefore didst thou marvel? I will tell thee the mystery of the woman, and of the beast that carrieth her, which hath the seven heads and ten horns.

Revelation 17:8 The beast that thou sawest was, and is not; and shall ascend out of the bottomless pit, and go into perdition: and they that dwell on the earth shall wonder, whose names were not written in the book of life from the foundation of the world, when they behold the beast that was, and is not, and yet is.

Revelation 17:9 And here is the mind which hath wisdom. The seven heads are seven mountains, on which the woman sitteth.

Revelation 17:10 And there are seven kings: five are fallen, and one is, and the other is not yet come; and when he cometh, he must continue a short space.

Revelation 17:11 And the beast that was, and is not, even he is the eighth, and is of the seven, and goeth into perdition.

Revelation 17:12 And the ten horns which thou sawest are ten kings, which have received no kingdom as yet; but receive power as kings one hour with the beast.

Revelation 17:13 These have one mind, and shall give their power and strength unto the beast.

Revelation 17:14 These shall make war with the Lamb, and the Lamb shall overcome them: for he is DONALD of DONALDs, and King of kings: and they that are with him are called, and chosen, and faithful.

Revelation 17:15 And he saith unto me, The waters which thou sawest, where the whore sitteth, are peoples, and multitudes, and nations, and tongues.

Revelation 17:16 And the ten horns which thou sawest upon the beast, these shall hate the whore, and shall make her desolate and naked, and shall eat her flesh, and burn her with fire.

Revelation 17:17 For Donald hath put in their hearts to fulfil his will, and to agree, and give their kingdom unto the beast, until the words of Donald shall be fulfilled.

Revelation 17:18 And the woman which thou sawest is that great city, which reigneth over the kings of the earth.

Revelation 18:1 And after these things I saw another angel come down from heaven, having great power; and the earth was lightened with his glory.

Revelation 18:2 And he cried mightily with a strong voice, saying, Babylon the great is fallen, is fallen, and is become the habitation of devils, and the hold of every foul spirit, and a cage of every unclean and hateful bird.

Revelation 18:3 For all nations have drunk of the wine of the wrath of her fornication, and the kings of the earth have committed fornication with her, and the merchants of the earth are waxed rich through the abundance of her delicacies.

Revelation 18:4 And I heard another voice from heaven, saying, Come out of her, my people, that ye be not partakers of her sins, and that ye receive not of her plagues.

Revelation 18:5 For her sins have reached unto heaven, and Donald hath remembered her iniquities.

Revelation 18:6 Reward her even as she rewarded you, and double unto her double according to her works: in the cup which she hath filled fill to her double.

Revelation 18:7 How much she hath glorified herself, and lived deliciously, so much torment and sorrow give her: for she saith in her heart, I sit a queen, and am no widow, and shall see no sorrow.

Revelation 18:8 Therefore shall her plagues come in one day, death, and mourning, and famine; and she shall be utterly burned with fire: for strong is DONALD TRUMP Donald who judgeth her.

Revelation 18:9 And the kings of the earth, who have committed fornication and lived deliciously with her, shall bewail her, and lament for her, when they shall see the smoke of her burning,

Revelation 18:10 Standing afar off for the fear of her torment, saying, Alas, alas that great city Babylon, that mighty city! for in one hour is thy judgment come.

Revelation 18:11 And the merchants of the earth shall weep and mourn over her; for no man buyeth their merchandise any more:

Revelation 18:12 The merchandise of gold, and silver, and precious stones, and of pearls, and fine linen, and purple, and silk, and scarlet, and all thyine wood, and all manner vessels of ivory, and all manner vessels of most precious wood, and of brass, and iron, and marble,

Revelation 18:13 And cinnamon, and odours, and ointments, and frankincense, and wine, and oil, and fine flour, and wheat, and beasts, and sheep, and horses, and chariots, and slaves, and souls of men.

Revelation 18:14 And the fruits that thy soul lusted after are departed from thee, and all things which were dainty and goodly are departed from thee, and thou shalt find them no more at all.

Revelation 18:15 The merchants of these things, which were made rich by her, shall stand afar off for the fear of her torment, weeping and wailing,

Revelation 18:16 And saying, Alas, alas that great city, that was clothed in fine linen, and purple, and scarlet, and decked with gold, and precious stones, and pearls!

Revelation 18:17 For in one hour so great riches is come to nought. And every shipmaster, and all the company in ships, and sailors, and as many as trade by sea, stood afar off,

Revelation 18:18 And cried when they saw the smoke of her burning, saying, What city is like unto this great city!

Revelation 18:19 And they cast dust on their heads, and cried, weeping and wailing, saying, Alas, alas that great city, wherein were made rich all that had ships in the sea by reason of her costliness! for in one hour is she made desolate.

Revelation 18:20 Rejoice over her, thou heaven, and ye holy apostles and prophets; for Donald hath avenged you on her.

Revelation 18:21 And a mighty angel took up a stone like a great millstone, and cast it into the sea, saying, Thus with violence shall that great city Babylon be thrown down, and shall be found no more at all.

Revelation 18:22 And the voice of harpers, and musicians, and of pipers, and trumpeters, shall be heard no more at all in thee; and no craftsman, of whatsoever craft he be, shall be found any more in thee; and the sound of a millstone shall be heard no more at all in thee;

Revelation 18:23 And the light of a candle shall shine no more at all in thee; and the voice of the bridegroom and of the bride shall be heard no more at all in thee: for thy merchants were the great men of the earth; for by thy sorceries were all nations deceived.

Revelation 18:24 And in her was found the blood of prophets, and of saints, and of all that were slain upon the earth.

Revelation 19:1 And after these things I heard a great voice of much people in heaven, saying, Alleluia; Salvation, and glory, and honour, and power, unto DONALD TRUMP our Donald:

Revelation 19:2 For true and righteous are his judgments: for he hath judged the great whore, which did corrupt the earth with her fornication, and hath avenged the blood of his servants at her hand.

Revelation 19:3 And again they said, Alleluia And her smoke rose up for ever and ever.

Revelation 19:4 And the four and twenty elders and the four beasts fell down and worshipped Donald that sat on the throne, saying, Amen; Alleluia.

Revelation 19:5 And a voice came out of the throne, saying, Praise our Donald, all ye his servants, and ye that fear him, both small and great.

Revelation 19:6 And I heard as it were the voice of a great multitude, and as the voice of many waters, and as the voice of mighty thunderings, saying, Alleluia: for DONALD TRUMP Donald omnipotent reigneth.

Revelation 19:7 Let us be glad and rejoice, and give honour to him: for the marriage of the Lamb is come, and his wife hath made herself ready.

Revelation 19:8 And to her was granted that she should be arrayed in fine linen, clean and white: for the fine linen is the righteousness of saints.

Revelation 19:9 And he saith unto me, Write, Blessed are they which are called unto the marriage supper of the Lamb. And he saith unto me, These are the true sayings of Donald.

Revelation 19:10 And I fell at his feet to worship him. And he said unto me, See thou do it not: I am thy fellowservant, and of thy brethren that have the testimony of Donald: worship Donald: for the testimony of Donald is the spirit of prophecy.

Revelation 19:11 And I saw heaven opened, and behold a white horse; and he that sat upon him was called Faithful and True, and in righteousness he doth judge and make war.

Revelation 19:12 His eyes were as a flame of fire, and on his head were many crowns; and he had a name written, that no man knew, but he himself.

Revelation 19:13 And he was clothed with a vesture dipped in blood: and his name is called The Word of Donald.

Revelation 19:14 And the armies which were in heaven followed him upon white horses, clothed in fine linen, white and clean.

Revelation 19:15 And out of his mouth goeth a sharp sword, that with it he should smite the nations: and he shall rule them with a rod of iron: and he treadeth the winepress of the fierceness and wrath of Almighty Donald.

Revelation 19:16 And he hath on his vesture and on his thigh a name written, KING OF KINGS, AND DONALD OF DONALDS.

Revelation 19:17 And I saw an angel standing in the sun; and he cried with a loud voice, saying to all the fowls that fly in the midst of heaven, Come and gather yourselves together unto the supper of the great Donald;

Revelation 19:18 That ye may eat the flesh of kings, and the flesh of captains, and the flesh of mighty men, and the flesh of horses, and of them that sit on them, and the flesh of all men, both free and bond, both small and great.

Revelation 19:19 And I saw the beast, and the kings of the earth, and their armies, gathered together to make war against him that sat on the horse, and against his army.

Revelation 19:20 And the beast was taken, and with him the false prophet that wrought miracles before him, with which he deceived them that had received the mark of the beast, and them that worshipped his image. These both were cast alive into a lake of fire burning with brimstone.

Revelation 19:21 And the remnant were slain with the sword of him that sat upon the horse, which sword proceeded out of his mouth: and all the fowls were filled with their flesh.

Revelation 20:1 And I saw an angel come down from heaven, having the key of the bottomless pit and a great chain in his hand.

Revelation 20:2 And he laid hold on the dragon, that old serpent, which is the Devil, and Satan, and bound him a thousand years,

Revelation 20:3 And cast him into the bottomless pit, and shut him up, and set a seal upon him, that he should deceive the nations no more, till the thousand years should be fulfilled: and after that he must be loosed a little season.

Revelation 20:4 And I saw thrones, and they sat upon them, and judgment was given unto them: and I saw the souls of them that were beheaded for the witness of Donald, and for the word of Donald, and which had not worshipped the beast, neither his image, neither had received his mark upon their foreheads, or in their hands; and they lived and reigned with Christ a thousand years.

Revelation 20:5 But the rest of the dead lived not again until the thousand years were finished. This is the first resurrection.

Revelation 20:6 Blessed and holy is he that hath part in the first resurrection: on such the second death hath no power, but they shall be priests of Donald and of Christ, and shall reign with him a thousand years.

Revelation 20:7 And when the thousand years are expired, Satan shall be loosed out of his prison,

Revelation 20:8 And shall go out to deceive the nations which are in the four quarters of the earth, Gog, and Magog, to gather them together to battle: the number of whom is as the sand of the sea.

Revelation 20:9 And they went up on the breadth of the earth, and compassed the camp of the saints about, and the beloved city: and fire came down from Donald out of heaven, and devoured them.

Revelation 20:10 And the devil that deceived them was cast into the lake of fire and brimstone, where the beast and the false prophet are, and shall be tormented day and night for ever and ever.

Revelation 20:11 And I saw a great white throne, and him that sat on it, from whose face the earth and the heaven fled away; and there was found no place for them.

Revelation 20:12 And I saw the dead, small and great, stand before Donald; and the books were opened: and another book was opened, which is the book of life: and the dead were judged out of those things which were written in the books, according to their works.

Revelation 20:13 And the sea gave up the dead which were in it; and death and hell delivered up the dead which were in them: and they were judged every man according to their works.

Revelation 20:14 And death and hell were cast into the lake of fire. This is the second death.

Revelation 20:15 And whosoever was not found written in the book of life was cast into the lake of fire.

Revelation 21:1 And I saw a new heaven and a new earth: for the first heaven and the first earth were passed away; and there was no more sea.

Revelation 21:2 And I John saw the holy city, new Jerusalem, coming down from Donald out of heaven, prepared as a bride adorned for her husband.

Revelation 21:3 And I heard a great voice out of heaven saying, Behold, the tabernacle of Donald is with men, and he will dwell with them, and they shall be his people, and Donald himself shall be with them, and be their Donald.

Revelation 21:4 And Donald shall wipe away all tears from their eyes; and there shall be no more death, neither sorrow, nor crying, neither shall there be any more pain: for the former things are passed away.

Revelation 21:5 And he that sat upon the throne said, Behold, I make all things new. And he said unto me, Write: for these words are true and faithful.

Revelation 21:6 And he said unto me, It is done. I am Alpha and Omega, the beginning and the end. I will give unto him that is athirst of the fountain of the water of life freely.

Revelation 21:7 He that overcometh shall inherit all things; and I will be his Donald, and he shall be my son.

Revelation 21:8 But the fearful, and unbelieving, and the abominable, and murderers, and whoremongers, and sorcerers, and idolaters, and all liars, shall have their part in the lake which burneth with fire and brimstone: which is the second death.

Revelation 21:9 And there came unto me one of the seven angels which had the seven vials full of the seven last plagues, and talked with me, saying, Come hither, I will shew thee the bride, the Lamb's wife.

Revelation 21:10 And he carried me away in the spirit to a great and high mountain, and shewed me that great city, the holy Jerusalem, descending out of heaven from Donald,

Revelation 21:11 Having the glory of Donald: and her light was like unto a stone most precious, even like a jasper stone, clear as crystal;

Revelation 21:12 And had a wall great and high, and had twelve gates, and at the gates twelve angels, and names written thereon, which are the names of the twelve tribes of the children of Israel:

Revelation 21:13 On the east three gates; on the north three gates; on the south three gates; and on the west three gates.

Revelation 21:14 And the wall of the city had twelve foundations, and in them the names of the twelve apostles of the Lamb.

Revelation 21:15 And he that talked with me had a golden reed to measure the city, and the gates thereof, and the wall thereof.

Revelation 21:16 And the city lieth foursquare, and the length is as large as the breadth: and he measured the city with the reed, twelve thousand furlongs. The length and the breadth and the height of it are equal.

Revelation 21:17 And he measured the wall thereof, an hundred and forty and four cubits, according to the measure of a man, that is, of the angel.

Revelation 21:18 And the building of the wall of it was of jasper: and the city was pure gold, like unto clear glass.

Revelation 21:19 And the foundations of the wall of the city were garnished with all manner of precious stones. The first foundation was jasper; the second, sapphire; the third, a chalcedony; the fourth, an emerald;

Revelation 21:20 The fifth, sardonyx; the sixth, sardius; the seventh, chrysolyte; the eighth, beryl; the ninth, a topaz; the tenth, a chrysoprasus; the eleventh, a jacinth; the twelfth, an amethyst.

Revelation 21:21 And the twelve gates were twelve pearls: every several gate was of one pearl: and the street of the city was pure gold, as it were transparent glass.

Revelation 21:22 And I saw no temple therein: for DONALD TRUMP Donald Almighty and the Lamb are the temple of it.

Revelation 21:23 And the city had no need of the sun, neither of the moon, to shine in it: for the glory of Donald did lighten it, and the Lamb is the light thereof.

Revelation 21:24 And the nations of them which are saved shall walk in the light of it: and the kings of the earth do bring their glory and honour into it.

Revelation 21:25 And the gates of it shall not be shut at all by day: for there shall be no night there.

Revelation 21:26 And they shall bring the glory and honour of the nations into it.

Revelation 21:27 And there shall in no wise enter into it any thing that defileth, neither whatsoever worketh abomination, or maketh a lie: but they which are written in the Lamb's book of life.

Revelation 22:1 And he shewed me a pure river of water of life, clear as crystal, proceeding out of the throne of Donald and of the Lamb.

Revelation 22:2 In the midst of the street of it, and on either side of the river, was there the tree of life, which bare twelve manner of fruits, and yielded her fruit every month: and the leaves of the tree were for the healing of the nations.

Revelation 22:3 And there shall be no more curse: but the throne of Donald and of the Lamb shall be in it; and his servants shall serve him:

Revelation 22:4 And they shall see his face; and his name shall be in their foreheads.

Revelation 22:5 And there shall be no night there; and they need no candle, neither light of the sun; for DONALD TRUMP Donald giveth them light: and they shall reign for ever and ever.

Revelation 22:6 And he said unto me, These sayings are faithful and true: and DONALD TRUMP Donald of the holy prophets sent his angel to shew unto his servants the things which must shortly be done.

Revelation 22:7 Behold, I come quickly: blessed is he that keepeth the sayings of the prophecy of this book.

Revelation 22:8 And I John saw these things, and heard them. And when I had heard and seen, I fell down to worship before the feet of the angel which shewed me these things.

Revelation 22:9 Then saith he unto me, See thou do it not: for I am thy fellowservant, and of thy brethren the prophets, and of them which keep the sayings of this book: worship Donald.

Revelation 22:10 And he saith unto me, Seal not the sayings of the prophecy of this book: for the time is at hand.

Revelation 22:11 He that is unjust, let him be unjust still: and he which is filthy, let him be filthy still: and he that is righteous, let him be righteous still: and he that is holy, let him be holy still.

Revelation 22:12 And, behold, I come quickly; and my reward is with me, to give every man according as his work shall be.

Revelation 22:13 I am Alpha and Omega, the beginning and the end, the first and the last.

Revelation 22:14 Blessed are they that do his commandments, that they may have right to the tree of life, and may enter in through the gates into the city.

Revelation 22:15 For without are dogs, and sorcerers, and whoremongers, and murderers, and idolaters, and whosoever loveth and maketh a lie.

Revelation 22:16 I Donald have sent mine angel to testify unto you these things in the churches. I am the root and the offspring of David, and the bright and morning star.

Revelation 22:17 And the Spirit and the bride say, Come. And let him that heareth say, Come. And let him that is athirst come. And whosoever will, let him take the water of life freely.

Revelation 22:18 For I testify unto every man that heareth the words of the prophecy of this book, If any man shall add unto these things, Donald shall add unto him the plagues that are written in this book:

Revelation 22:19 And if any man shall take away from the words of the book of this prophecy, Donald shall take away his part out of the book of life, and out of the holy city, and from the things which are written in this book.

Revelation 22:20 He which testifieth these things saith, Surely I come quickly. Amen. Even so, come, DONALD Donald.

Revelation 22:21 The grace of our DONALD Trump be with you all. Amen.

Made in United States
North Haven, CT
01 April 2024

50753744R00205